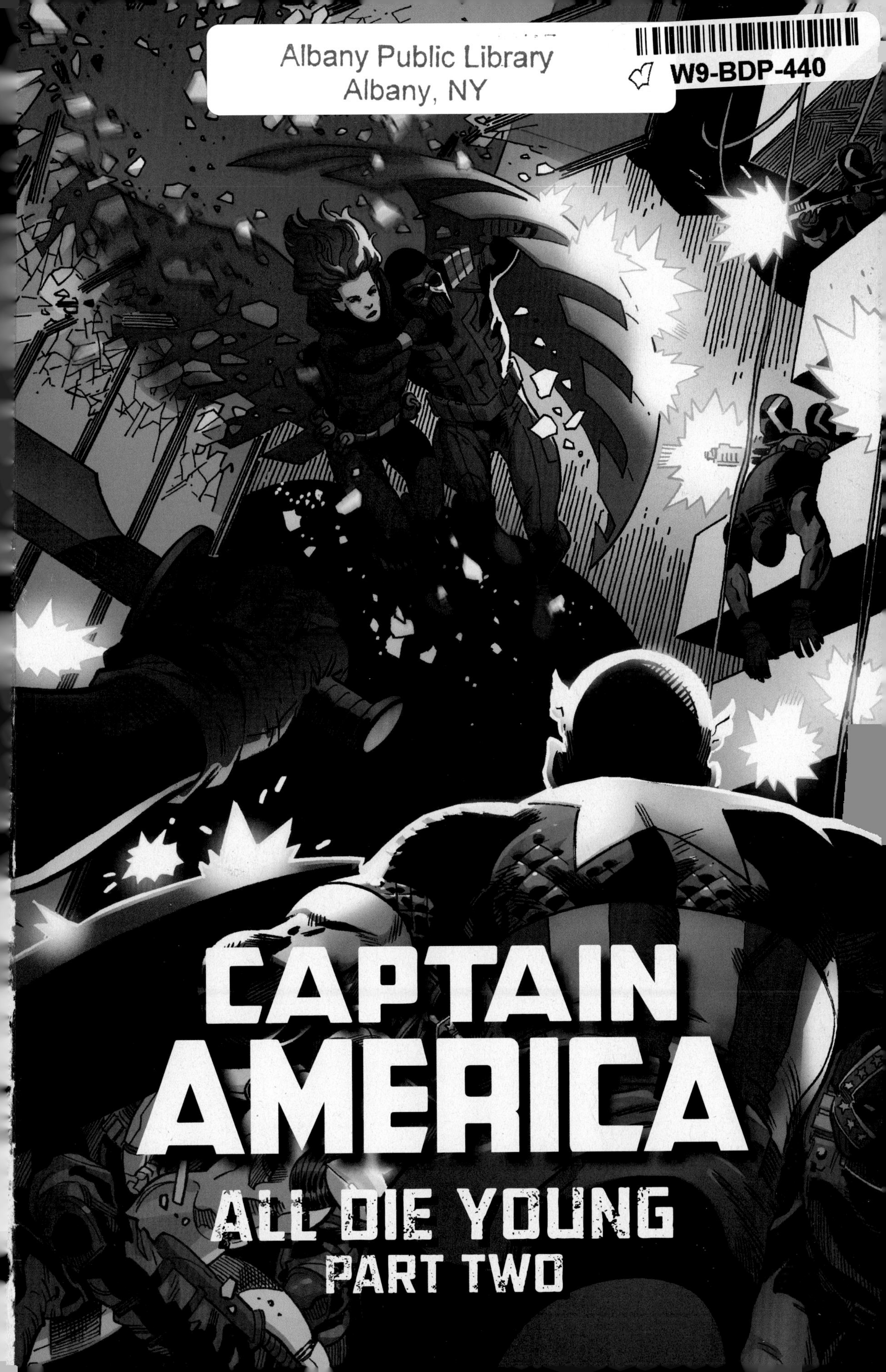
CAPTAIN AMERICA
ALL DIE YOUNG
PART TWO

CAPTAIN AMERICA, FALCON, THE WINTER SOLDIER AND SHARON CARTER (RECENTLY RESTORED TO HER PROPER AGE AND OUTFITTED WITH A NEW SUIT OF BODY ARMOR) TRAVELED TO MADRIPOOR. THEIR MISSION: RESCUE MEMBERS OF THE DAUGHTERS OF LIBERTY, INCLUDING PEGGY CARTER, AS WELL AS THUNDERBOLT ROSS. THE GROUP WAS BEING HELD PRISONER BY THE RED SKULL AND ALEXA LUKIN OF THE POWER ELITE. WHILE CAPTAIN AMERICA AND HIS ALLIES BATTLED THEIR WAY THROUGH THE POWER ELITE'S FORCES, PEGGY MANAGED TO FREE HERSELF AND PURSUED THE DEPARTING RED SKULL AND ALEXA.

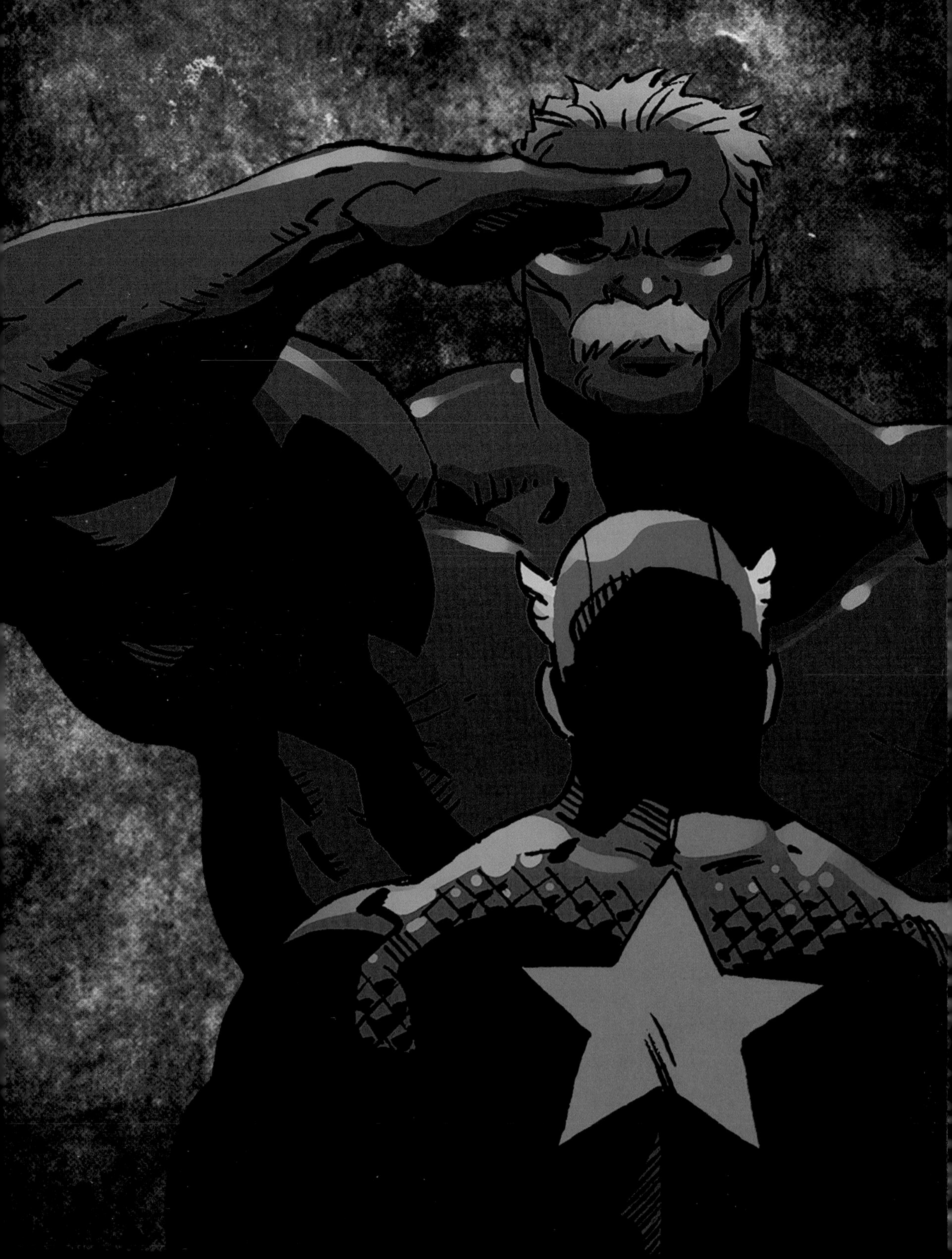

CAPTAIN AMERICA

ALL DIE YOUNG
PART TWO

Ta-Nehisi Coates
WRITER

Leonard Kirk
ARTIST

Matt Milla
COLOR ARTIST

VC's Joe Caramagna
LETTERER

Alex Ross
COVER ART

Martin Biro
ASSISTANT EDITOR

Alanna Smith
ASSOCIATE EDITOR

Tom Brevoort
EDITOR

CAPTAIN AMERICA CREATED BY JOE SIMON & JACK KIRBY

COLLECTION EDITOR **DANIEL KIRCHHOFFER**
ASSISTANT MANAGING EDITOR **MAIA LOY**
ASSISTANT MANAGING EDITOR **LISA MONTALBANO**
SENIOR EDITOR, SPECIAL PROJECTS: **JENNIFER GRÜNWALD**

VP PRODUCTION & SPECIAL PROJECTS **JEFF YOUNGQUIST**
BOOK DESIGNER **ADAM DEL RE**
SVP PRINT, SALES & MARKETING **DAVID GABRIEL**
EDITOR IN CHIEF **C.B. CEBULSKI**

CAPTAIN AMERICA BY TA-NEHISI COATES VOL. 5: ALL DIE YOUNG PART TWO. Contains material originally published in magazine form as CAPTAIN AMERICA (2018) #26-30. First printing 2021. ISBN 978-1-302-92041-8. Published by MARVEL WORLDWIDE, INC., a subsidiary of MARVEL ENTERTAINMENT, LLC. OFFICE OF PUBLICATION: 1290 Avenue of the Americas, New York, NY 10104. © 2021 MARVEL. No similarity between any of the names, characters, persons, and/or institutions in this magazine with those of any living or dead person or institution is intended, and any such similarity which may exist is purely coincidental. **Printed in Canada.** KEVIN FEIGE, Chief Creative Officer; DAN BUCKLEY, President, Marvel Entertainment; JOE QUESADA, EVP & Creative Director; DAVID BOGART, Associate Publisher & SVP of Talent Affairs; TOM BREVOORT, VP, Executive Editor; NICK LOWE, Executive Editor, VP of Content, Digital Publishing; DAVID GABRIEL, VP of Print & Digital Publishing; JEFF YOUNGQUIST, VP of Production & Special Projects; ALEX MORALES, Director of Publishing Operations; DAN EDINGTON, Managing Editor; RICKEY PURDIN, Director of Talent Relations; JENNIFER GRUNWALD, Senior Editor, Special Projects; SUSAN CRESPI, Production Manager; STAN LEE, Chairman Emeritus. For information regarding advertising in Marvel Comics or on Marvel.com, please contact Vit DeBellis, Custom Solutions & Integrated Advertising Manager, at vdebellis@marvel.com. For Marvel subscription inquiries, please call 888-511-5480. **Manufactured between 7/9/2021 and 8/10/2021 by SOLISCO PRINTERS, SCOTT, QC, CANADA.**

10 9 8 7 6 5 4 3 2 1

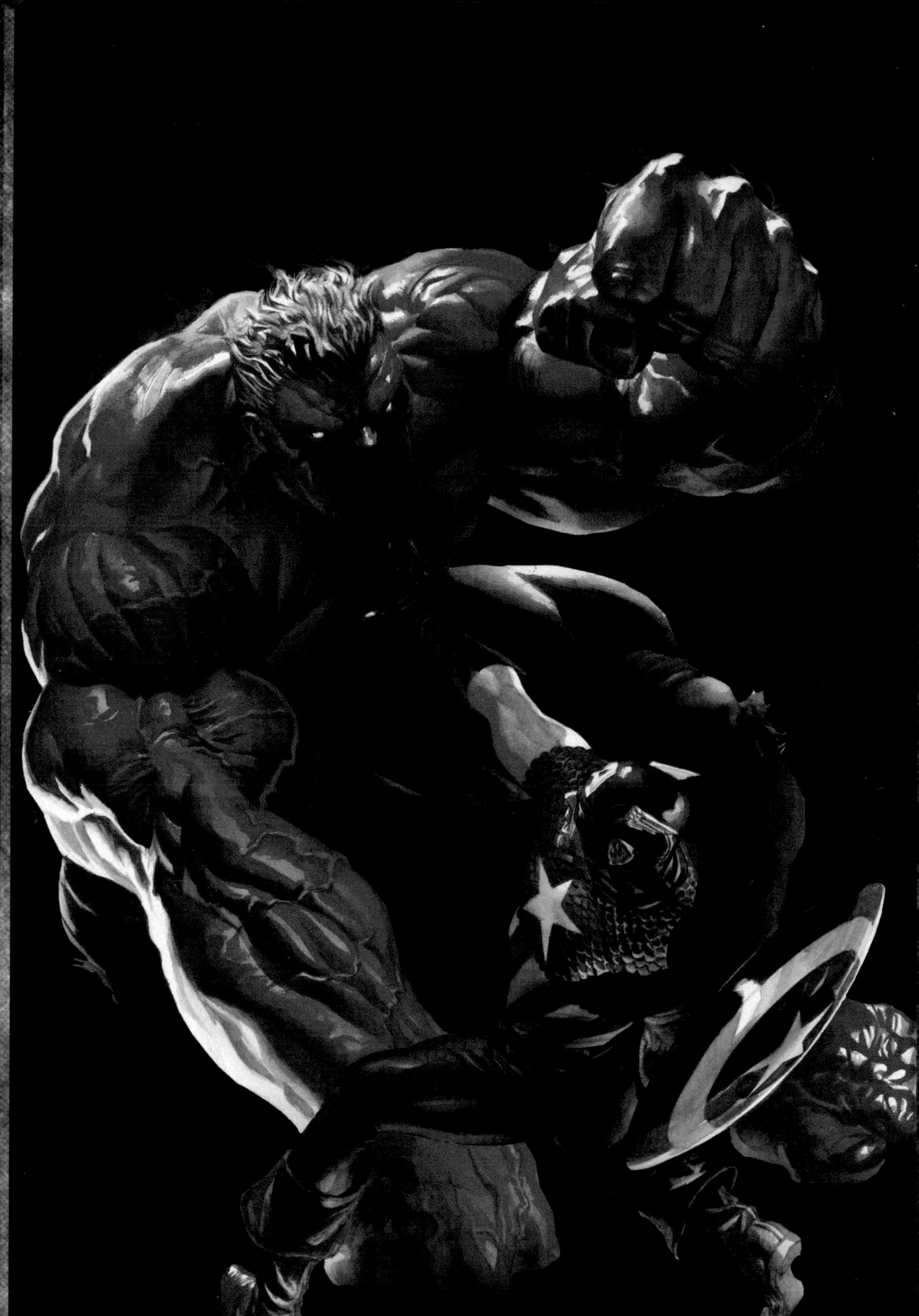

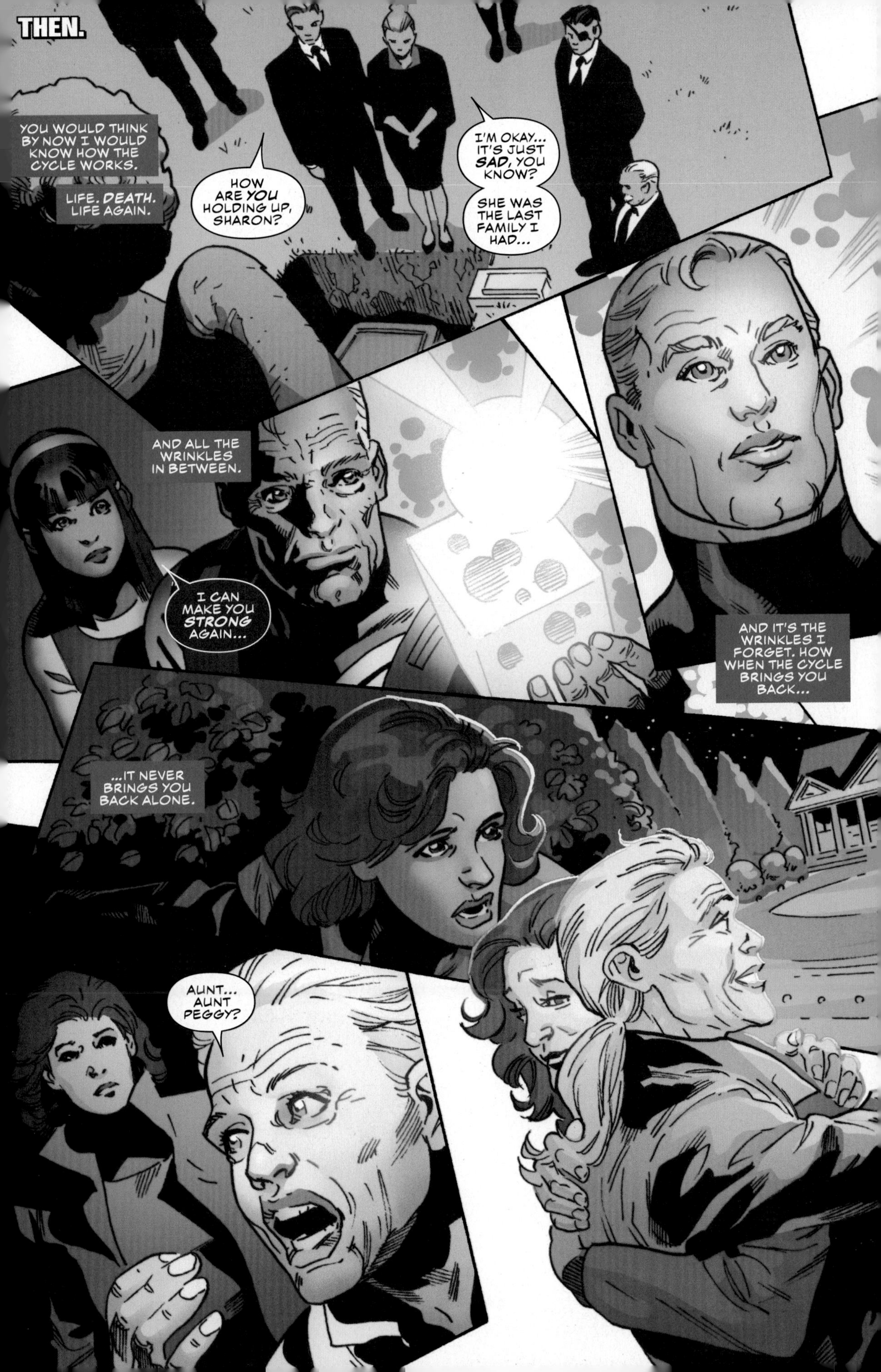
THEN.
YOU WOULD THINK BY NOW I WOULD KNOW HOW THE CYCLE WORKS.
LIFE. DEATH. LIFE AGAIN.
HOW ARE YOU HOLDING UP, SHARON?
I'M OKAY... IT'S JUST SAD, YOU KNOW?
SHE WAS THE LAST FAMILY I HAD...
AND ALL THE WRINKLES IN BETWEEN.
I CAN MAKE YOU STRONG AGAIN...
AND IT'S THE WRINKLES I FORGET. HOW WHEN THE CYCLE BRINGS YOU BACK...
...IT NEVER BRINGS YOU BACK ALONE.
AUNT... AUNT PEGGY?

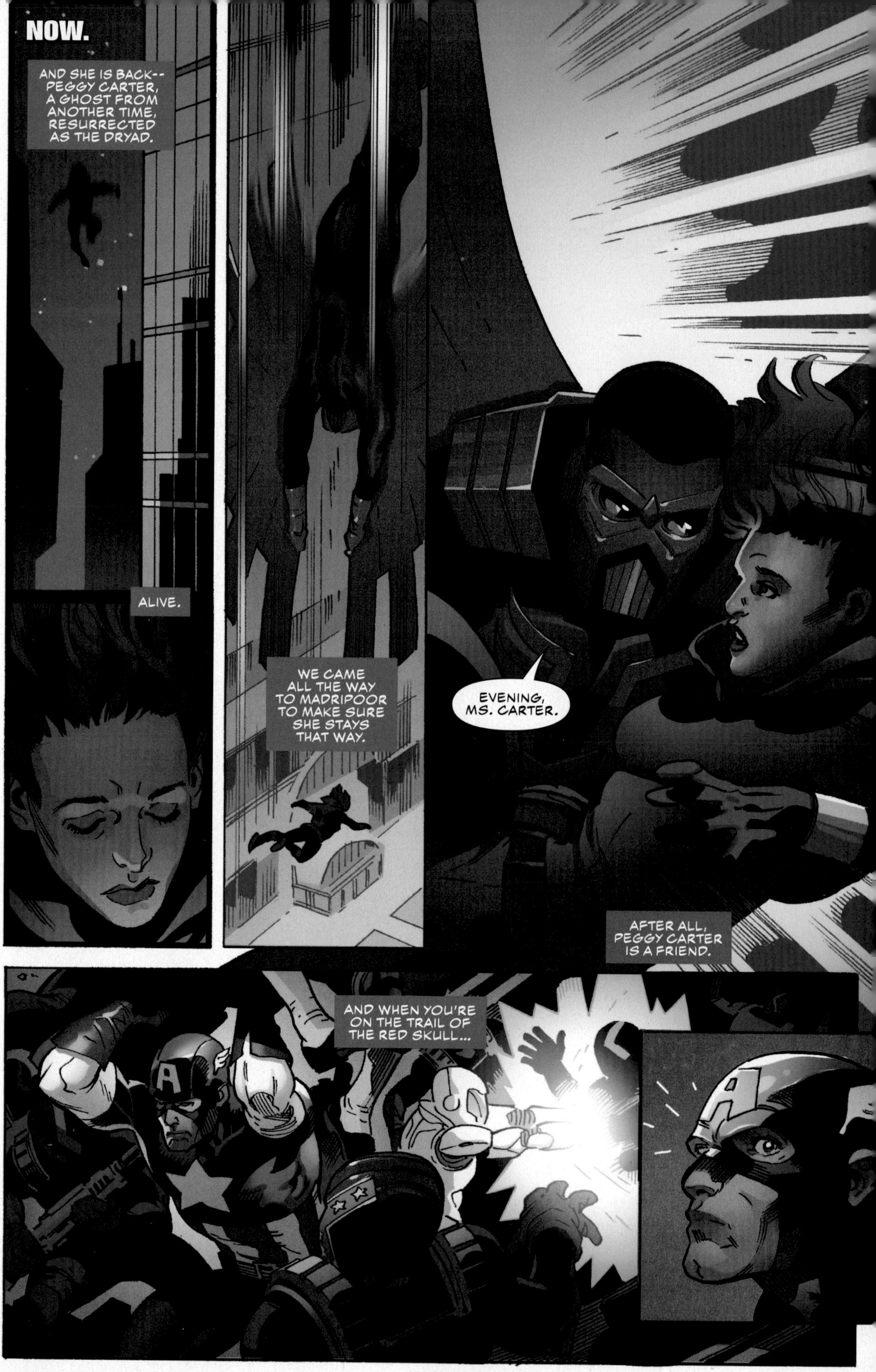
NOW.
AND SHE IS BACK-- PEGGY CARTER, A GHOST FROM ANOTHER TIME, RESURRECTED AS THE DRYAD.
ALIVE.
WE CAME ALL THE WAY TO MADRIPOOR TO MAKE SURE SHE STAYS THAT WAY.
EVENING, MS. CARTER.
AFTER ALL, PEGGY CARTER IS A FRIEND.
AND WHEN YOU'RE ON THE TRAIL OF THE RED SKULL...

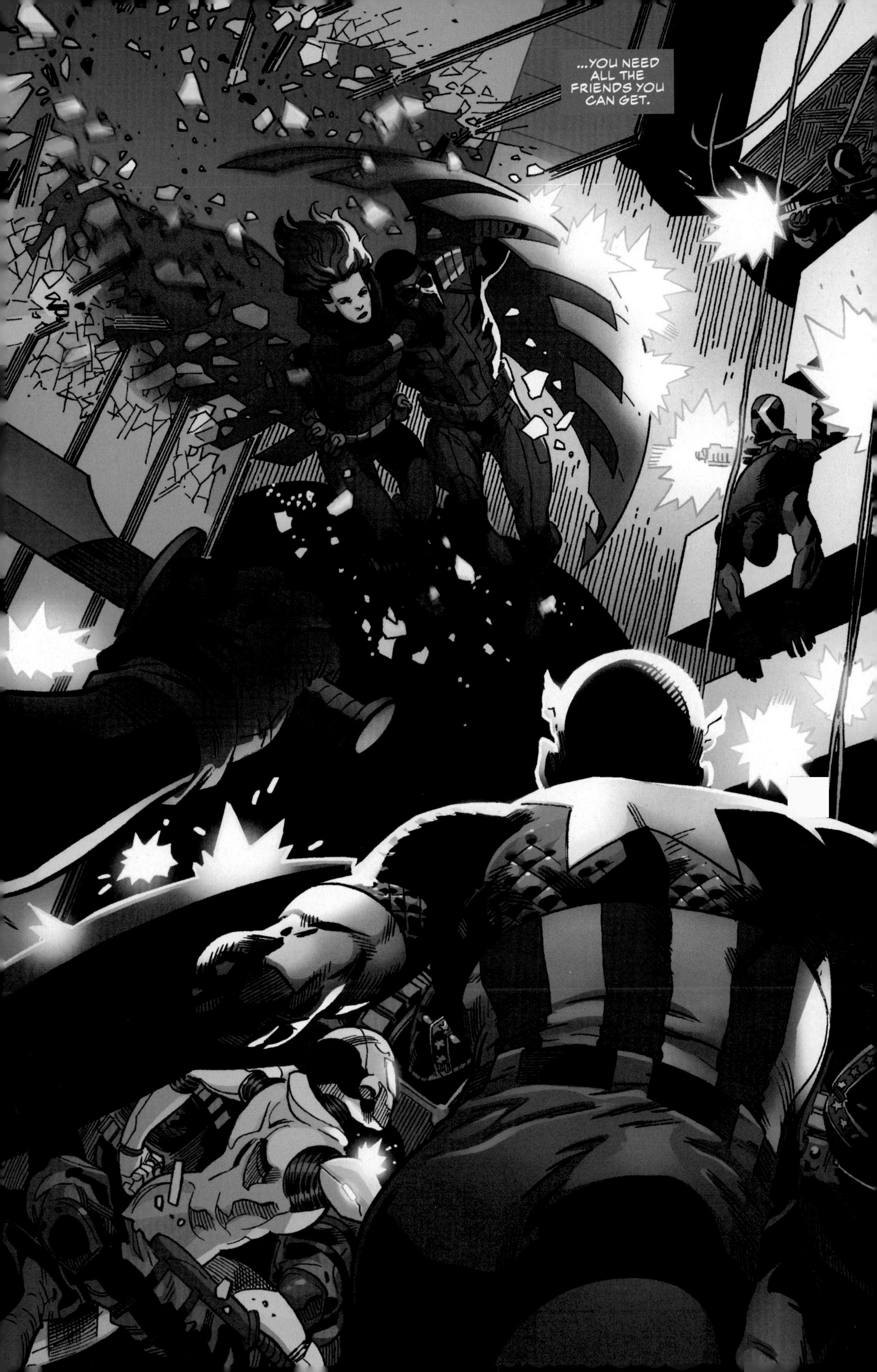
...YOU NEED ALL THE FRIENDS YOU CAN GET.

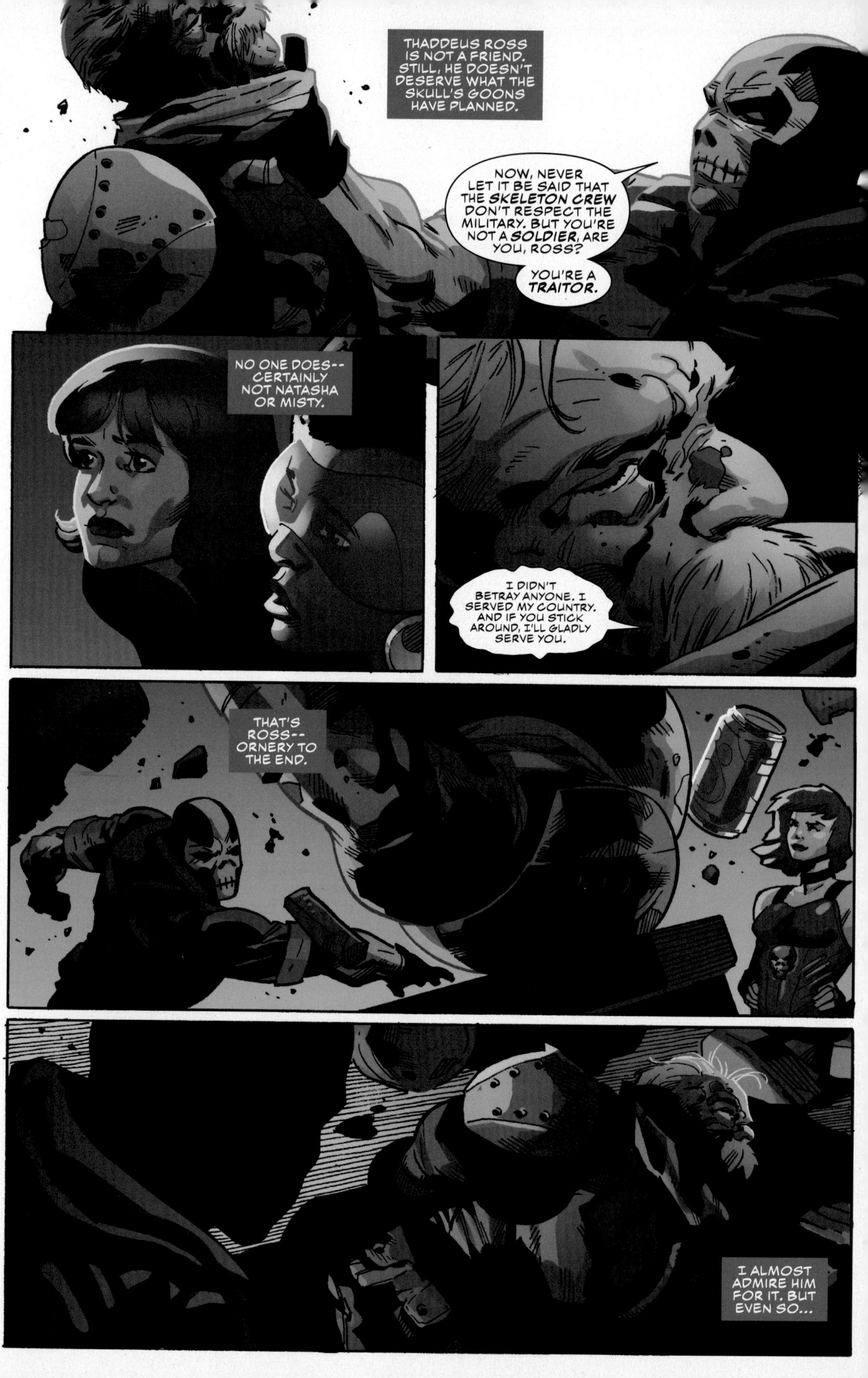
THADDEUS ROSS IS NOT A FRIEND. STILL, HE DOESN'T DESERVE WHAT THE SKULL'S GOONS HAVE PLANNED.
NOW, NEVER LET IT BE SAID THAT THE **SKELETON CREW** DON'T RESPECT THE MILITARY. BUT YOU'RE NOT A **SOLDIER**, ARE YOU, ROSS?
YOU'RE A **TRAITOR.**
NO ONE DOES-- CERTAINLY NOT NATASHA OR MISTY.
I DIDN'T BETRAY ANYONE. I SERVED MY COUNTRY. AND IF YOU STICK AROUND, I'LL GLADLY SERVE YOU.
THAT'S ROSS-- ORNERY TO THE END.
I ALMOST ADMIRE HIM FOR IT. BUT EVEN SO...

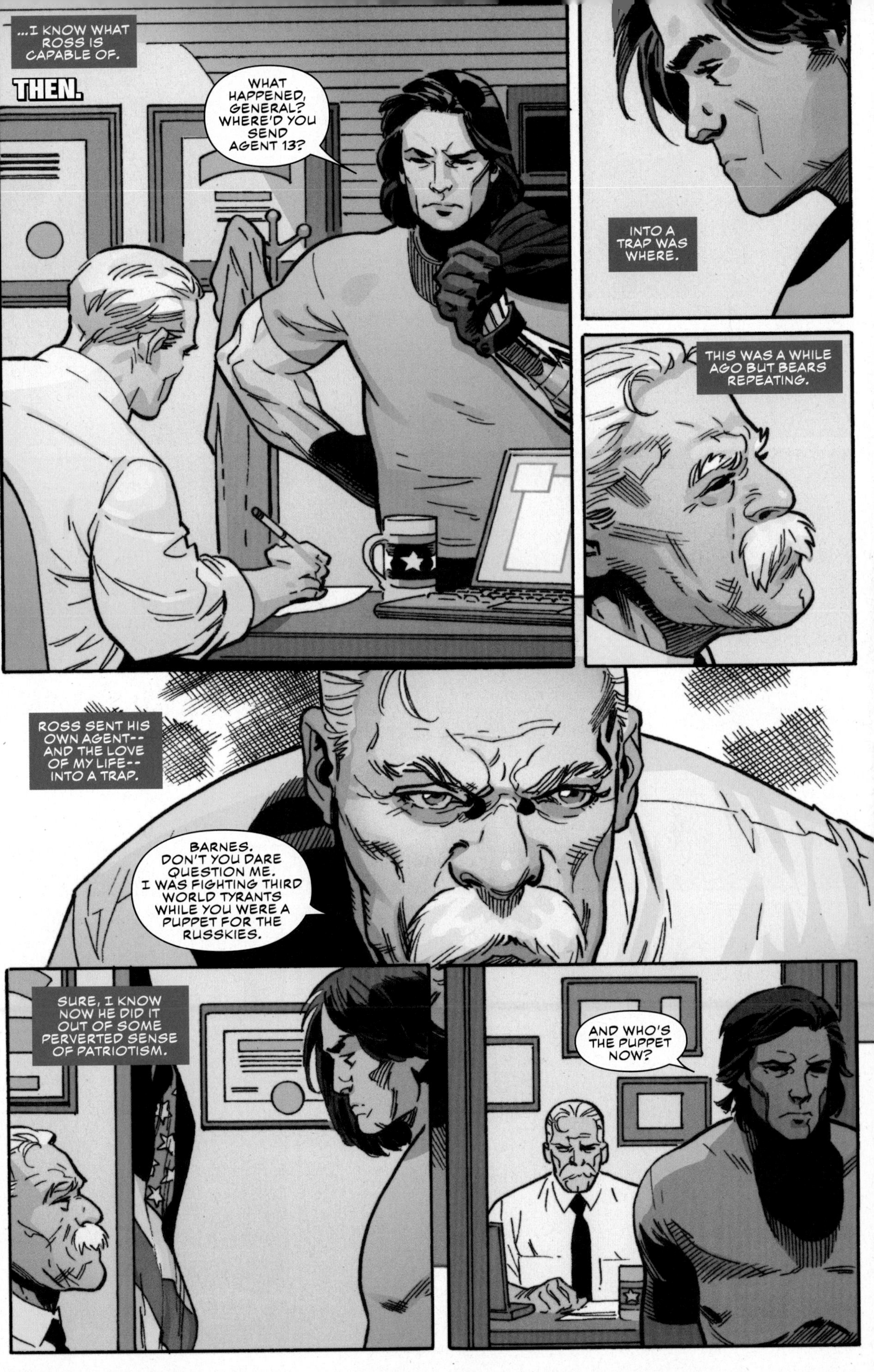
...I KNOW WHAT ROSS IS CAPABLE OF.
THEN.
WHAT HAPPENED, GENERAL? WHERE'D YOU SEND AGENT 13?
INTO A TRAP WAS WHERE.
THIS WAS A WHILE AGO BUT BEARS REPEATING.
ROSS SENT HIS OWN AGENT-- AND THE LOVE OF MY LIFE-- INTO A TRAP.
BARNES. DON'T YOU DARE QUESTION ME. I WAS FIGHTING THIRD WORLD TYRANTS WHILE YOU WERE A PUPPET FOR THE RUSSKIES.
SURE, I KNOW NOW HE DID IT OUT OF SOME PERVERTED SENSE OF PATRIOTISM.
AND WHO'S THE PUPPET NOW?

NOW.

THE TRUTH IS WE'VE ALL BEEN PUPPETS.

LET'S SEE WHAT WE HAVE.

TOYS PLAYED WITH BY HYDRA, OUR WORST INSTINCTS USED AGAINST US.

OKAY, THEN.

WHAT CAN WE FIND OUT FROM THIS...?

AMONG THOSE INSTINCTS: BLIND LOYALTY-- LOYALTY TO ME.

THOSE CHARGES SHOULD HAVE TAKEN OUT MADRIPOOR'S AIRPOWER... AND YET...

"IT'S NOT YOUR FAULT," SHARON WOULD SAY.

TRUE.

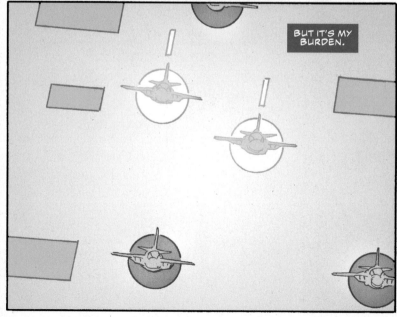

BUT IT'S MY BURDEN.

DAMMIT.

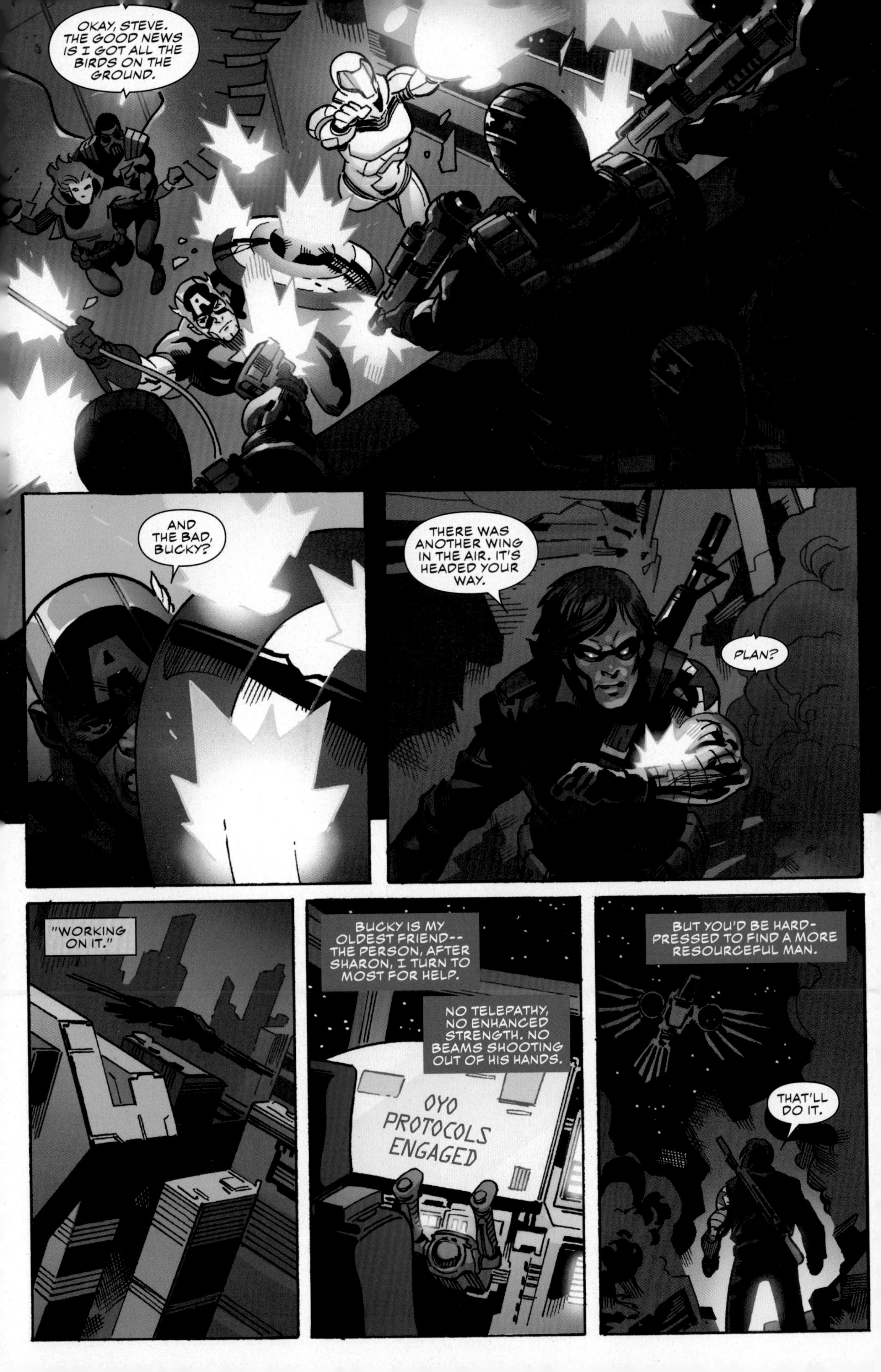
OKAY, STEVE. THE GOOD NEWS IS I GOT ALL THE BIRDS ON THE GROUND.
AND THE BAD, BUCKY?
THERE WAS ANOTHER WING IN THE AIR. IT'S HEADED YOUR WAY.
PLAN?
"WORKING ON IT."
BUCKY IS MY OLDEST FRIEND-- THE PERSON, AFTER SHARON, I TURN TO MOST FOR HELP.
NO TELEPATHY, NO ENHANCED STRENGTH. NO BEAMS SHOOTING OUT OF HIS HANDS.
OYO PROTOCOLS ENGAGED
BUT YOU'D BE HARD-PRESSED TO FIND A MORE RESOURCEFUL MAN.
THAT'LL DO IT.

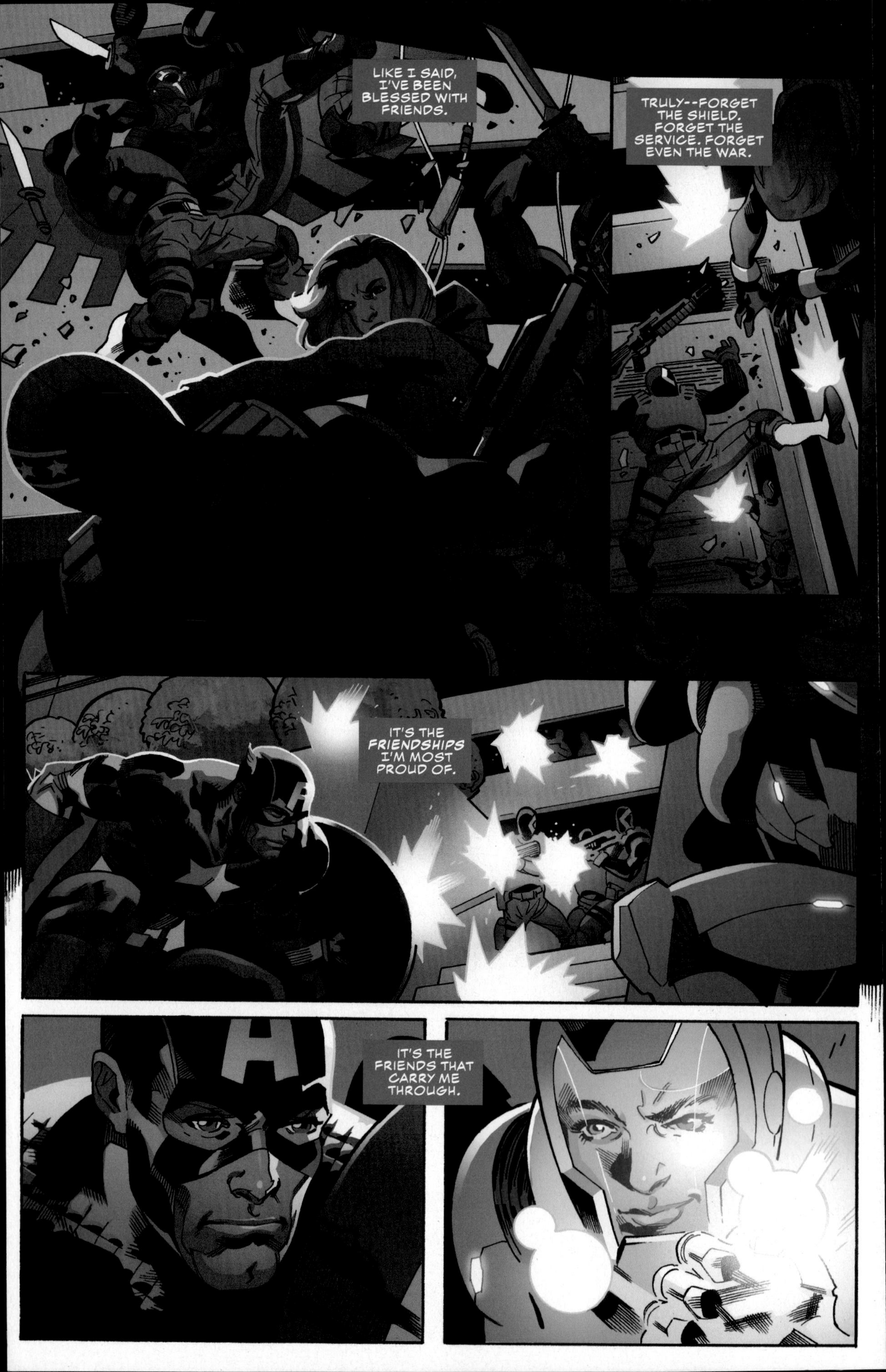
LIKE I SAID, I'VE BEEN BLESSED WITH FRIENDS.
TRULY--FORGET THE SHIELD. FORGET THE SERVICE. FORGET EVEN THE WAR.
IT'S THE FRIENDSHIPS I'M MOST PROUD OF.
IT'S THE FRIENDS THAT CARRY ME THROUGH.

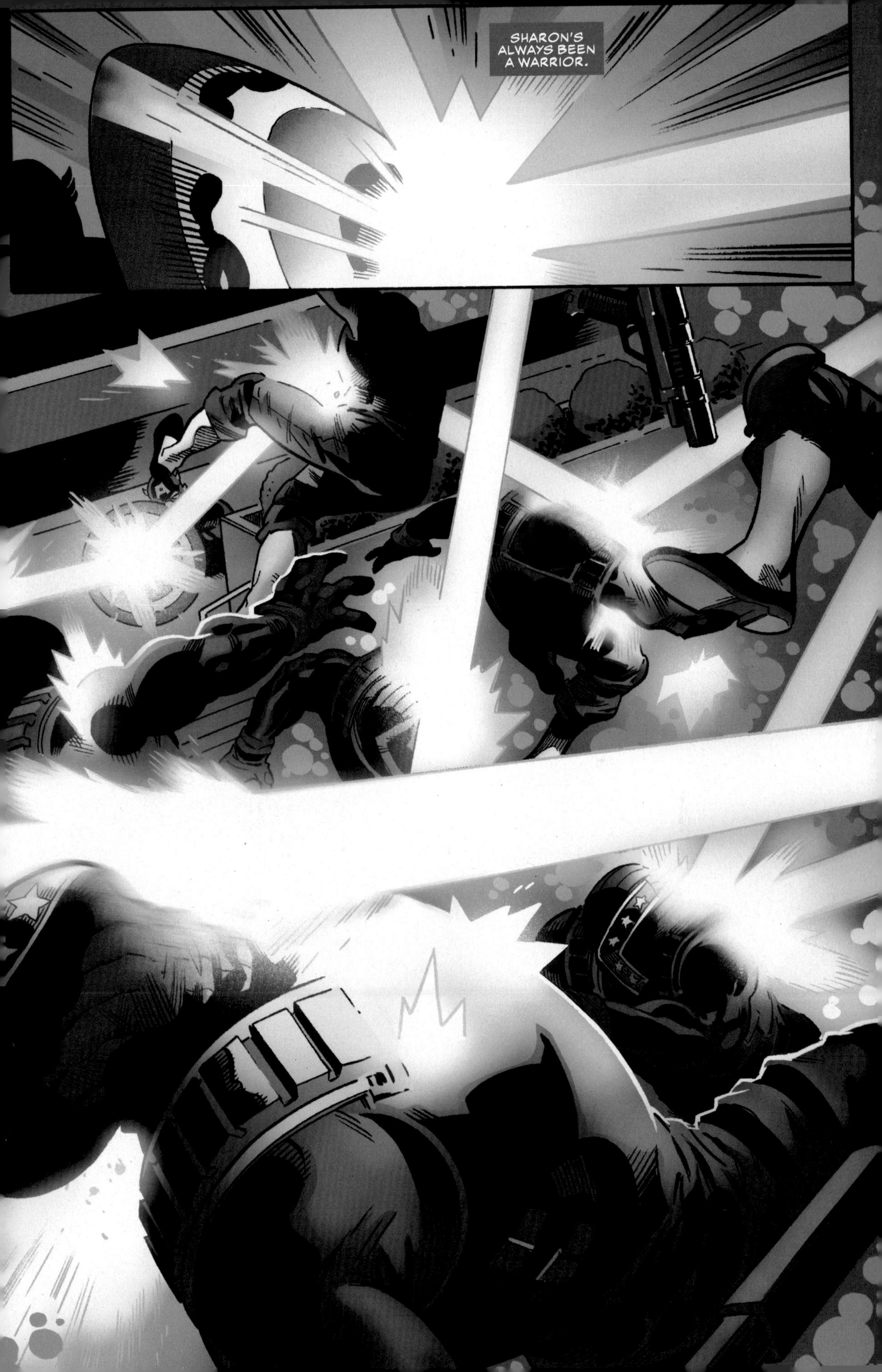
SHARON'S ALWAYS BEEN A WARRIOR.

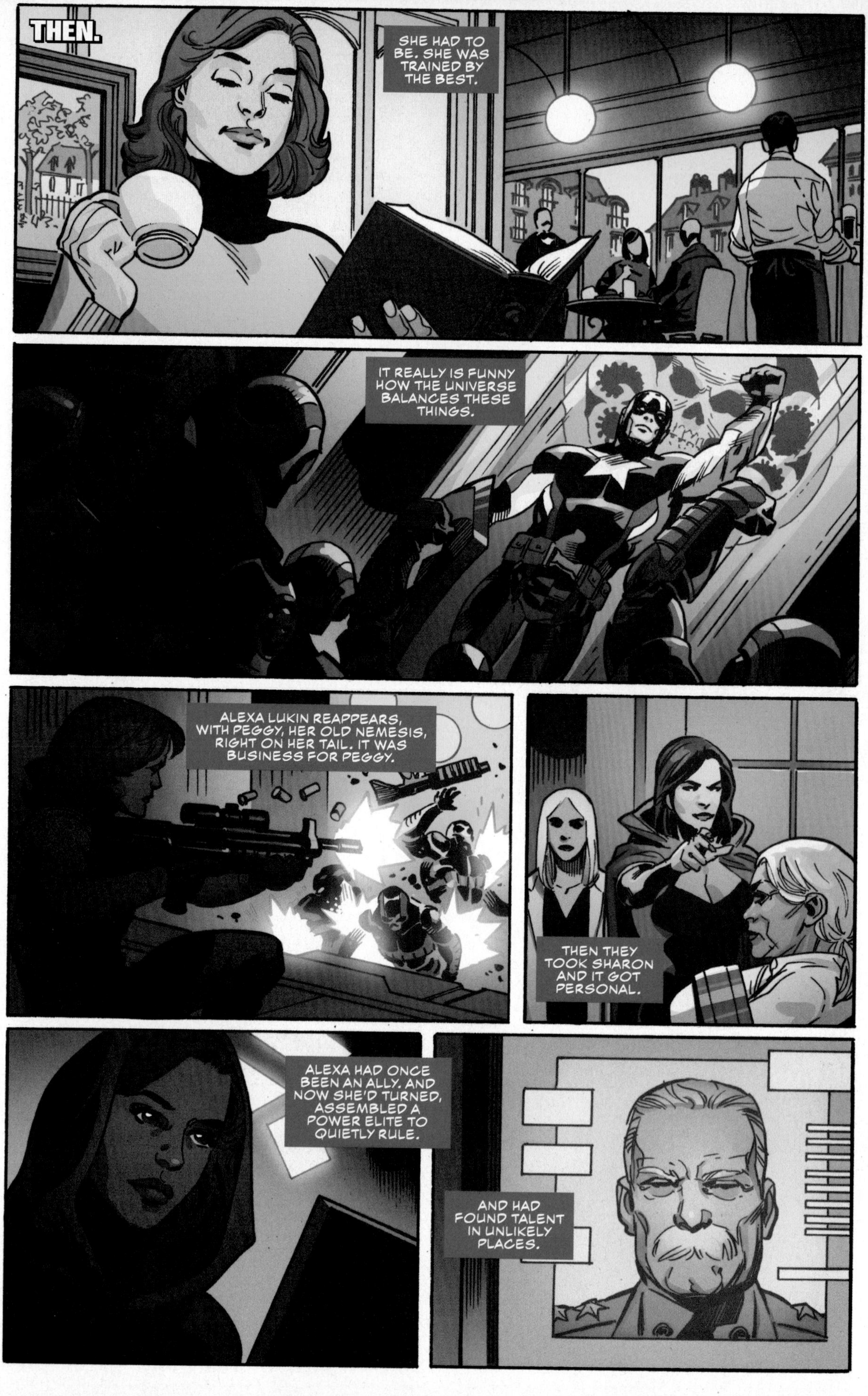
THEN.
SHE HAD TO BE. SHE WAS TRAINED BY THE BEST.
IT REALLY IS FUNNY HOW THE UNIVERSE BALANCES THESE THINGS.
ALEXA LUKIN REAPPEARS, WITH PEGGY, HER OLD NEMESIS, RIGHT ON HER TAIL. IT WAS BUSINESS FOR PEGGY.
THEN THEY TOOK SHARON AND IT GOT PERSONAL.
ALEXA HAD ONCE BEEN AN ALLY, AND NOW SHE'D TURNED, ASSEMBLED A POWER ELITE TO QUIETLY RULE.
AND HAD FOUND TALENT IN UNLIKELY PLACES.

YOU'RE S-S'POSED TO BE SOME KIND OF KILLER...

C-COME ON, CROSSBONES. T-THAT ALL YOU GOT?

NOT EVEN CLOSE.

IS ROSS TRYING TO GET KILLED?

NO. HE IS TRYING TO BE REBORN.

BROCK! THE PLANES ARE ON THE WAY.

TIME TO JET, SWEET CHEEKS!

YOU'RE S-S'POSED TO BE SOME

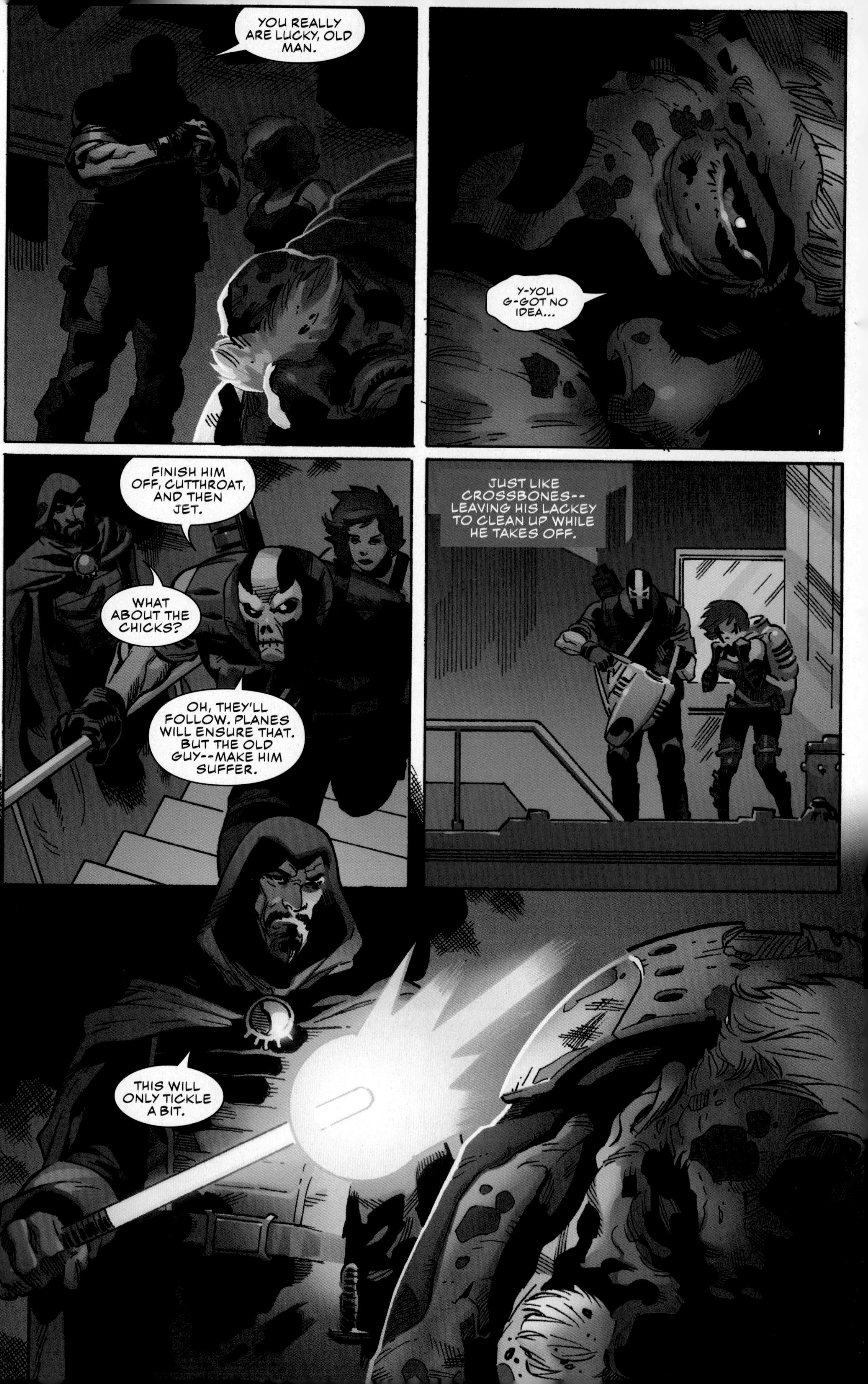

YOU REALLY ARE LUCKY, OLD MAN.
Y-YOU G-GOT NO IDEA...
FINISH HIM OFF, CUTTHROAT, AND THEN JET.
WHAT ABOUT THE CHICKS?
OH, THEY'LL FOLLOW. PLANES WILL ENSURE THAT. BUT THE OLD GUY--MAKE HIM SUFFER.
JUST LIKE CROSSBONES--LEAVING HIS LACKEY TO CLEAN UP WHILE HE TAKES OFF.
THIS WILL ONLY TICKLE A BIT.

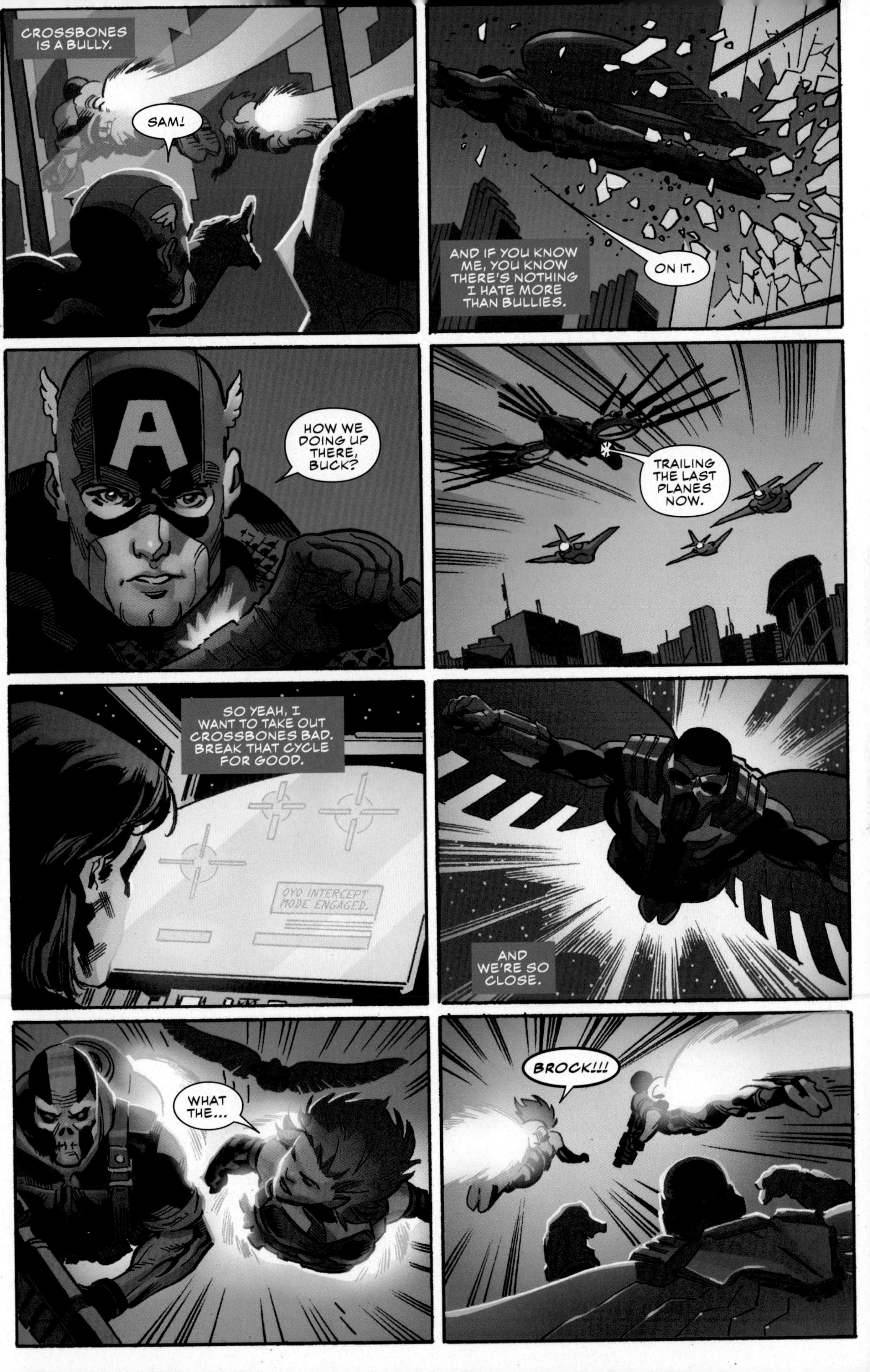
CROSSBONES IS A BULLY.
SAM!
AND IF YOU KNOW ME, YOU KNOW THERE'S NOTHING I HATE MORE THAN BULLIES.
ON IT.
HOW WE DOING UP THERE, BUCK?
TRAILING THE LAST PLANES NOW.
SO YEAH, I WANT TO TAKE OUT CROSSBONES BAD. BREAK THAT CYCLE FOR GOOD.
OYO INTERCEPT MODE ENGAGED.
AND WE'RE SO CLOSE.
WHAT THE...
BROCK!!!

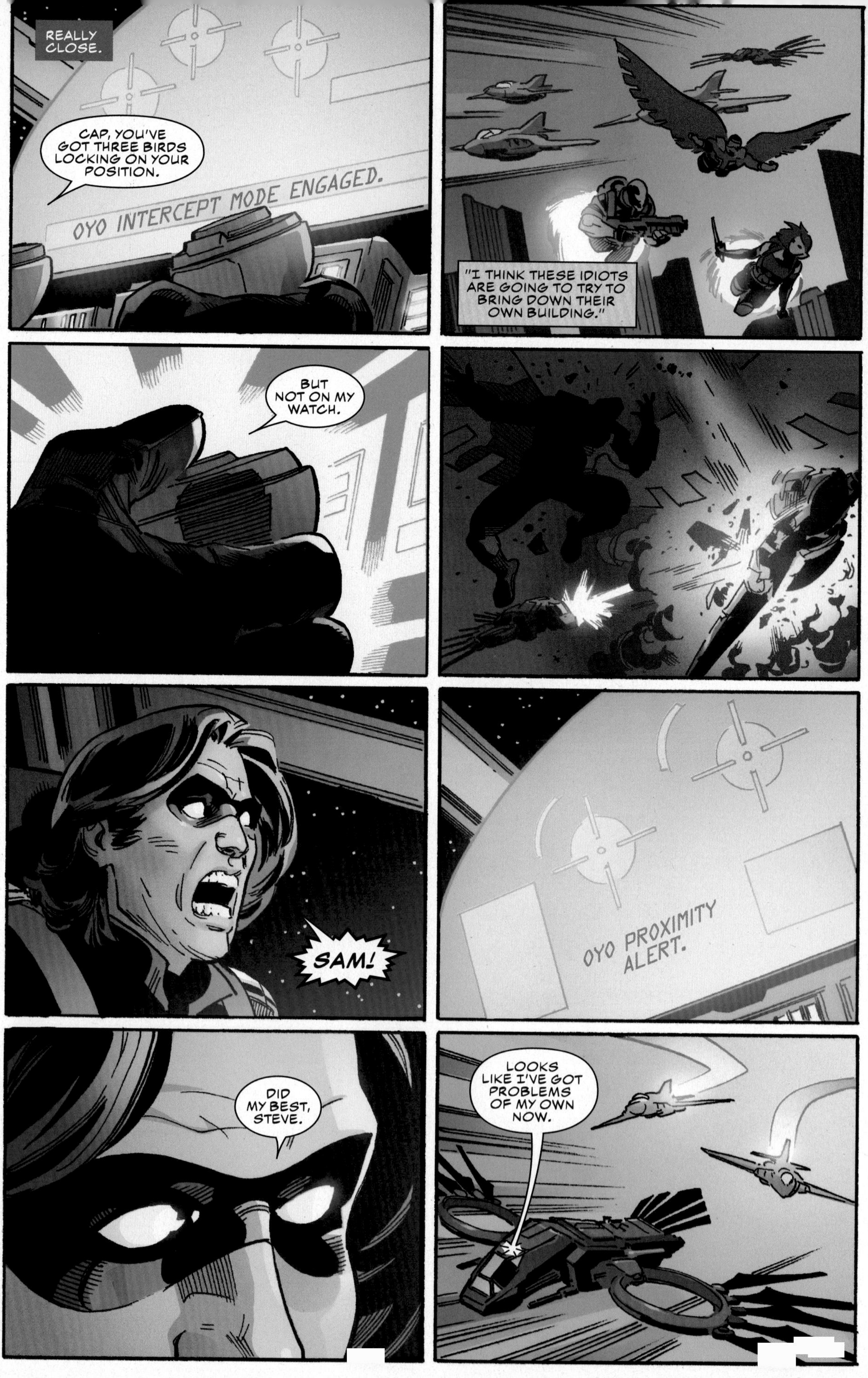
REALLY CLOSE.
CAP, YOU'VE GOT THREE BIRDS LOCKING ON YOUR POSITION.
OYO INTERCEPT MODE ENGAGED.
"I THINK THESE IDIOTS ARE GOING TO TRY TO BRING DOWN THEIR OWN BUILDING."
BUT NOT ON MY WATCH.
SAM!
OYO PROXIMITY ALERT.
DID MY BEST, STEVE.
LOOKS LIKE I'VE GOT PROBLEMS OF MY OWN NOW.

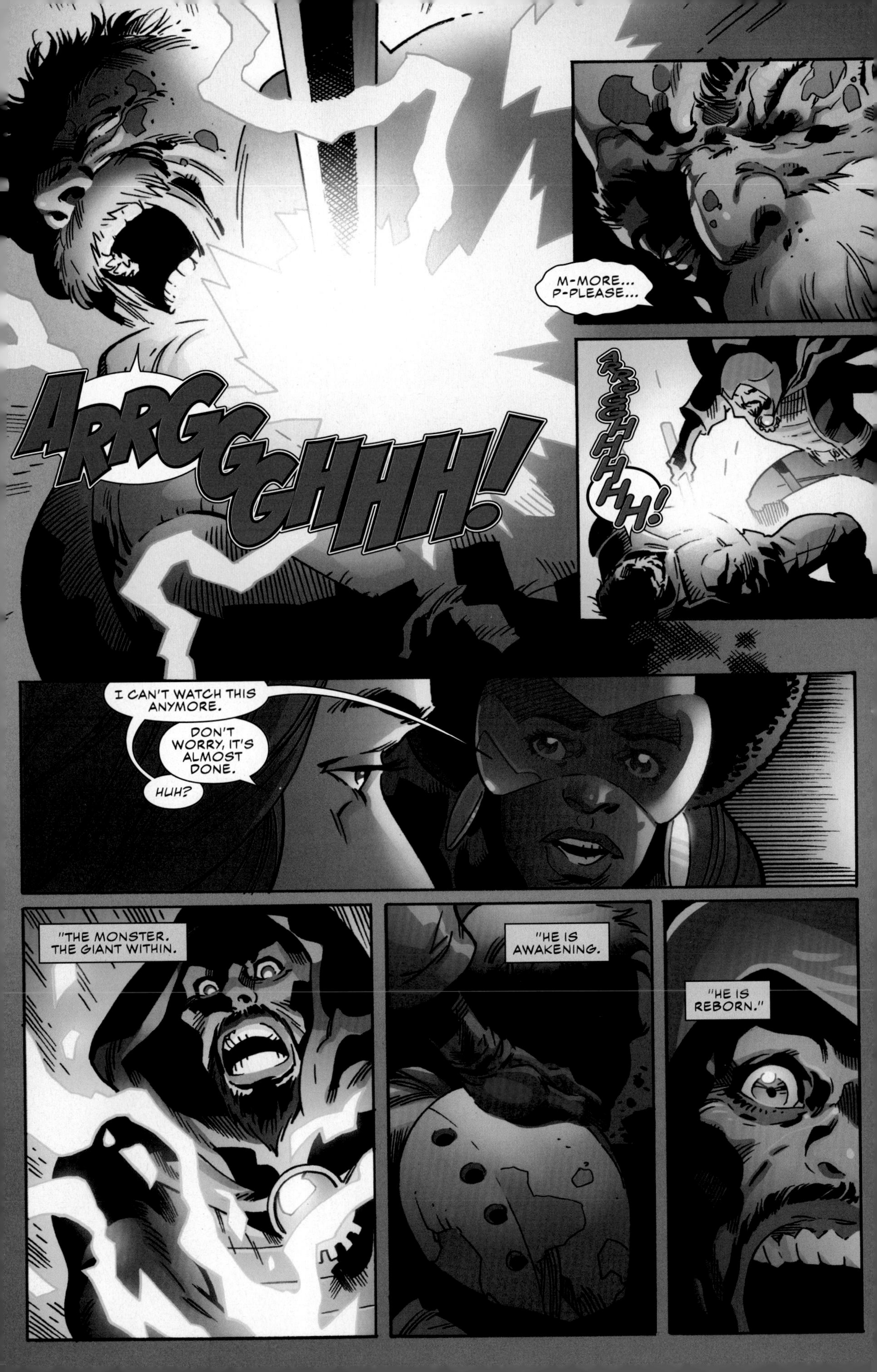
ARRGGGHHHH!
M-MORE... P-PLEASE...
ARGGHHHHHH!
I CAN'T WATCH THIS ANYMORE.
DON'T WORRY, IT'S ALMOST DONE.
HUH?
"THE MONSTER. THE GIANT WITHIN.
"HE IS AWAKENING.
"HE IS REBORN."

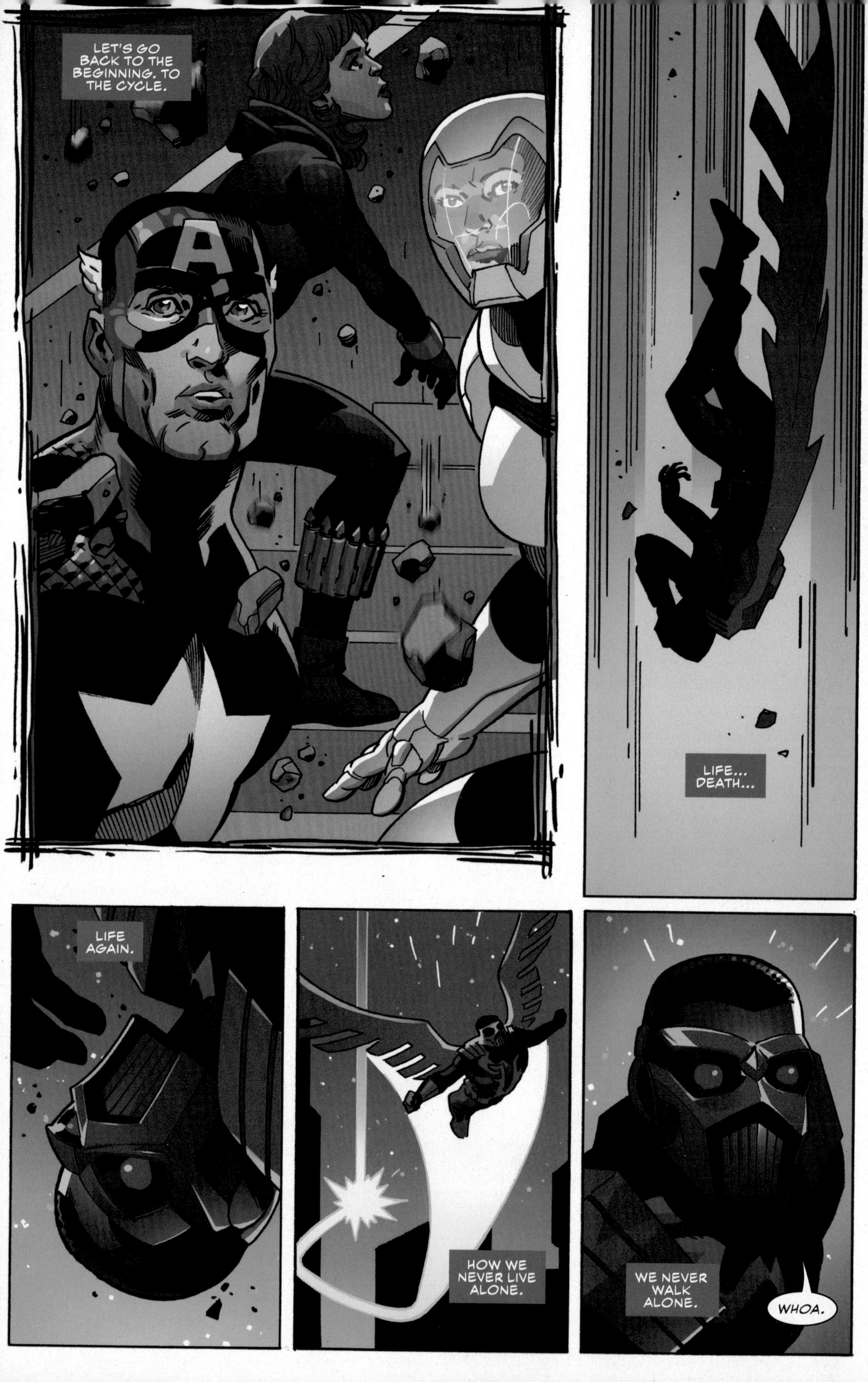
LET'S GO BACK TO THE BEGINNING. TO THE CYCLE.
LIFE... DEATH...
LIFE AGAIN.
HOW WE NEVER LIVE ALONE.
WE NEVER WALK ALONE.
WHOA.

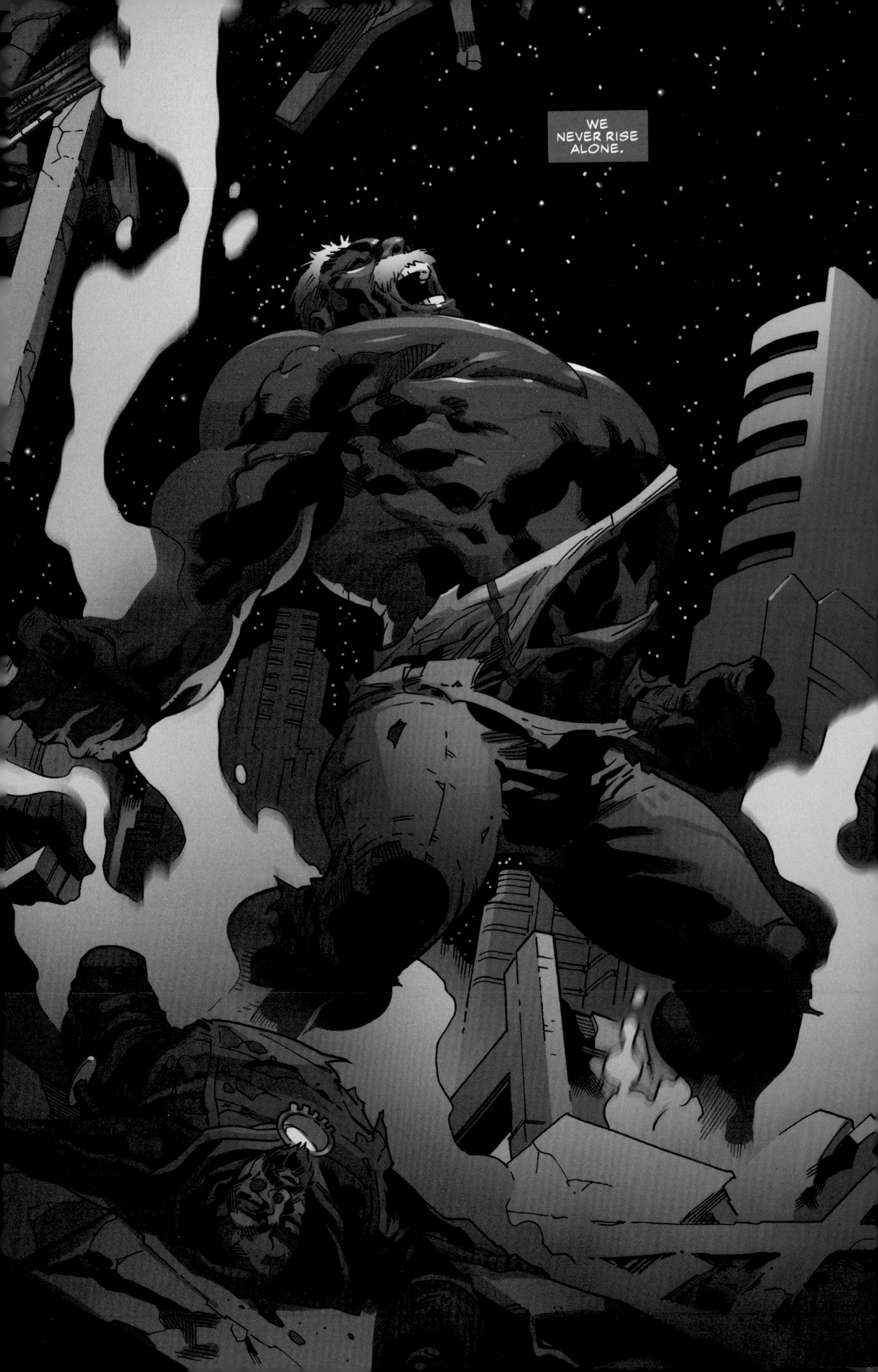
WE NEVER RISE ALONE.

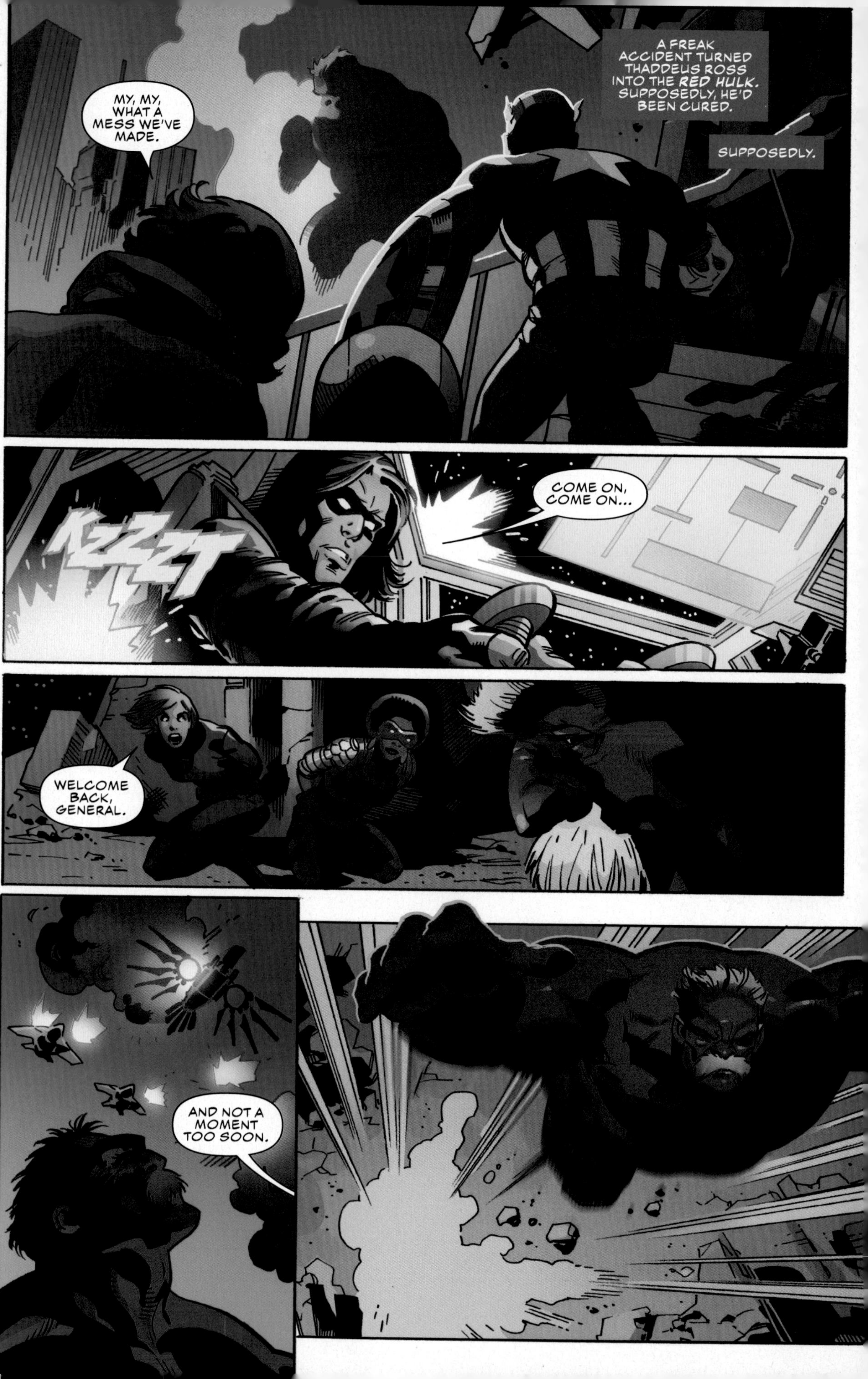
A FREAK ACCIDENT TURNED THADDEUS ROSS INTO THE RED HULK. SUPPOSEDLY, HE'D BEEN CURED.
MY, MY, WHAT A MESS WE'VE MADE.
SUPPOSEDLY.
KZZZZT
COME ON, COME ON...
WELCOME BACK, GENERAL.
AND NOT A MOMENT TOO SOON.

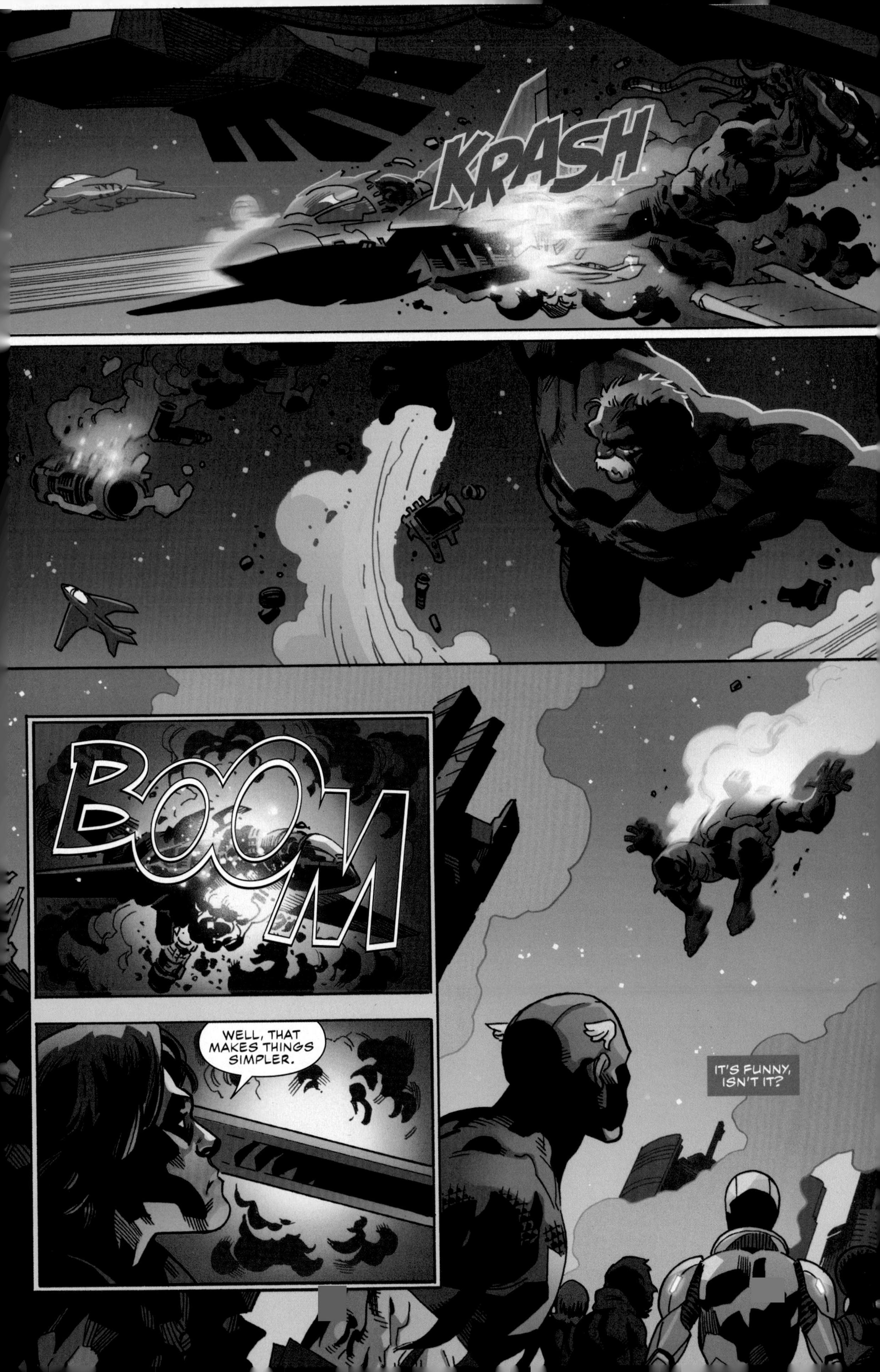
KRASH
BOOM
WELL, THAT MAKES THINGS SIMPLER.
IT'S FUNNY, ISN'T IT?

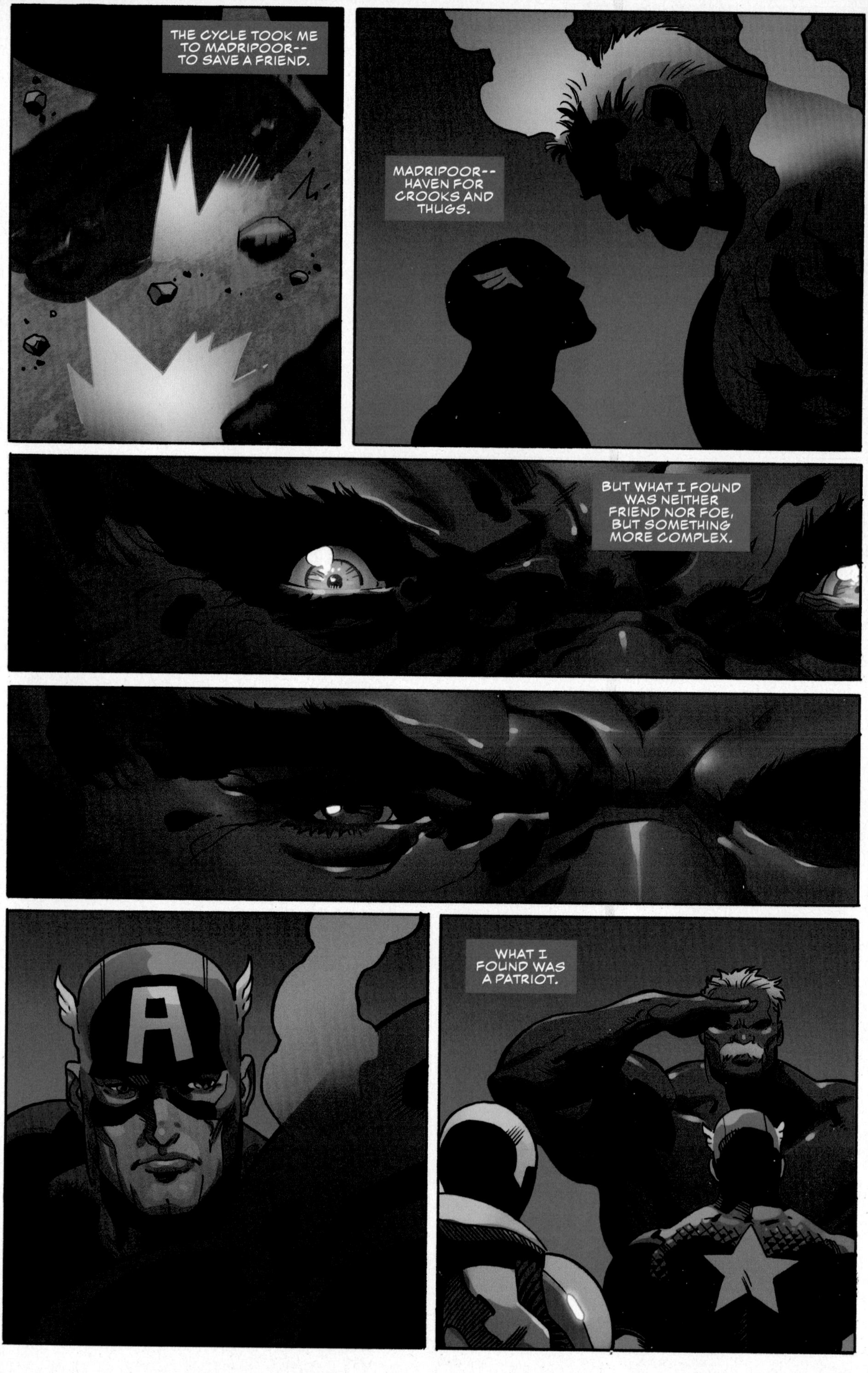
THE CYCLE TOOK ME TO MADRIPOOR-- TO SAVE A FRIEND.
MADRIPOOR-- HAVEN FOR CROOKS AND THUGS.
BUT WHAT I FOUND WAS NEITHER FRIEND NOR FOE, BUT SOMETHING MORE COMPLEX.
WHAT I FOUND WAS A PATRIOT.

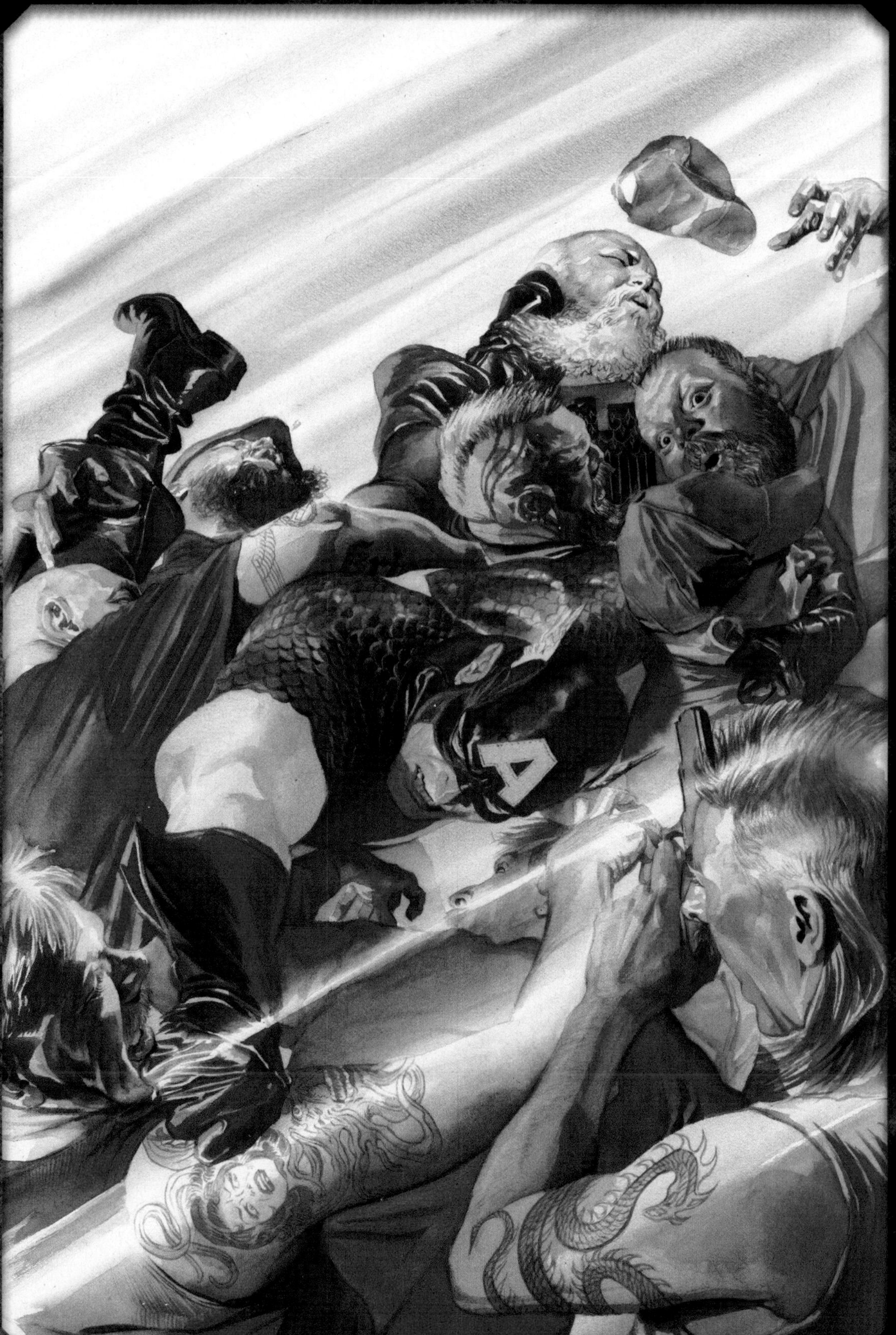

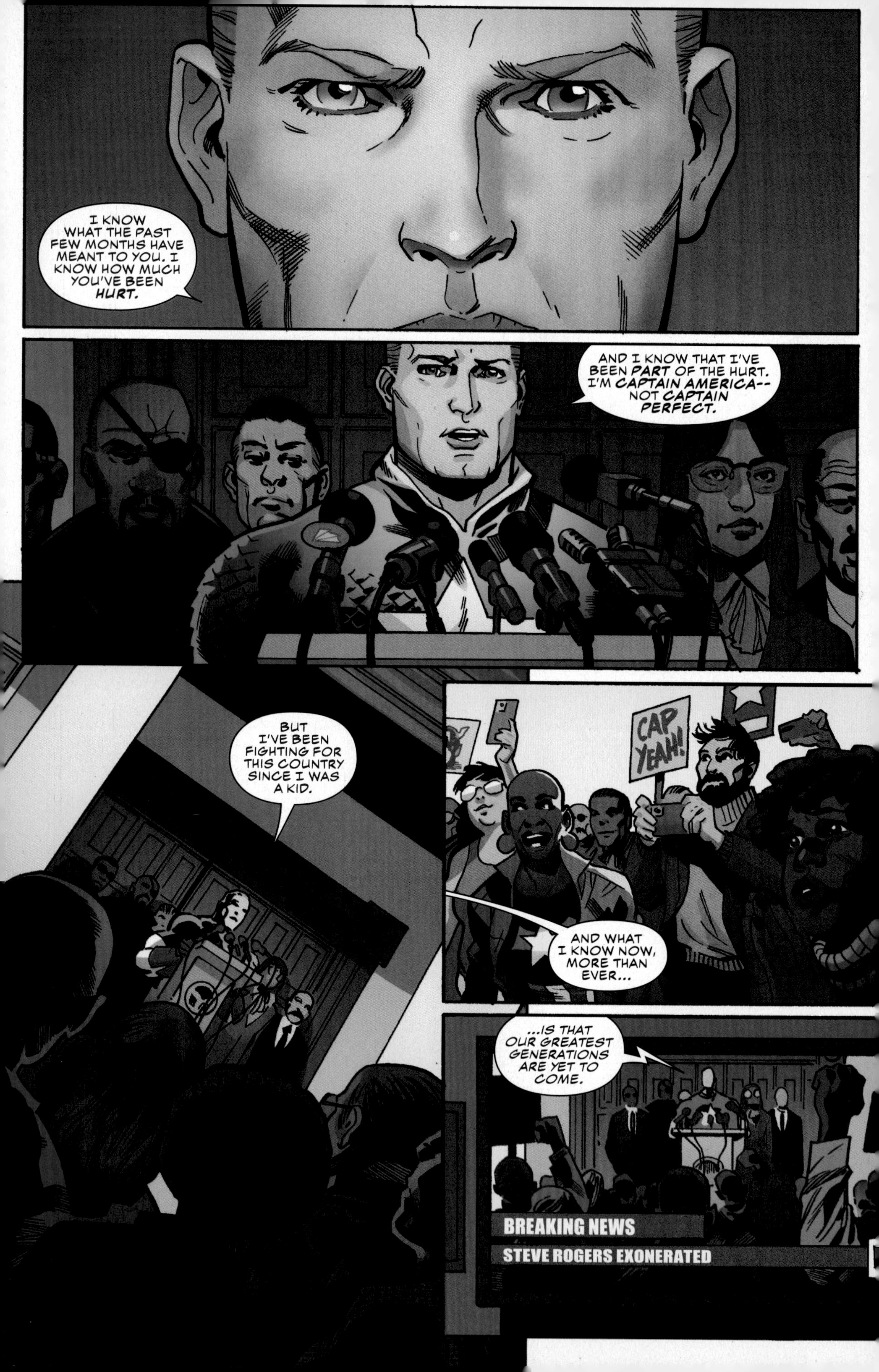
I KNOW WHAT THE PAST FEW MONTHS HAVE MEANT TO YOU. I KNOW HOW MUCH YOU'VE BEEN HURT.
AND I KNOW THAT I'VE BEEN PART OF THE HURT. I'M CAPTAIN AMERICA-- NOT CAPTAIN PERFECT.
BUT I'VE BEEN FIGHTING FOR THIS COUNTRY SINCE I WAS A KID.
CAP YEAH!
AND WHAT I KNOW NOW, MORE THAN EVER...
...IS THAT OUR GREATEST GENERATIONS ARE YET TO COME.
BREAKING NEWS
STEVE ROGERS EXONERATED

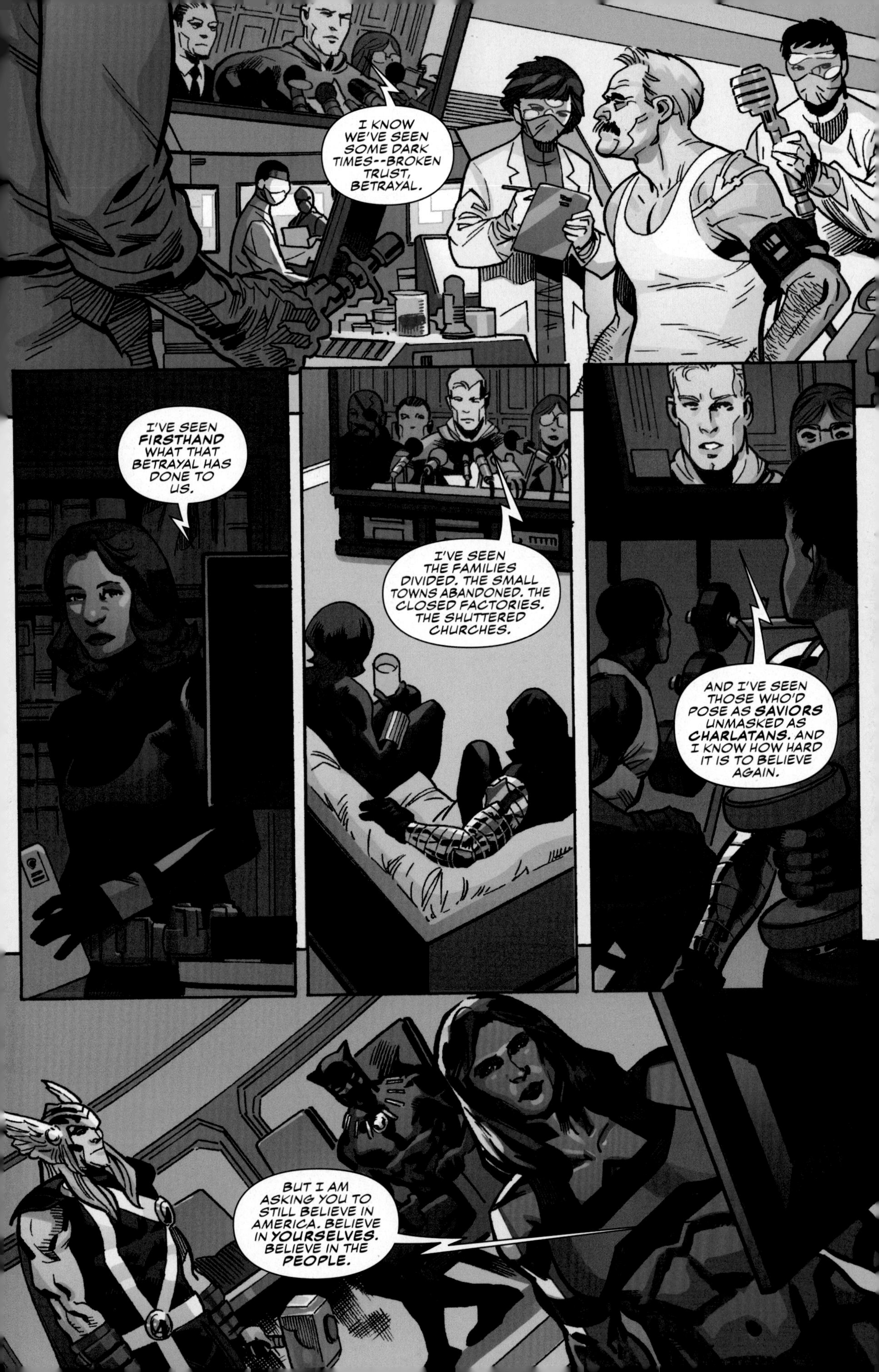
I KNOW WE'VE SEEN SOME DARK TIMES--BROKEN TRUST, BETRAYAL.
I'VE SEEN **FIRSTHAND** WHAT THAT BETRAYAL HAS DONE TO US.
I'VE SEEN THE FAMILIES DIVIDED. THE SMALL TOWNS ABANDONED. THE CLOSED FACTORIES. THE SHUTTERED CHURCHES.
AND I'VE SEEN THOSE WHO'D POSE AS **SAVIORS** UNMASKED AS **CHARLATANS.** AND I KNOW HOW HARD IT IS TO BELIEVE AGAIN.
BUT I AM ASKING YOU TO STILL BELIEVE IN AMERICA. BELIEVE IN **YOURSELVES.** BELIEVE IN THE **PEOPLE.**

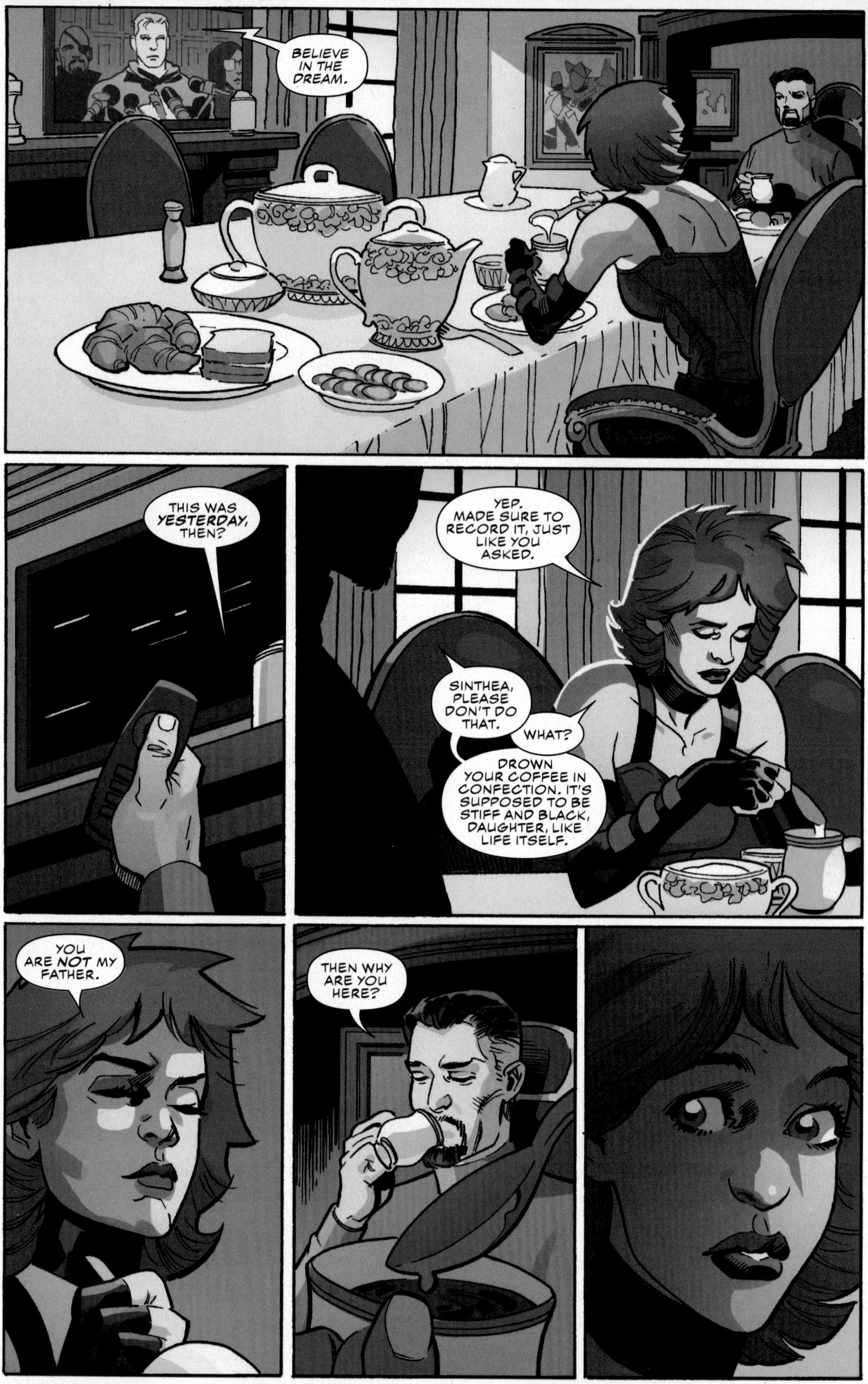
BELIEVE IN THE DREAM.
THIS WAS YESTERDAY, THEN?
YEP. MADE SURE TO RECORD IT, JUST LIKE YOU ASKED.
SINTHEA, PLEASE DON'T DO THAT.
WHAT?
DROWN YOUR COFFEE IN CONFECTION. IT'S SUPPOSED TO BE STIFF AND BLACK, DAUGHTER, LIKE LIFE ITSELF.
YOU ARE NOT MY FATHER.
THEN WHY ARE YOU HERE?

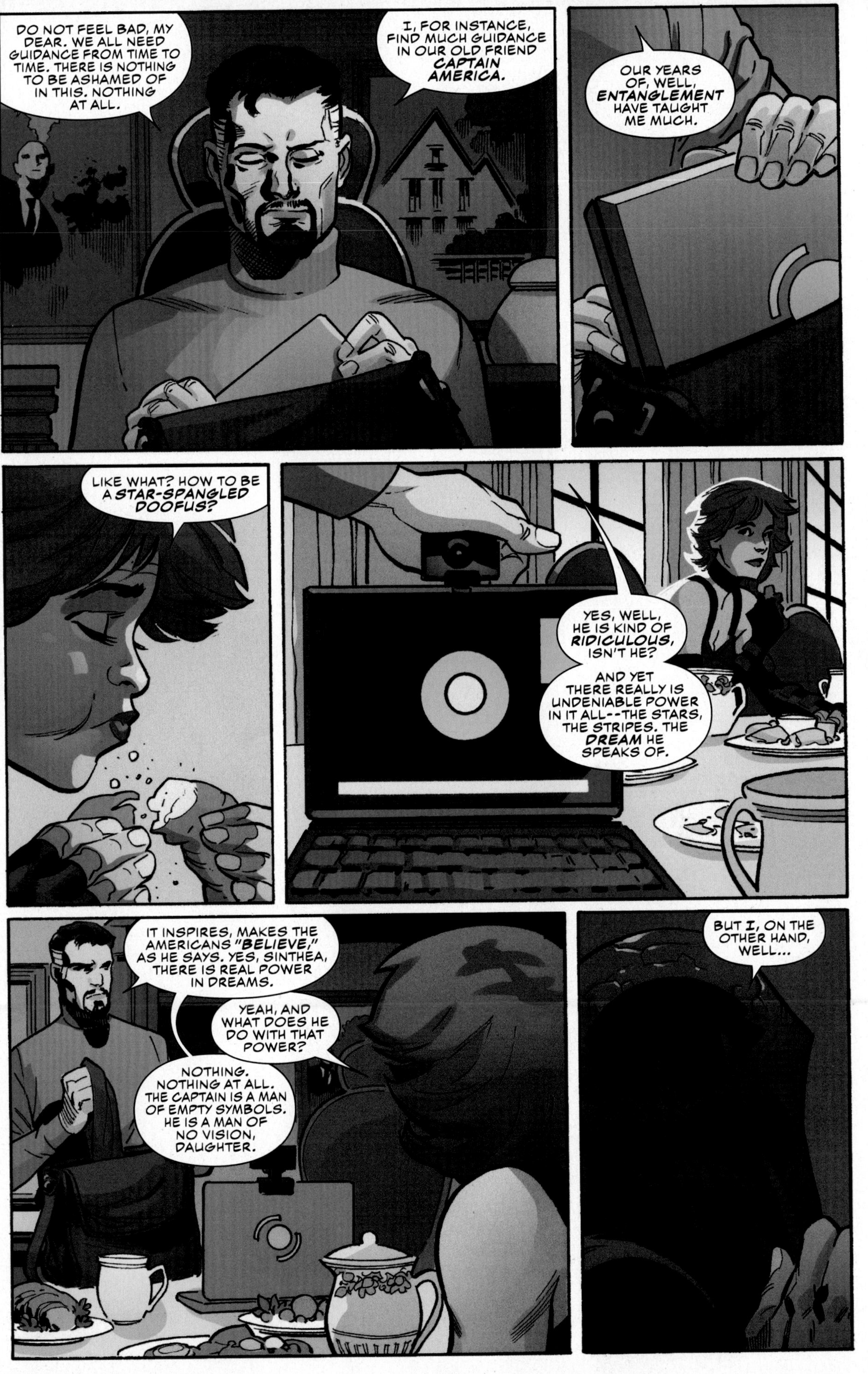
DO NOT FEEL BAD, MY DEAR. WE ALL NEED GUIDANCE FROM TIME TO TIME. THERE IS NOTHING TO BE ASHAMED OF IN THIS. NOTHING AT ALL.
I, FOR INSTANCE, FIND MUCH GUIDANCE IN OUR OLD FRIEND CAPTAIN AMERICA.
OUR YEARS OF, WELL, ENTANGLEMENT HAVE TAUGHT ME MUCH.
LIKE WHAT? HOW TO BE A STAR-SPANGLED DOOFUS?
YES, WELL, HE IS KIND OF RIDICULOUS, ISN'T HE?
AND YET THERE REALLY IS UNDENIABLE POWER IN IT ALL--THE STARS, THE STRIPES. THE DREAM HE SPEAKS OF.
IT INSPIRES, MAKES THE AMERICANS "BELIEVE," AS HE SAYS. YES, SINTHEA, THERE IS REAL POWER IN DREAMS.
YEAH, AND WHAT DOES HE DO WITH THAT POWER?
NOTHING. NOTHING AT ALL. THE CAPTAIN IS A MAN OF EMPTY SYMBOLS. HE IS A MAN OF NO VISION, DAUGHTER.
BUT I, ON THE OTHER HAND, WELL...

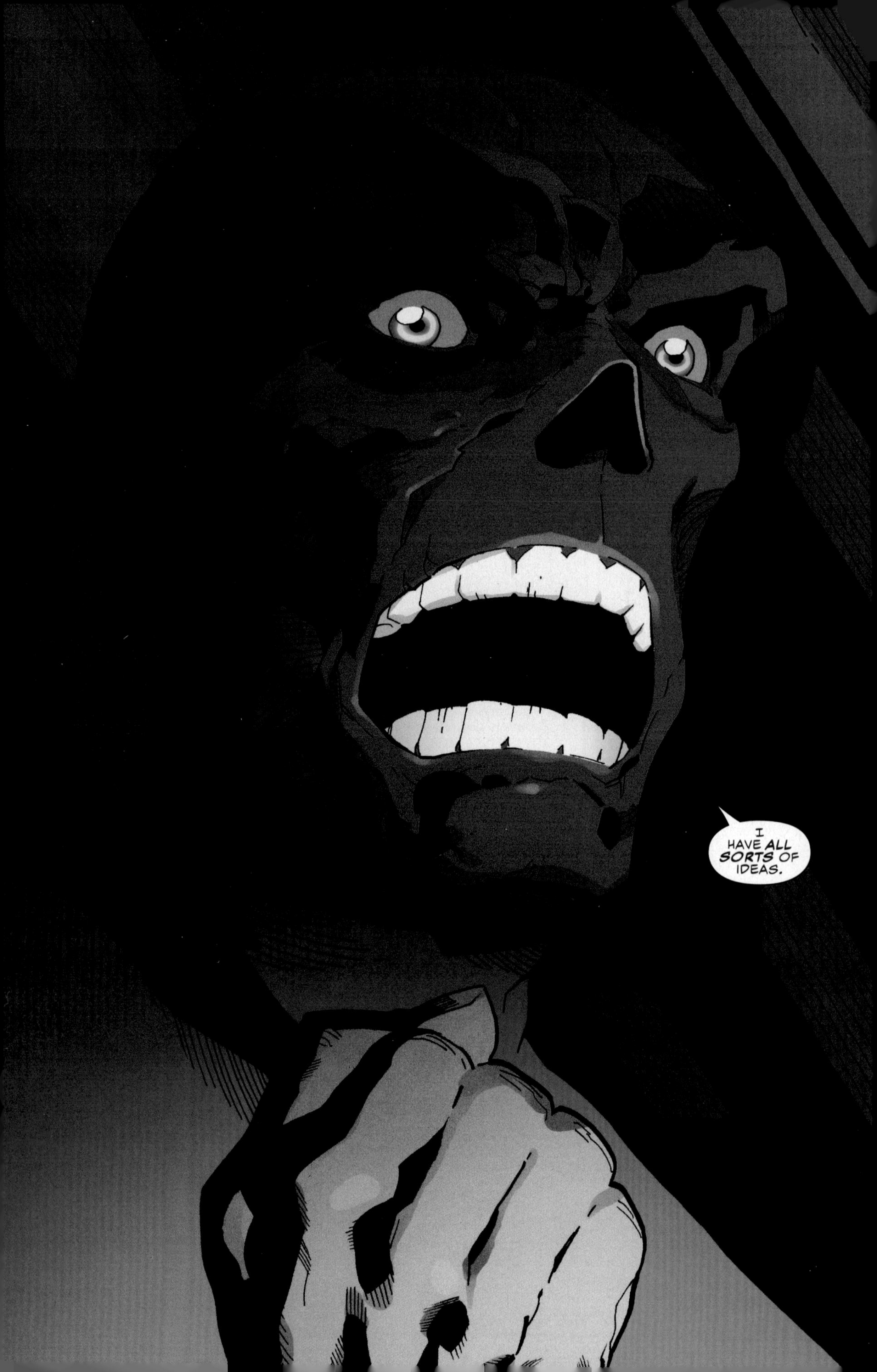
I HAVE ALL SORTS OF IDEAS.

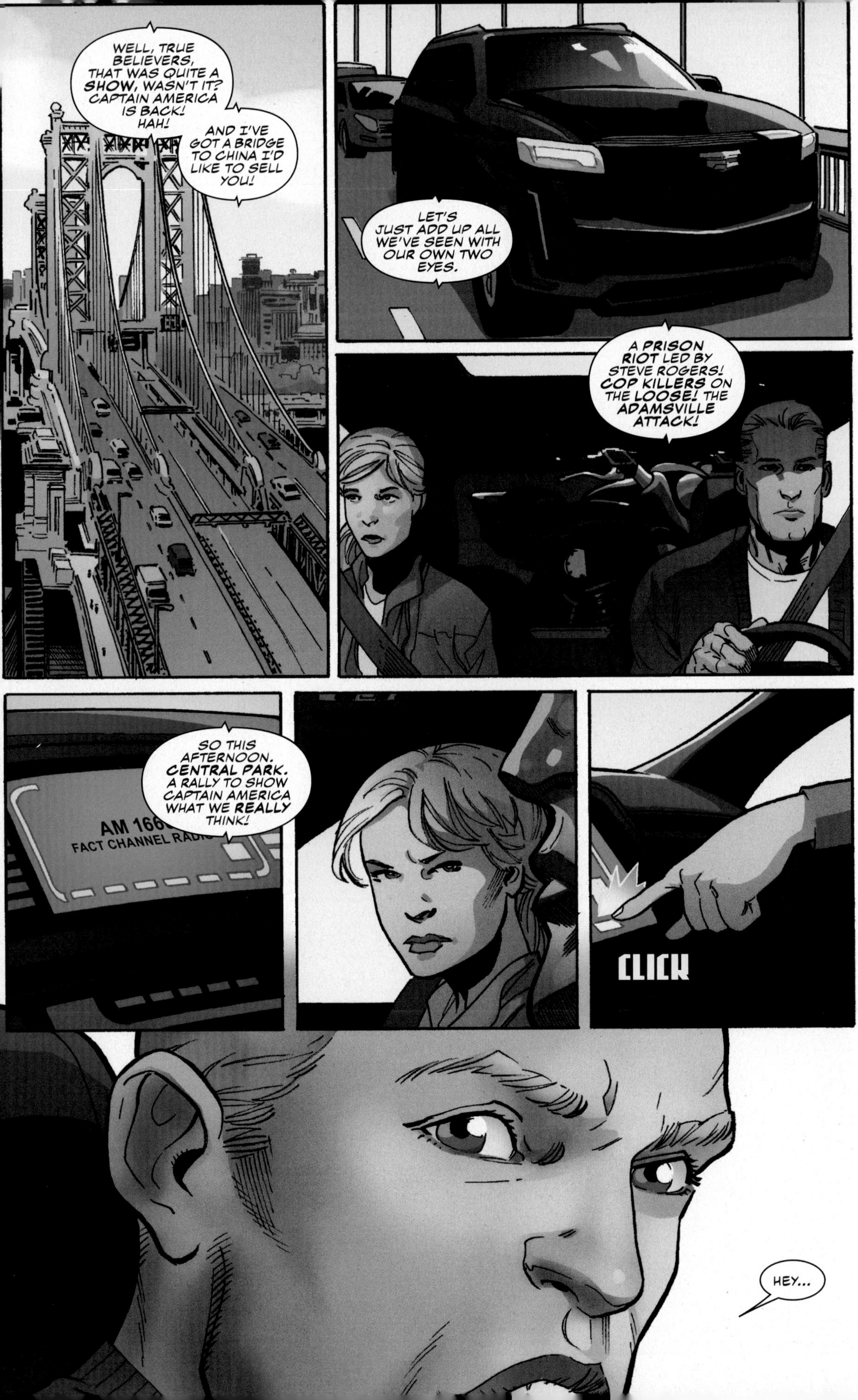
WELL, TRUE BELIEVERS, THAT WAS QUITE A SHOW, WASN'T IT? CAPTAIN AMERICA IS BACK! HAH!
AND I'VE GOT A BRIDGE TO CHINA I'D LIKE TO SELL YOU!
LET'S JUST ADD UP ALL WE'VE SEEN WITH OUR OWN TWO EYES.
A PRISON RIOT LED BY STEVE ROGERS! COP KILLERS ON THE LOOSE! THE ADAMSVILLE ATTACK!
SO THIS AFTERNOON. CENTRAL PARK. A RALLY TO SHOW CAPTAIN AMERICA WHAT WE REALLY THINK!
FACT CHANNEL RADIO
CLICK
HEY...

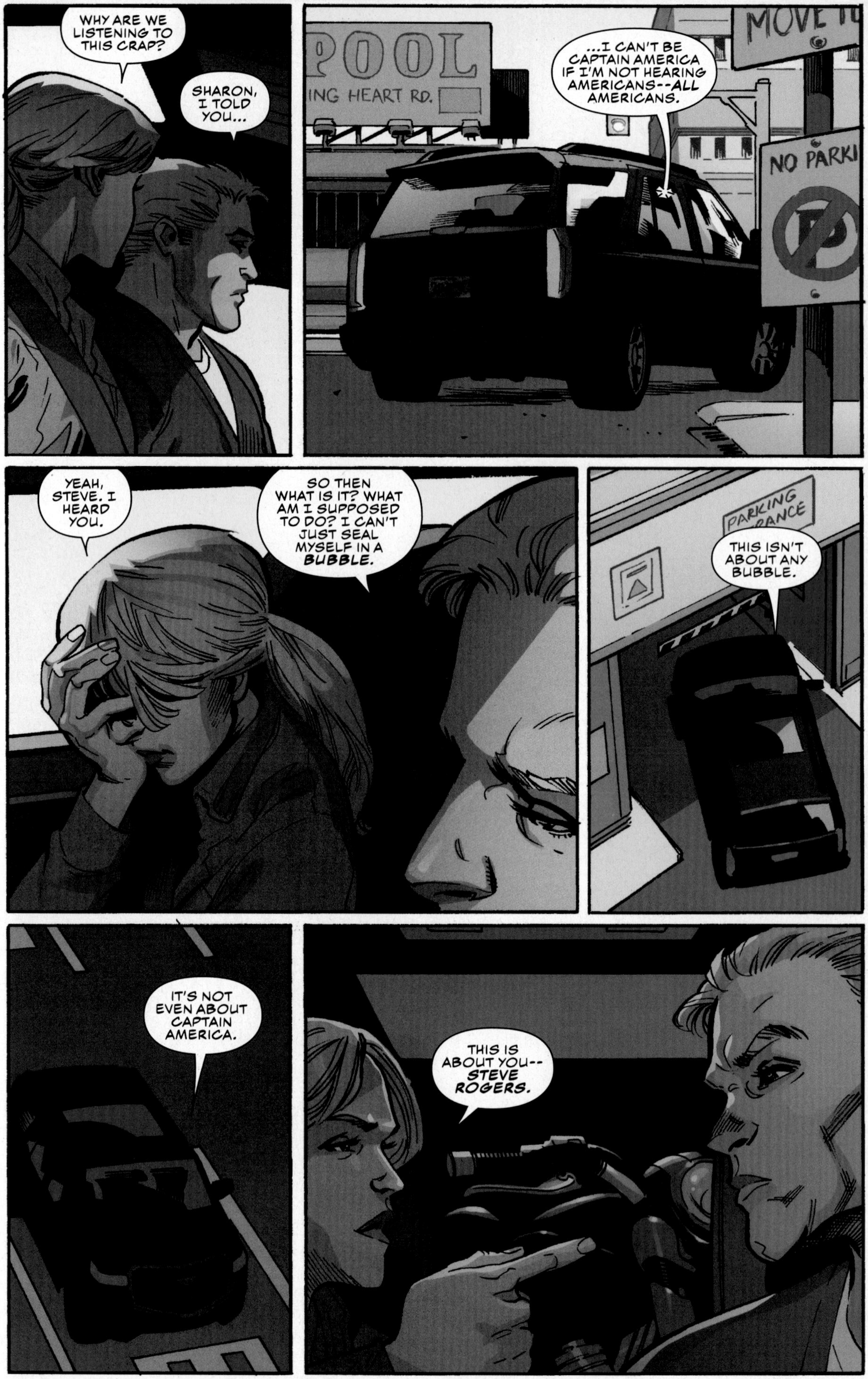
WHY ARE WE LISTENING TO THIS CRAP?
SHARON, I TOLD YOU...
POOL
ING HEART RD.
MOVE
...I CAN'T BE CAPTAIN AMERICA IF I'M NOT HEARING AMERICANS--ALL AMERICANS.
NO PARKI
YEAH, STEVE. I HEARD YOU.
SO THEN WHAT IS IT? WHAT AM I SUPPOSED TO DO? I CAN'T JUST SEAL MYSELF IN A BUBBLE.
PARKING
THIS ISN'T ABOUT ANY BUBBLE.
IT'S NOT EVEN ABOUT CAPTAIN AMERICA.
THIS IS ABOUT YOU--STEVE ROGERS.

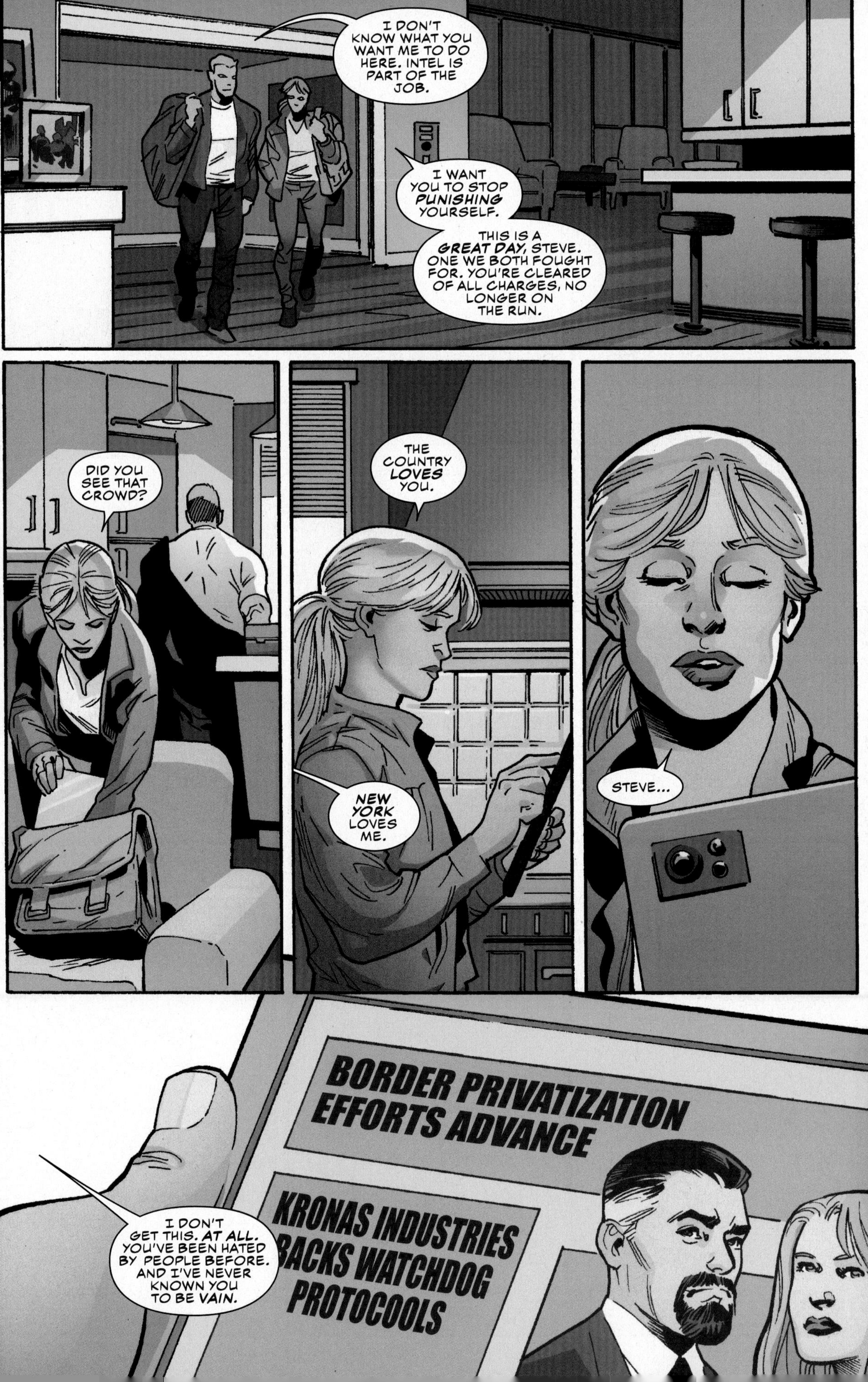
I DON'T KNOW WHAT YOU WANT ME TO DO HERE. INTEL IS PART OF THE JOB.
I WANT YOU TO STOP PUNISHING YOURSELF.
THIS IS A GREAT DAY, STEVE. ONE WE BOTH FOUGHT FOR. YOU'RE CLEARED OF ALL CHARGES, NO LONGER ON THE RUN.
DID YOU SEE THAT CROWD?
THE COUNTRY LOVES YOU.
NEW YORK LOVES ME.
STEVE...
BORDER PRIVATIZATION EFFORTS ADVANCE
KRONAS INDUSTRIES BACKS WATCHDOG PROTOCOOLS
I DON'T GET THIS. AT ALL. YOU'VE BEEN HATED BY PEOPLE BEFORE. AND I'VE NEVER KNOWN YOU TO BE VAIN.

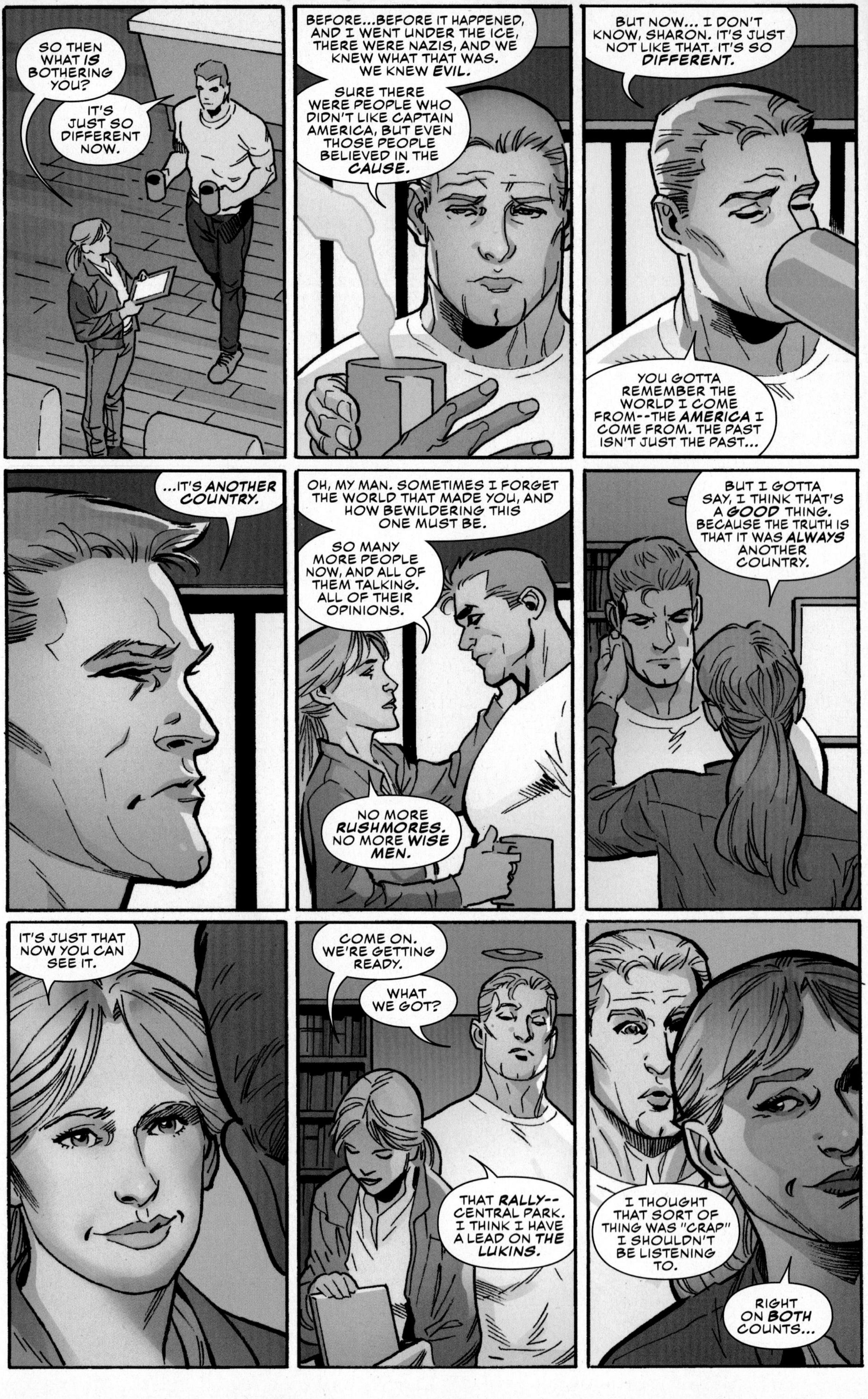
SO THEN WHAT IS BOTHERING YOU?
IT'S JUST SO DIFFERENT NOW.
BEFORE...BEFORE IT HAPPENED, AND I WENT UNDER THE ICE, THERE WERE NAZIS, AND WE KNEW WHAT THAT WAS. WE KNEW EVIL.
SURE THERE WERE PEOPLE WHO DIDN'T LIKE CAPTAIN AMERICA, BUT EVEN THOSE PEOPLE BELIEVED IN THE CAUSE.
BUT NOW... I DON'T KNOW, SHARON. IT'S JUST NOT LIKE THAT. IT'S SO DIFFERENT.
YOU GOTTA REMEMBER THE WORLD I COME FROM--THE AMERICA I COME FROM. THE PAST ISN'T JUST THE PAST...
...IT'S ANOTHER COUNTRY.
OH, MY MAN. SOMETIMES I FORGET THE WORLD THAT MADE YOU, AND HOW BEWILDERING THIS ONE MUST BE.
SO MANY MORE PEOPLE NOW, AND ALL OF THEM TALKING. ALL OF THEIR OPINIONS.
NO MORE RUSHMORES. NO MORE WISE MEN.
BUT I GOTTA SAY, I THINK THAT'S A GOOD THING. BECAUSE THE TRUTH IS THAT IT WAS ALWAYS ANOTHER COUNTRY.
IT'S JUST THAT NOW YOU CAN SEE IT.
COME ON. WE'RE GETTING READY.
WHAT WE GOT?
THAT RALLY-- CENTRAL PARK. I THINK I HAVE A LEAD ON THE LUKINS.
I THOUGHT THAT SORT OF THING WAS "CRAP" I SHOULDN'T BE LISTENING TO.
RIGHT ON BOTH COUNTS...

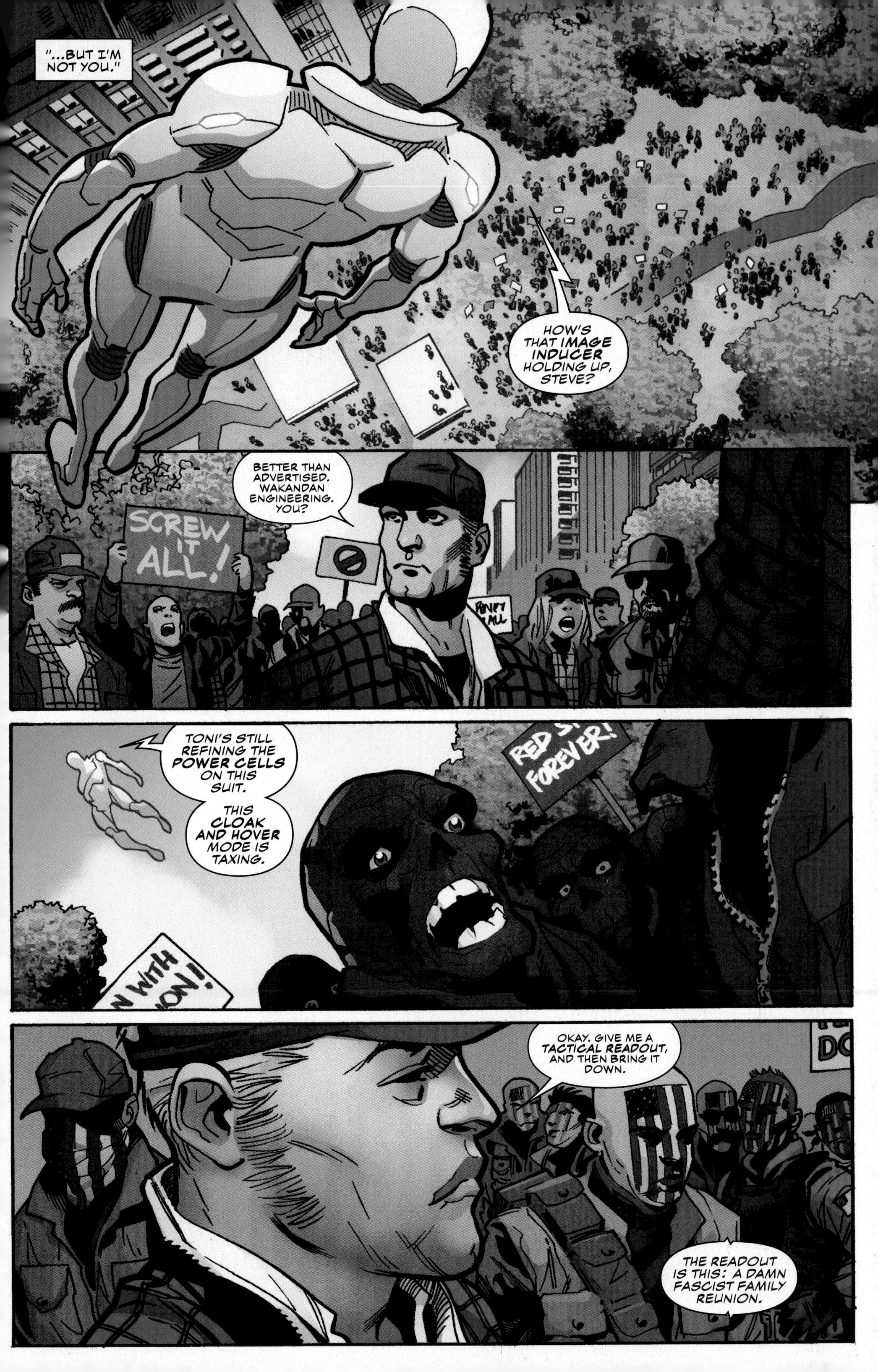
"...BUT I'M NOT YOU."
HOW'S THAT IMAGE INDUCER HOLDING UP, STEVE?
BETTER THAN ADVERTISED. WAKANDAN ENGINEERING. YOU?
SCREW IT ALL!
TONI'S STILL REFINING THE POWER CELLS ON THIS SUIT.
THIS CLOAK AND HOVER MODE IS TAXING.
FOREVER!
OKAY. GIVE ME A TACTICAL READOUT, AND THEN BRING IT DOWN.
THE READOUT IS THIS: A DAMN FASCIST FAMILY REUNION.

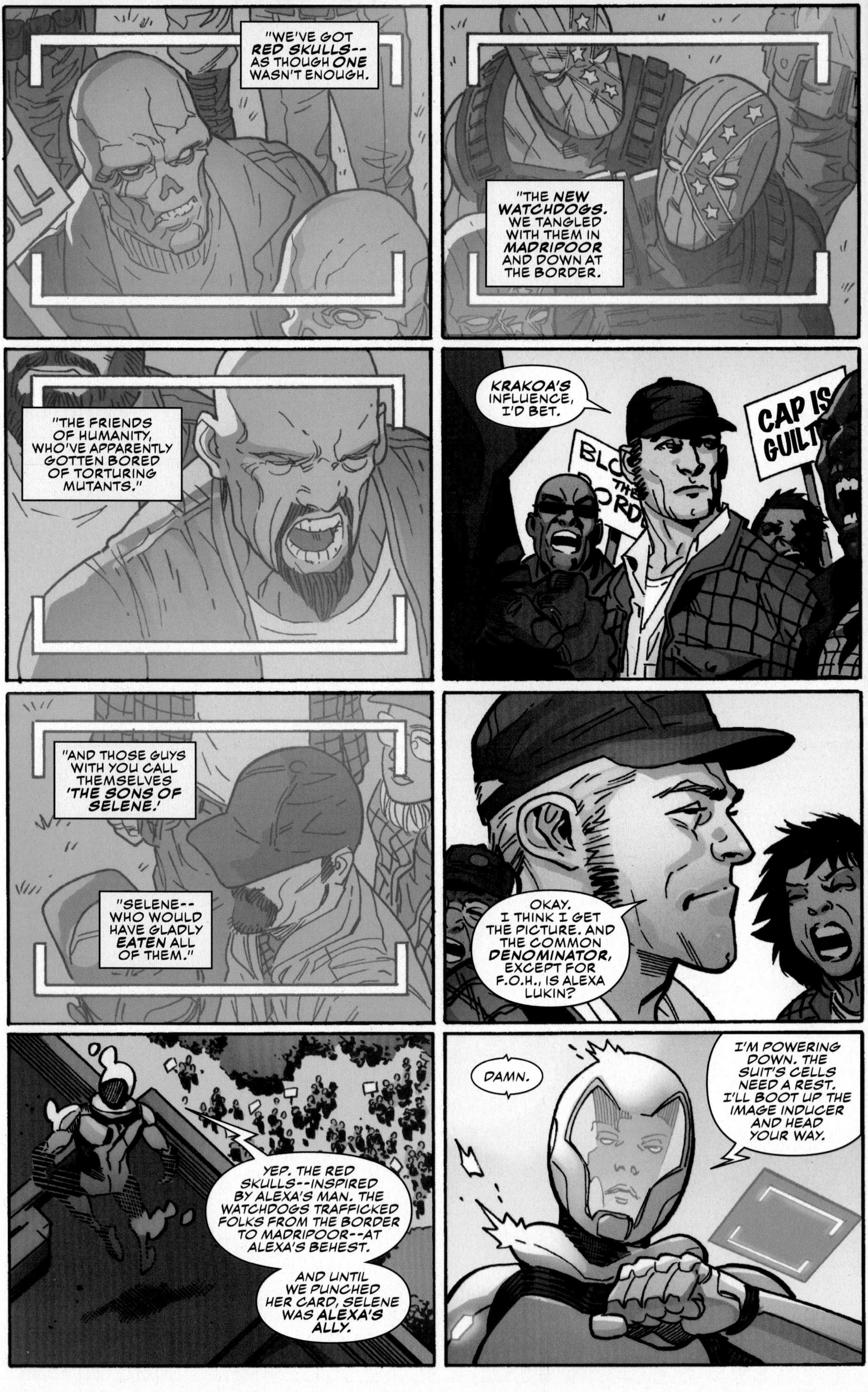
"WE'VE GOT RED SKULLS-- AS THOUGH ONE WASN'T ENOUGH.
"THE NEW WATCHDOGS. WE TANGLED WITH THEM IN MADRIPOOR AND DOWN AT THE BORDER.
"THE FRIENDS OF HUMANITY, WHO'VE APPARENTLY GOTTEN BORED OF TORTURING MUTANTS."
KRAKOA'S INFLUENCE, I'D BET.
CAP IS GUILT
"AND THOSE GUYS WITH YOU CALL THEMSELVES 'THE SONS OF SELENE.'
"SELENE-- WHO WOULD HAVE GLADLY EATEN ALL OF THEM."
OKAY. I THINK I GET THE PICTURE. AND THE COMMON DENOMINATOR, EXCEPT FOR F.O.H., IS ALEXA LUKIN?
YEP. THE RED SKULLS--INSPIRED BY ALEXA'S MAN. THE WATCHDOGS TRAFFICKED FOLKS FROM THE BORDER TO MADRIPOOR--AT ALEXA'S BEHEST.
AND UNTIL WE PUNCHED HER CARD, SELENE WAS ALEXA'S ALLY.
DAMN.
I'M POWERING DOWN. THE SUIT'S CELLS NEED A REST. I'LL BOOT UP THE IMAGE INDUCER AND HEAD YOUR WAY.

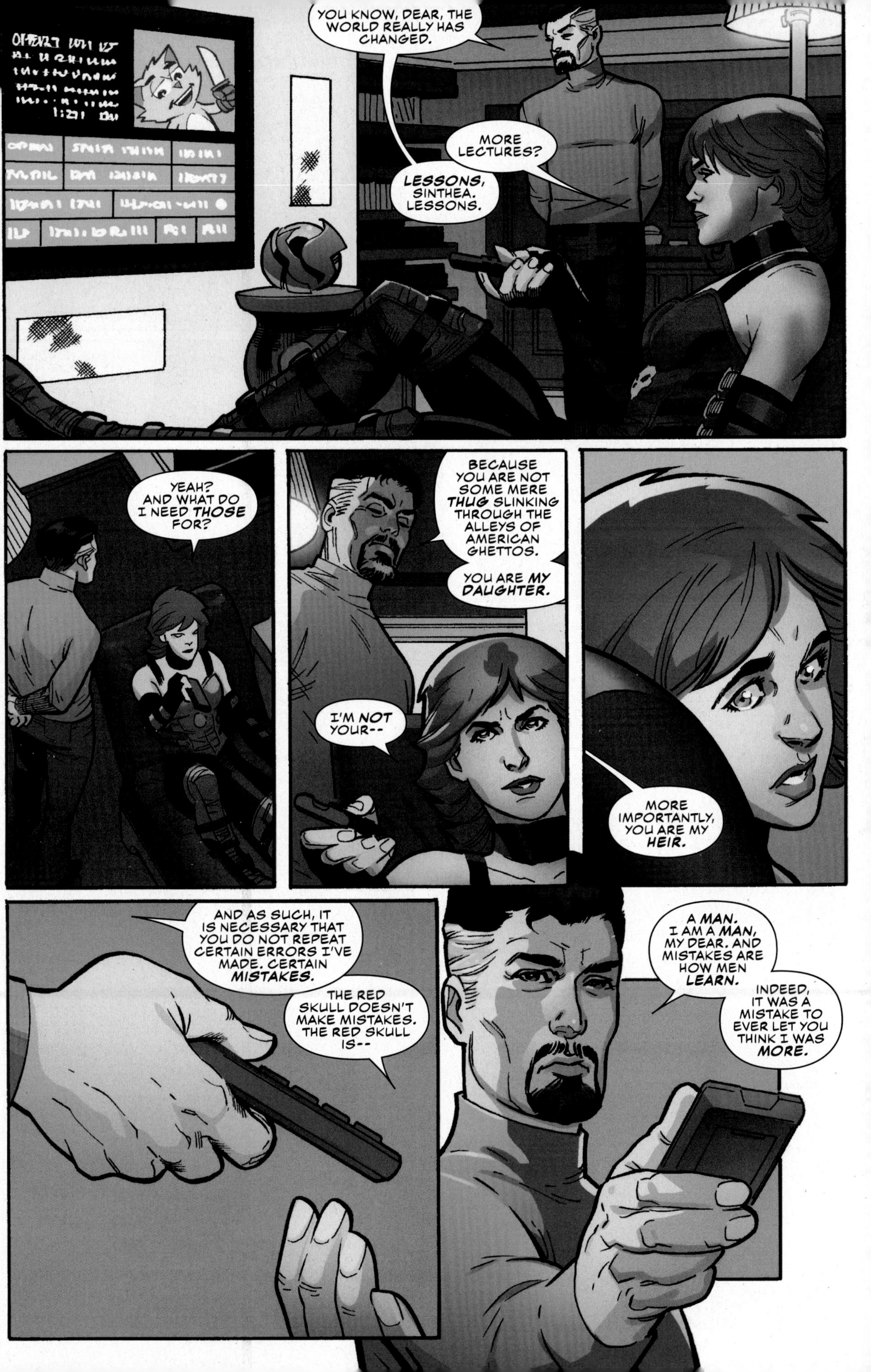

YOU KNOW, DEAR, THE WORLD REALLY HAS CHANGED.
MORE LECTURES?
LESSONS, SINTHEA. LESSONS.
YEAH? AND WHAT DO I NEED THOSE FOR?
BECAUSE YOU ARE NOT SOME MERE THUG SLINKING THROUGH THE ALLEYS OF AMERICAN GHETTOS.
YOU ARE MY DAUGHTER.
I'M NOT YOUR--
MORE IMPORTANTLY, YOU ARE MY HEIR.
AND AS SUCH, IT IS NECESSARY THAT YOU DO NOT REPEAT CERTAIN ERRORS I'VE MADE. CERTAIN MISTAKES.
THE RED SKULL DOESN'T MAKE MISTAKES. THE RED SKULL IS--
A MAN. I AM A MAN, MY DEAR. AND MISTAKES ARE HOW MEN LEARN.
INDEED, IT WAS A MISTAKE TO EVER LET YOU THINK I WAS MORE.

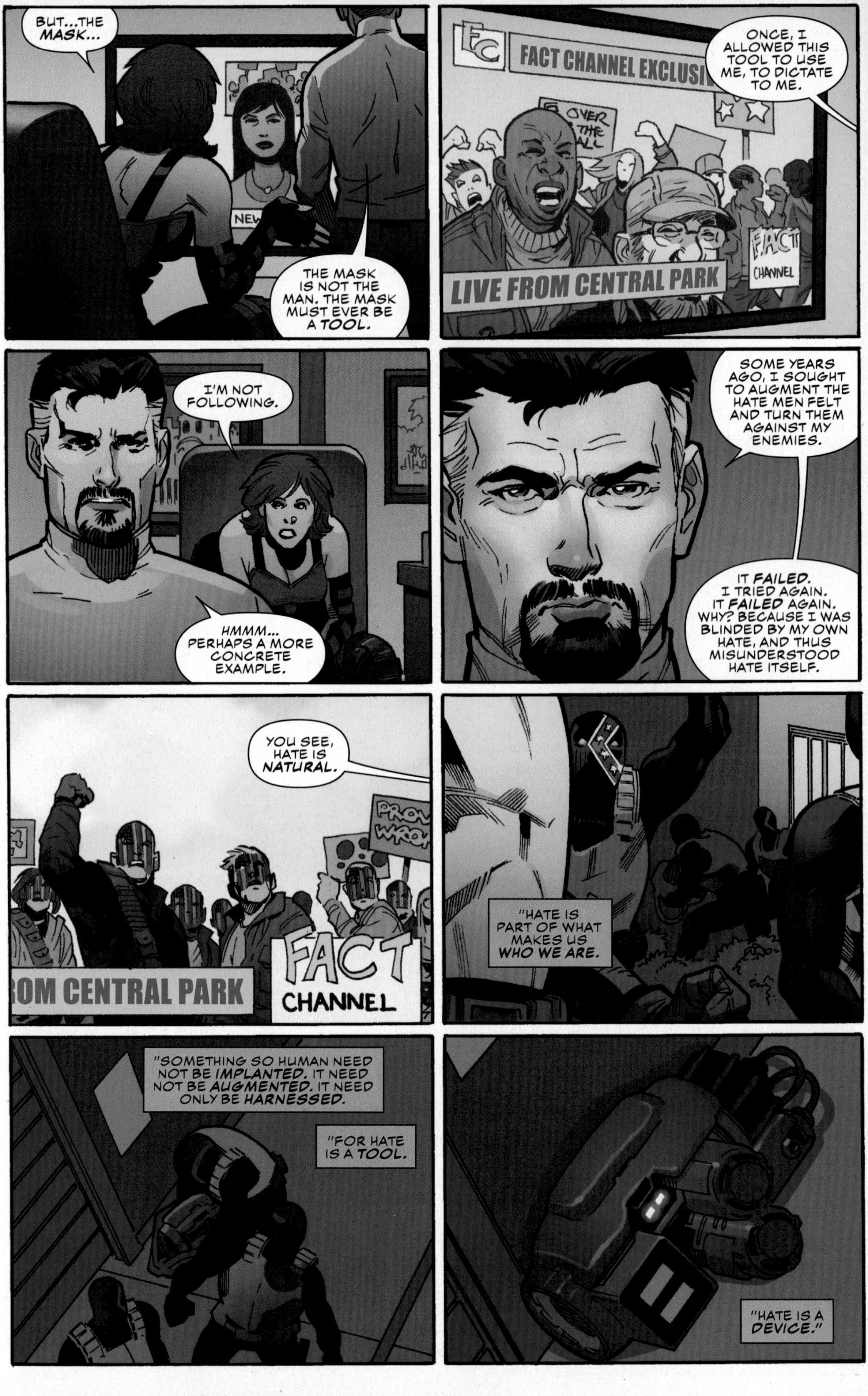
BUT...THE MASK...
NEW
THE MASK IS NOT THE MAN. THE MASK MUST EVER BE A TOOL.
FC
FACT CHANNEL EXCLUSIV
ONCE, I ALLOWED THIS TOOL TO USE ME, TO DICTATE TO ME.
LIVE FROM CENTRAL PARK
FACT CHANNEL
I'M NOT FOLLOWING.
HMMM... PERHAPS A MORE CONCRETE EXAMPLE.
SOME YEARS AGO, I SOUGHT TO AUGMENT THE HATE MEN FELT AND TURN THEM AGAINST MY ENEMIES.
IT FAILED. I TRIED AGAIN. IT FAILED AGAIN. WHY? BECAUSE I WAS BLINDED BY MY OWN HATE, AND THUS MISUNDERSTOOD HATE ITSELF.
YOU SEE, HATE IS NATURAL.
ROM CENTRAL PARK
FACT CHANNEL
"HATE IS PART OF WHAT MAKES US WHO WE ARE.
"SOMETHING SO HUMAN NEED NOT BE IMPLANTED. IT NEED NOT BE AUGMENTED. IT NEED ONLY BE HARNESSED.
"FOR HATE IS A TOOL.
"HATE IS A DEVICE."

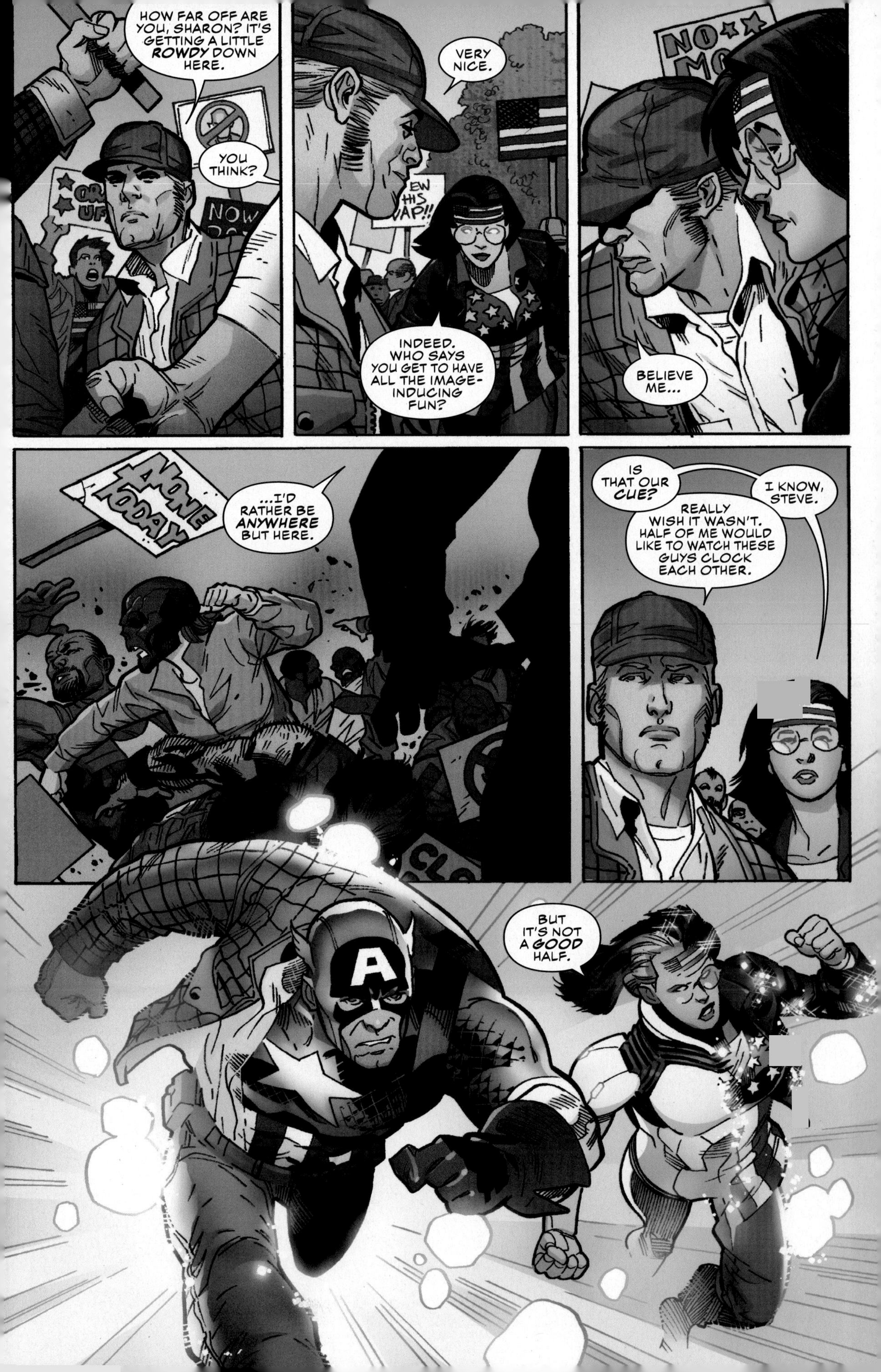
HOW FAR OFF ARE YOU, SHARON? IT'S GETTING A LITTLE ROWDY DOWN HERE.
YOU THINK?
VERY NICE.
INDEED. WHO SAYS YOU GET TO HAVE ALL THE IMAGE-INDUCING FUN?
BELIEVE ME...
...I'D RATHER BE ANYWHERE BUT HERE.
IS THAT OUR CUE?
I KNOW, STEVE.
REALLY WISH IT WASN'T. HALF OF ME WOULD LIKE TO WATCH THESE GUYS CLOCK EACH OTHER.
BUT IT'S NOT A GOOD HALF.

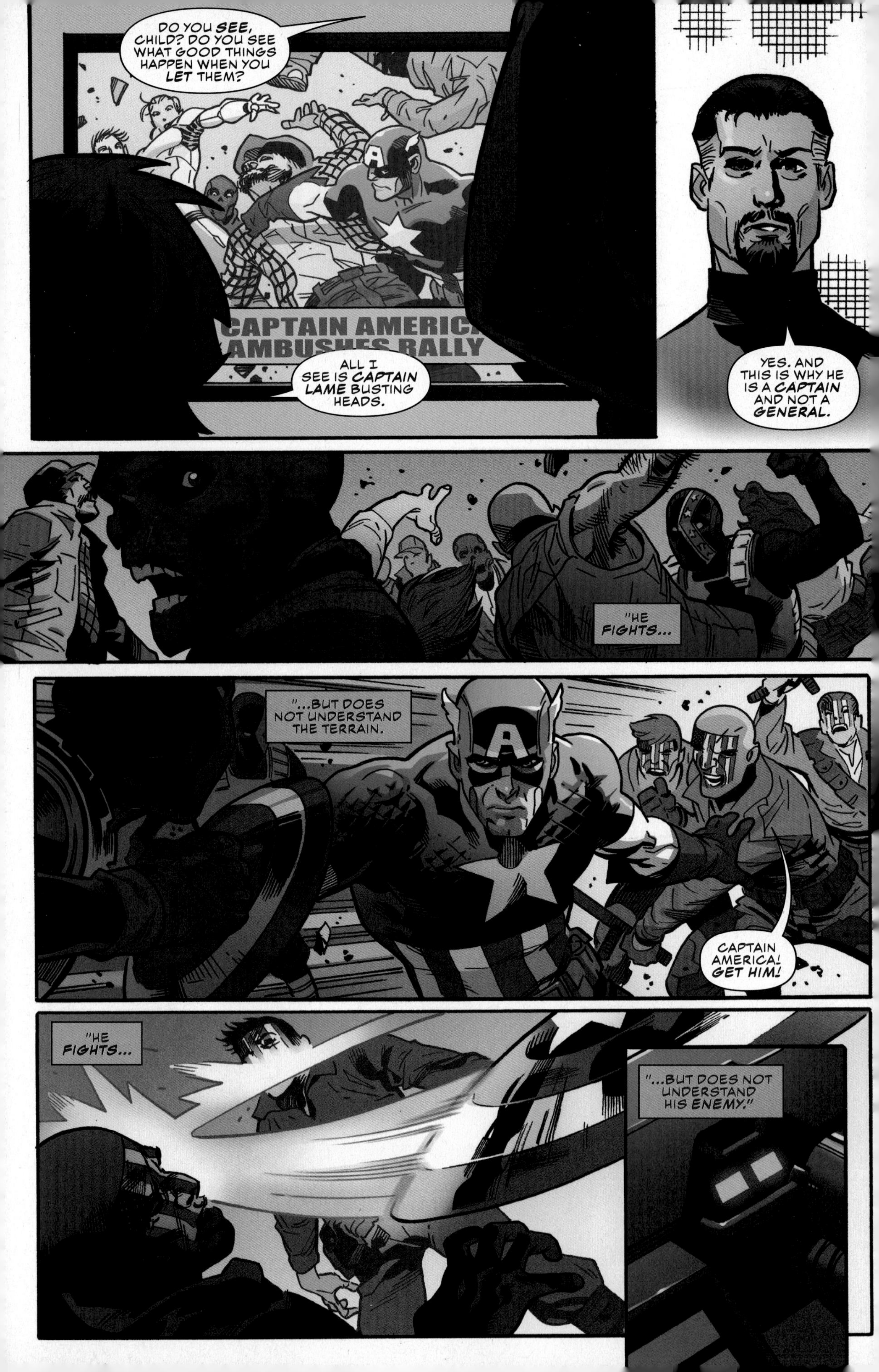
DO YOU SEE, CHILD? DO YOU SEE WHAT GOOD THINGS HAPPEN WHEN YOU LET THEM?
CAPTAIN AMERICA AMBUSHES RALLY
ALL I SEE IS CAPTAIN LAME BUSTING HEADS.
YES. AND THIS IS WHY HE IS A CAPTAIN AND NOT A GENERAL.
"HE FIGHTS...
"...BUT DOES NOT UNDERSTAND THE TERRAIN.
CAPTAIN AMERICA! GET HIM!
"HE FIGHTS...
"...BUT DOES NOT UNDERSTAND HIS ENEMY."

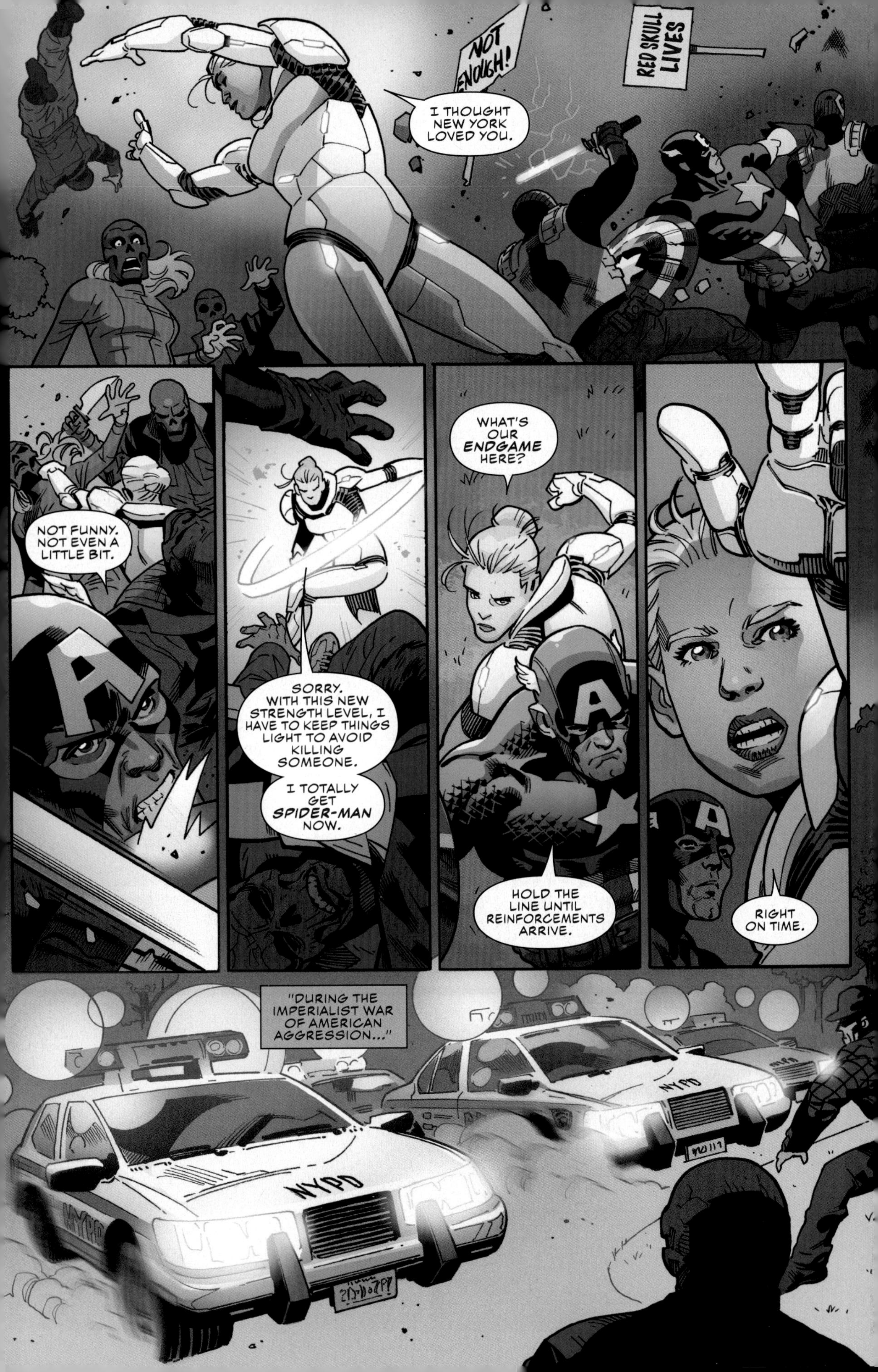
NOT ENOUGH!
RED SKULL LIVES
I THOUGHT NEW YORK LOVED YOU.
NOT FUNNY. NOT EVEN A LITTLE BIT.
SORRY. WITH THIS NEW STRENGTH LEVEL, I HAVE TO KEEP THINGS LIGHT TO AVOID KILLING SOMEONE.
I TOTALLY GET SPIDER-MAN NOW.
WHAT'S OUR ENDGAME HERE?
HOLD THE LINE UNTIL REINFORCEMENTS ARRIVE.
RIGHT ON TIME.
"DURING THE IMPERIALIST WAR OF AMERICAN AGGRESSION..."
NYPD

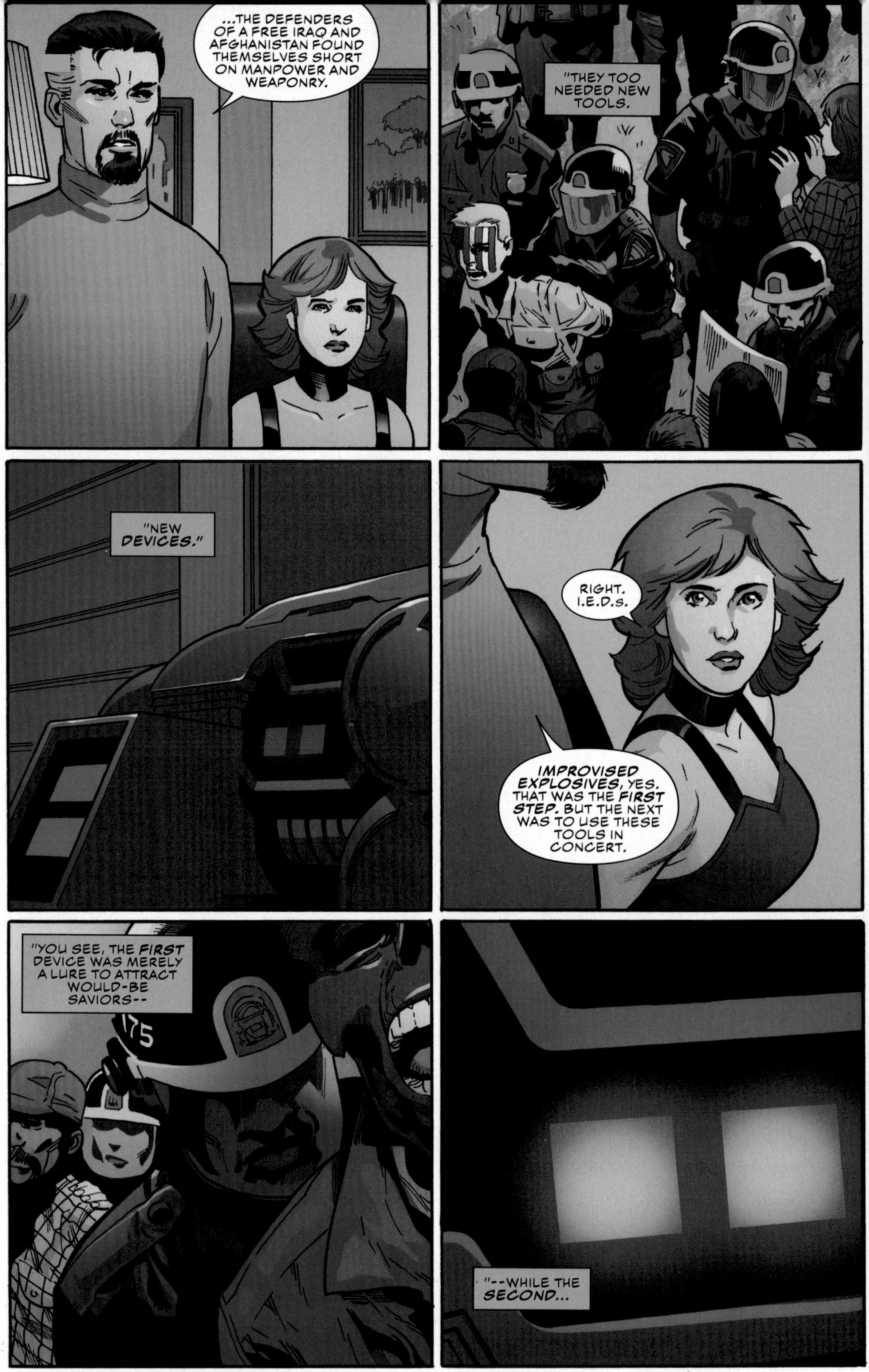
...THE DEFENDERS OF A FREE IRAQ AND AFGHANISTAN FOUND THEMSELVES SHORT ON MANPOWER AND WEAPONRY.
"THEY TOO NEEDED NEW TOOLS.
"NEW *DEVICES.*"
RIGHT. I.E.D.s.
IMPROVISED EXPLOSIVES, YES. THAT WAS THE *FIRST STEP.* BUT THE NEXT WAS TO USE THESE TOOLS IN CONCERT.
"YOU SEE, THE *FIRST* DEVICE WAS MERELY A LURE TO ATTRACT WOULD-BE SAVIORS--
175
"--WHILE THE *SECOND...*

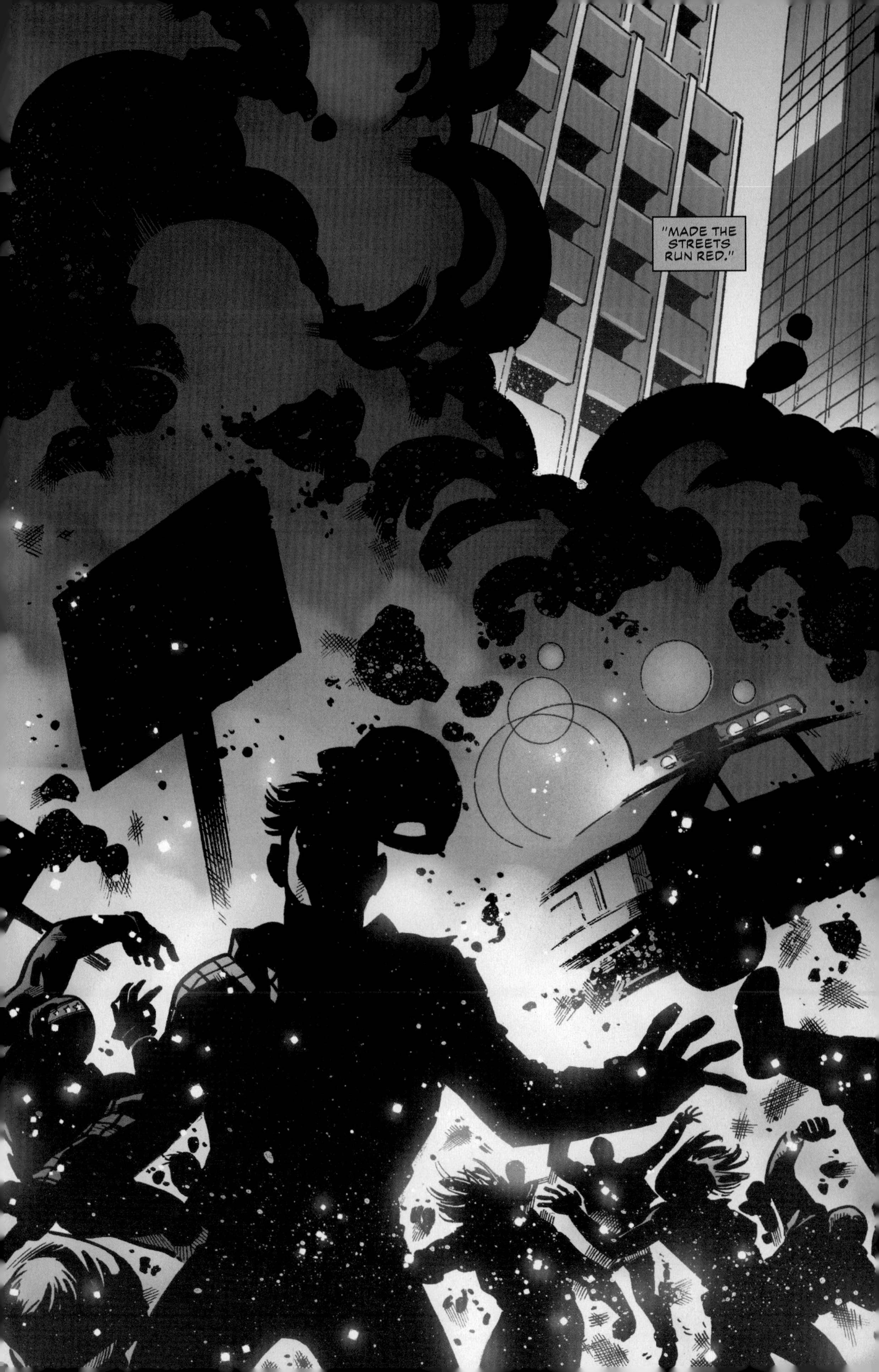
"MADE THE STREETS RUN RED."

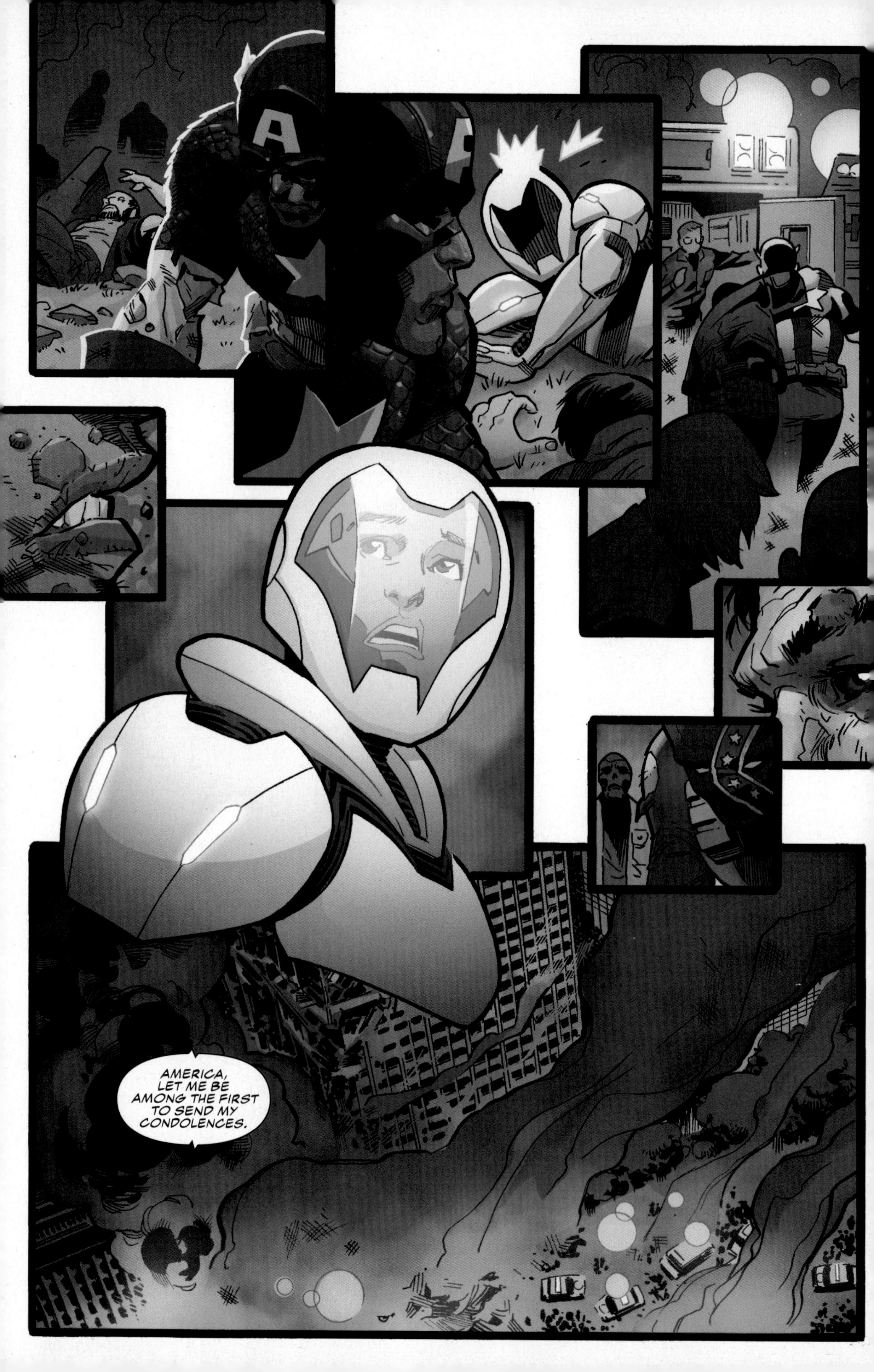
AMERICA, LET ME BE AMONG THE FIRST TO SEND MY CONDOLENCES.

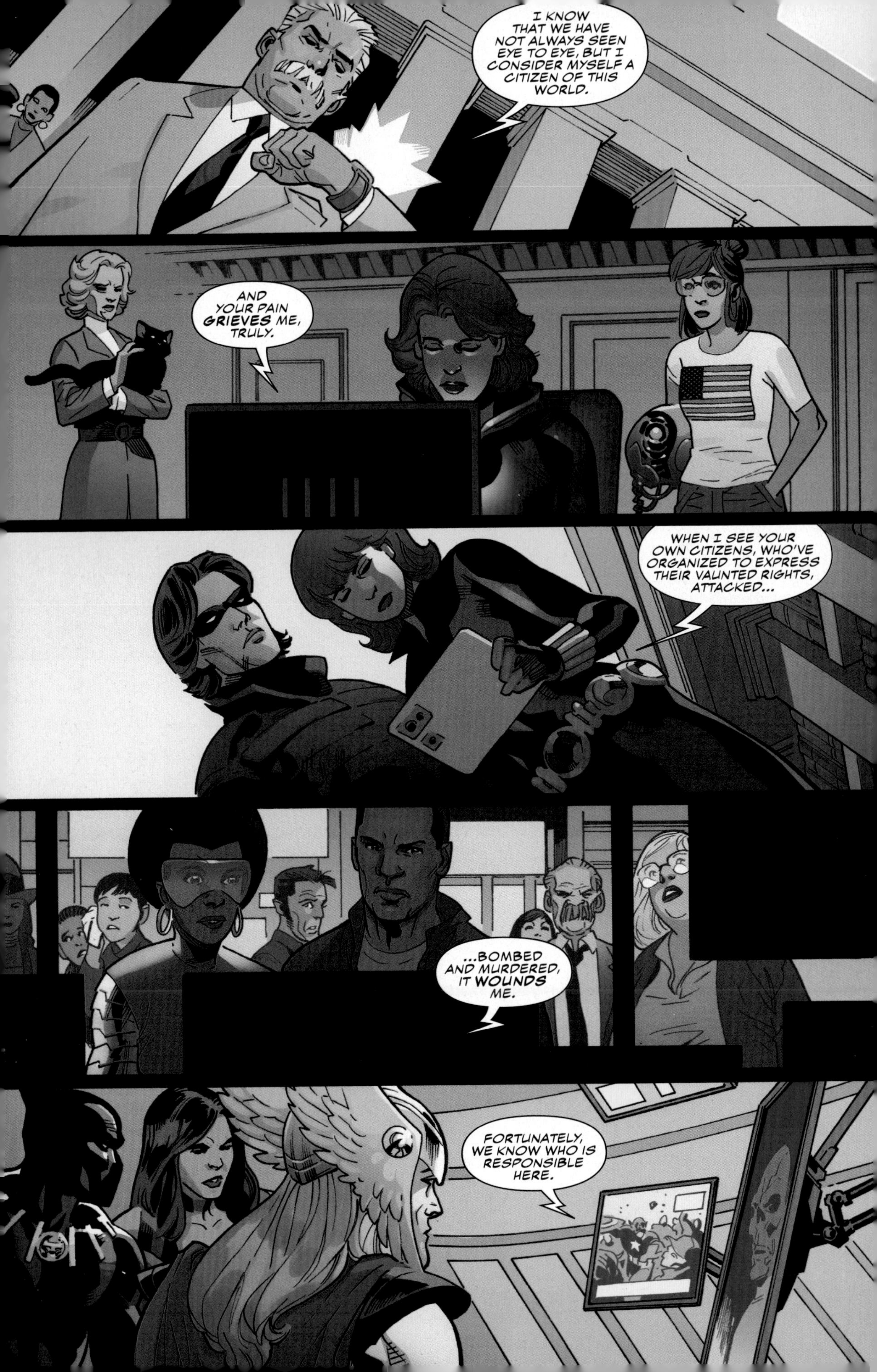
I KNOW THAT WE HAVE NOT ALWAYS SEEN EYE TO EYE, BUT I CONSIDER MYSELF A CITIZEN OF THIS WORLD.
AND YOUR PAIN GRIEVES ME, TRULY.
WHEN I SEE YOUR OWN CITIZENS, WHO'VE ORGANIZED TO EXPRESS THEIR VAUNTED RIGHTS, ATTACKED...
...BOMBED AND MURDERED, IT WOUNDS ME.
FORTUNATELY, WE KNOW WHO IS RESPONSIBLE HERE.

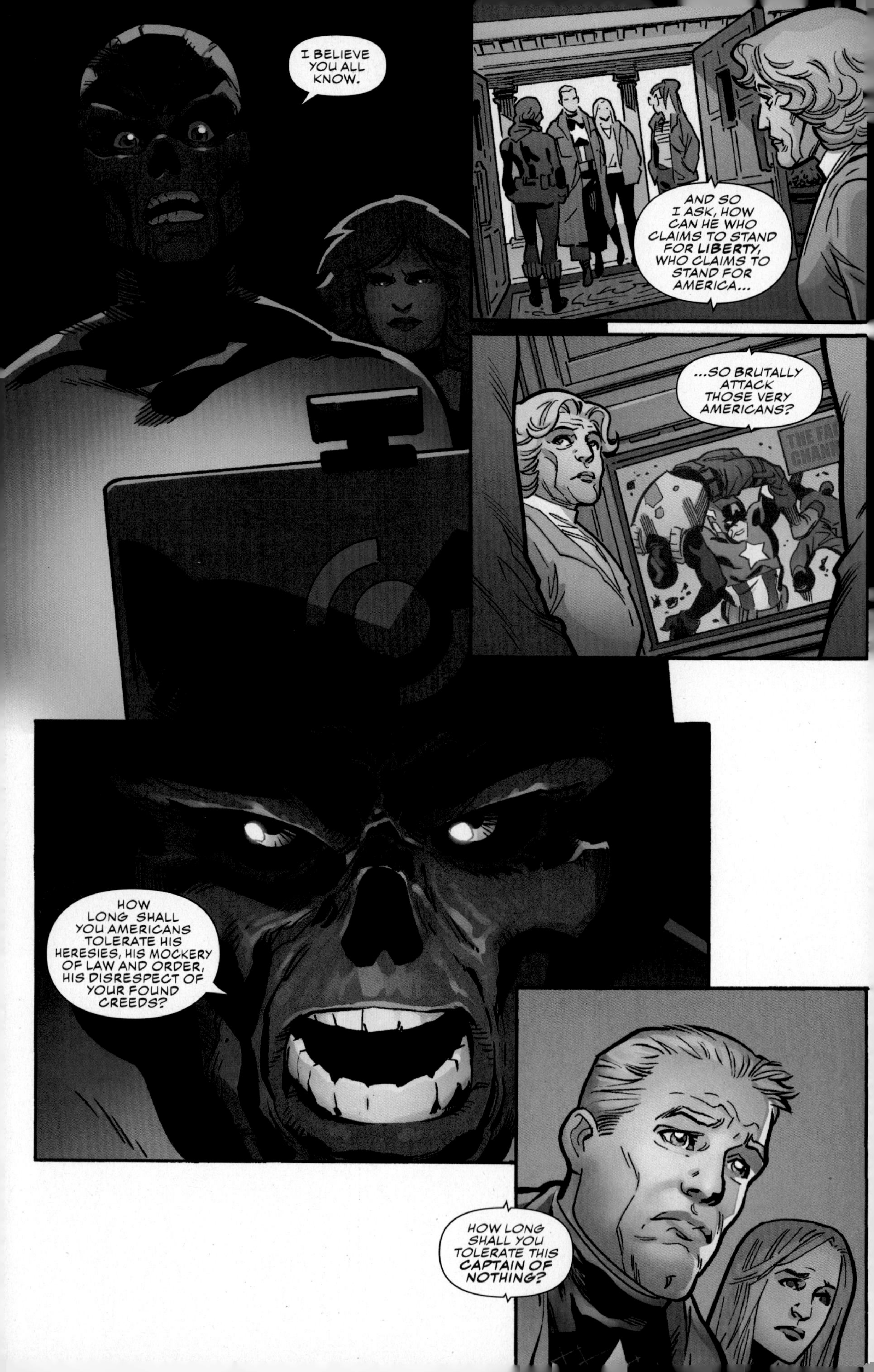
I BELIEVE YOU ALL KNOW.
AND SO I ASK, HOW CAN HE WHO CLAIMS TO STAND FOR LIBERTY, WHO CLAIMS TO STAND FOR AMERICA...
...SO BRUTALLY ATTACK THOSE VERY AMERICANS?
HOW LONG SHALL YOU AMERICANS TOLERATE HIS HERESIES, HIS MOCKERY OF LAW AND ORDER, HIS DISRESPECT OF YOUR FOUND CREEDS?
HOW LONG SHALL YOU TOLERATE THIS CAPTAIN OF NOTHING?

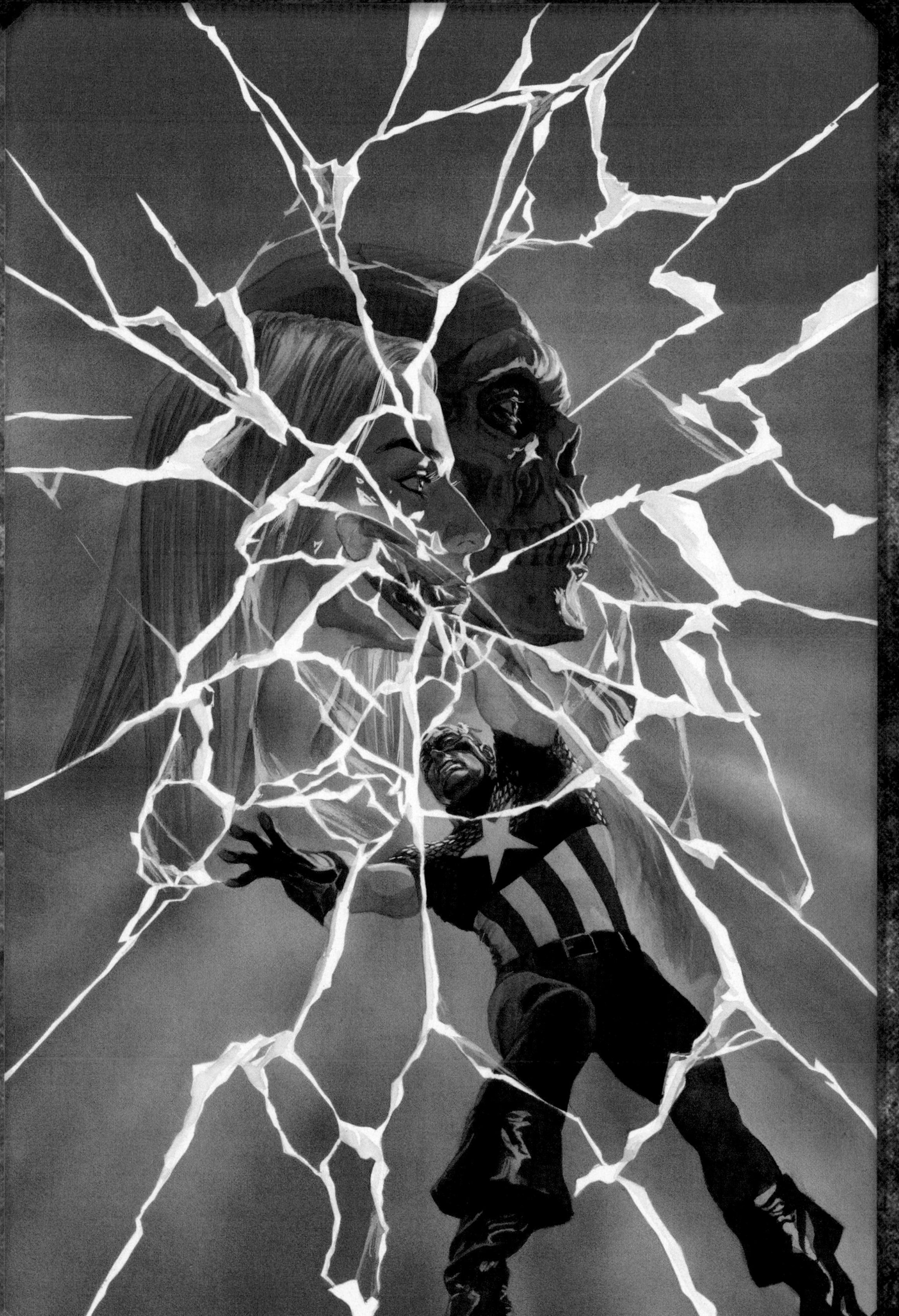

WHAT THE HELL DO YOU WANT, ALEXA? HERE TO GLOAT SOME MORE?

SINTHEA, I WISH YOU WOULD STOP THINKING OF ME AS COMPETITION. YOU THINK I'M TRYING TO DIVIDE YOU FROM YOUR FATHER...

"...WHEN, IN FACT, I'M TRYING TO BRING OUT THE BEST IN YOU.

"I AM TRYING TO SHOW YOU WHAT IT MEANS TO LIVE IN THIS WORLD OF TROGLODYTES AND BRUTES."

"THICK-WITTED MEN WHO LOOK AT YOU AND SEE ONE THING."

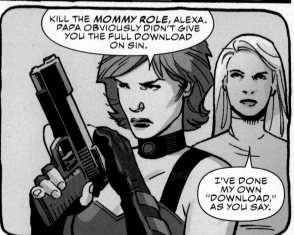

KILL THE *MOMMY ROLE*, ALEXA. PAPA OBVIOUSLY DIDN'T GIVE YOU THE FULL DOWNLOAD ON SIN.

I'VE DONE MY OWN "DOWNLOAD," AS YOU SAY.

HEARD THE RED SKULL NEEDED SOME MUSCLE IN HIS NEW *SKELETON CREW.*

DIDN'T KNOW HE WAS SENDING A SKIRT.

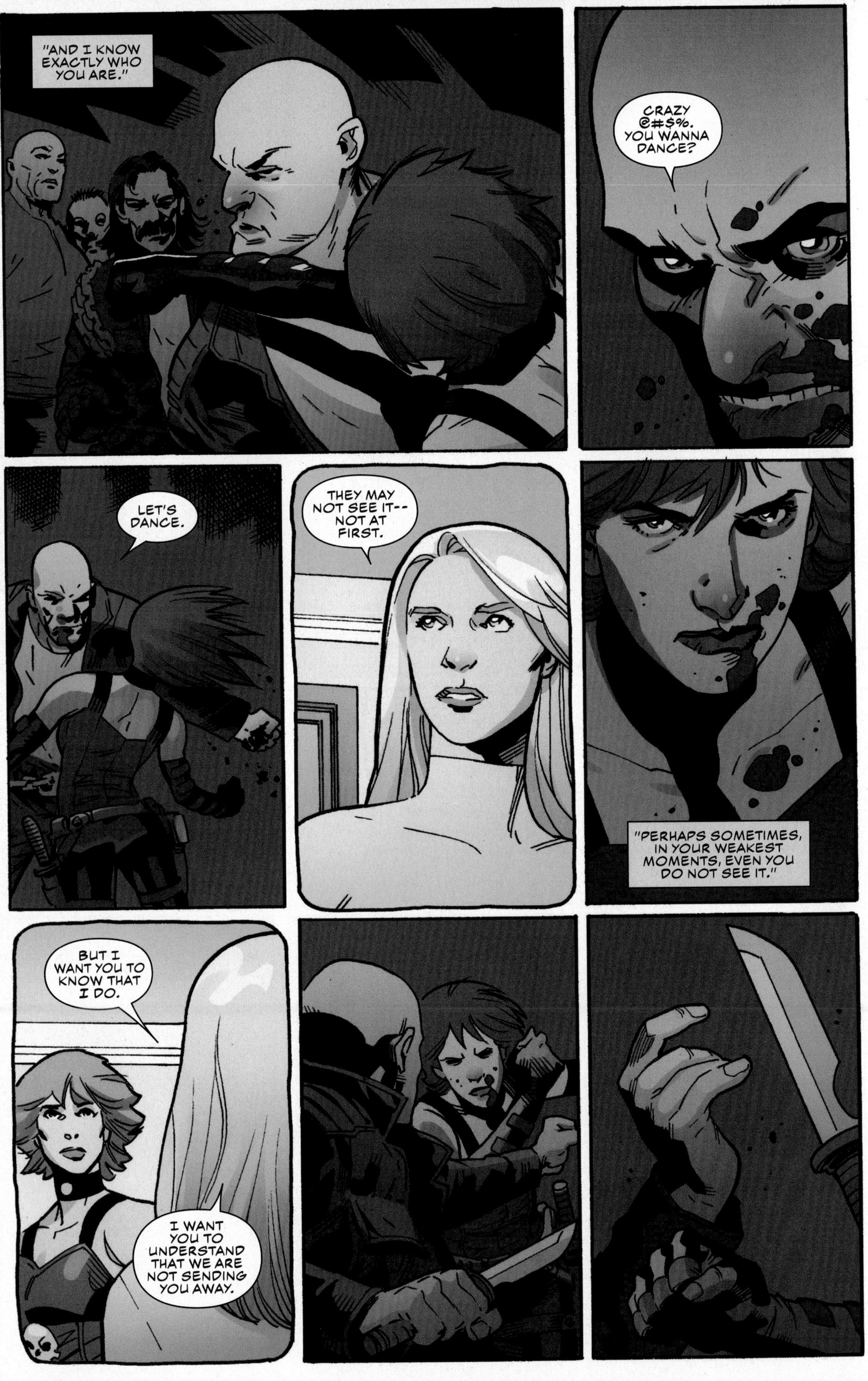
"AND I KNOW EXACTLY WHO YOU ARE."
CRAZY @#$%. YOU WANNA DANCE?
LET'S DANCE.
THEY MAY NOT SEE IT-- NOT AT FIRST.
"PERHAPS SOMETIMES, IN YOUR WEAKEST MOMENTS, EVEN YOU DO NOT SEE IT."
BUT I WANT YOU TO KNOW THAT I DO.
I WANT YOU TO UNDERSTAND THAT WE ARE NOT SENDING YOU AWAY.

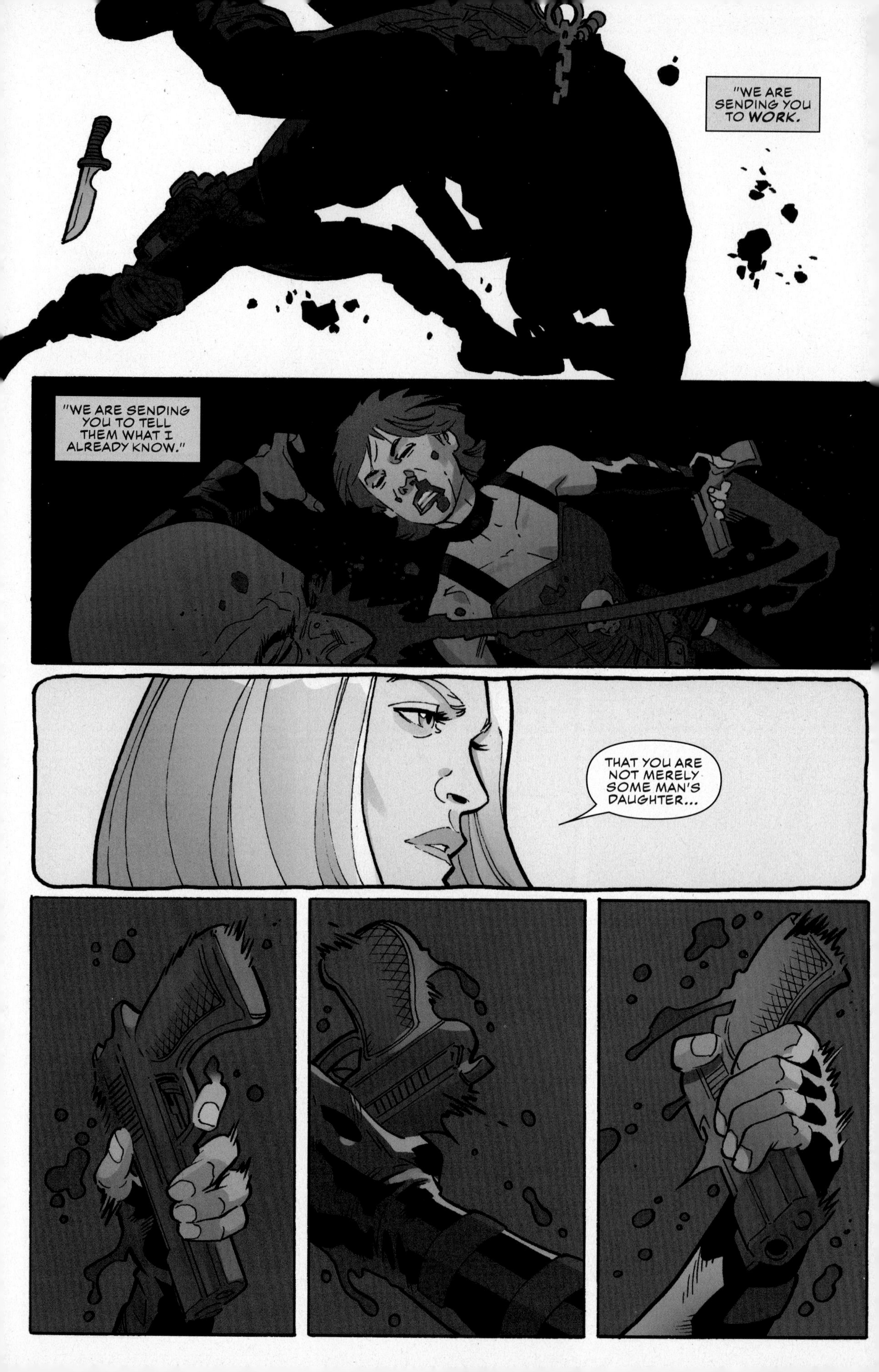
"WE ARE SENDING YOU TO WORK.
"WE ARE SENDING YOU TO TELL THEM WHAT I ALREADY KNOW."
THAT YOU ARE NOT MERELY SOME MAN'S DAUGHTER...

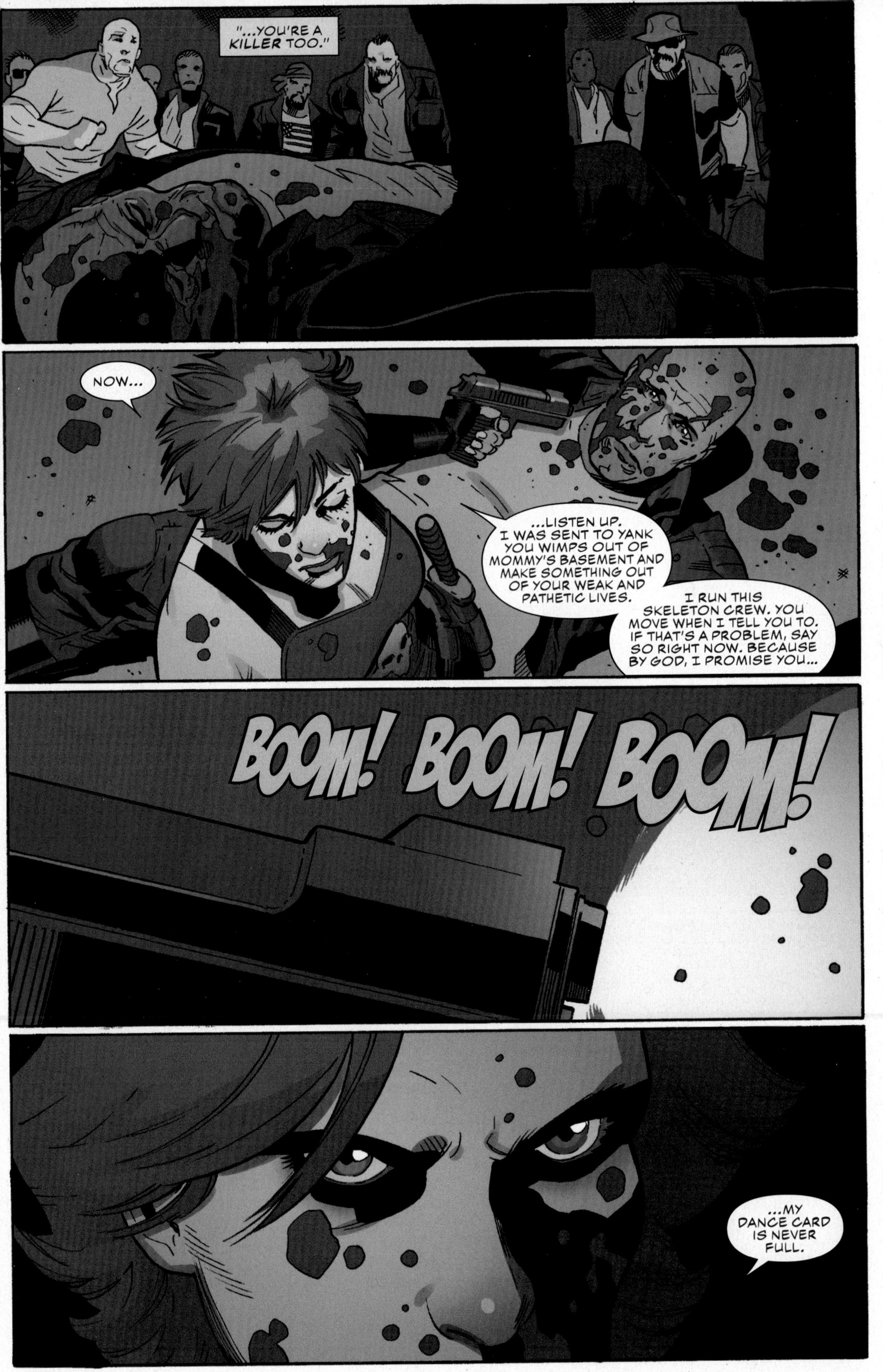
"...YOU'RE A KILLER TOO."
NOW...
...LISTEN UP. I WAS SENT TO YANK YOU WIMPS OUT OF MOMMY'S BASEMENT AND MAKE SOMETHING OUT OF YOUR WEAK AND PATHETIC LIVES.
I RUN THIS SKELETON CREW. YOU MOVE WHEN I TELL YOU TO. IF THAT'S A PROBLEM, SAY SO RIGHT NOW. BECAUSE BY GOD, I PROMISE YOU...
BOOM! BOOM! BOOM!
...MY DANCE CARD IS NEVER FULL.

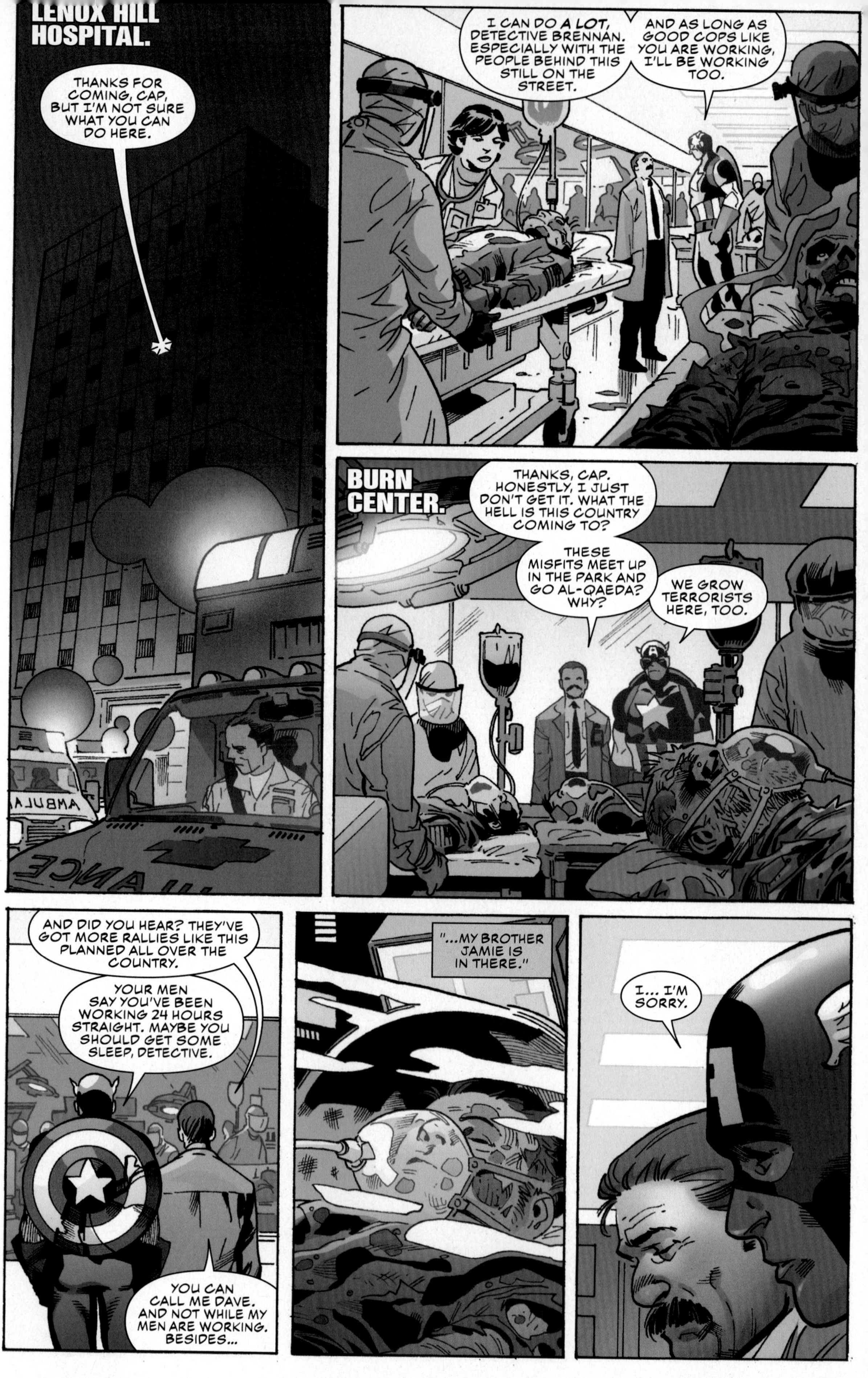
LENOX HILL HOSPITAL.
THANKS FOR COMING, CAP, BUT I'M NOT SURE WHAT YOU CAN DO HERE.
I CAN DO A LOT, DETECTIVE BRENNAN. ESPECIALLY WITH THE PEOPLE BEHIND THIS STILL ON THE STREET.
AND AS LONG AS GOOD COPS LIKE YOU ARE WORKING, I'LL BE WORKING TOO.
BURN CENTER.
THANKS, CAP. HONESTLY, I JUST DON'T GET IT. WHAT THE HELL IS THIS COUNTRY COMING TO?
THESE MISFITS MEET UP IN THE PARK AND GO AL-QAEDA? WHY?
WE GROW TERRORISTS HERE, TOO.
AND DID YOU HEAR? THEY'VE GOT MORE RALLIES LIKE THIS PLANNED ALL OVER THE COUNTRY.
YOUR MEN SAY YOU'VE BEEN WORKING 24 HOURS STRAIGHT. MAYBE YOU SHOULD GET SOME SLEEP, DETECTIVE.
YOU CAN CALL ME DAVE. AND NOT WHILE MY MEN ARE WORKING. BESIDES...
"...MY BROTHER JAMIE IS IN THERE."
I... I'M SORRY.

THEY SAY THE APPLE NEVER FALLS FAR FROM THE TREE. WELL, THAT'S A DAMN LIE. THERE'RE FIVE OF US, YOU KNOW. FIVE BOYS.

ALL NYPD. ALL EXCEPT JAMIE.

HE WAS ALWAYS THE SCREWUP. BUMMING THROUGH LIFE. LIVING OFF MY FOLKS.

TOTAL DISAPPOINTMENT TO EVERYONE. AND AS BAD AS THAT WAS, YOU KNOW WHAT THE WORST PART WAS?

HE WAS A DISAPPOINTMENT TO HIMSELF.

HOW'D YOU KNOW?

I'VE GOT A LITTLE EXPERIENCE HERE.

YOU'RE A *COP*, BUT THAT ISN'T JUST YOUR *JOB*, IT'S YOUR *MISSION*. AND THE NYPD ISN'T JUST A CAREER, IT'S A FRATERNITY.

I KNOW. BACK DURING THE WAR, IT WASN'T JUST THE WAR ITSELF, IT WAS THE *CAUSE*. WE WERE FIGHTING THE GREATEST EVIL IN HISTORY. HOW GRAND WAS THAT?

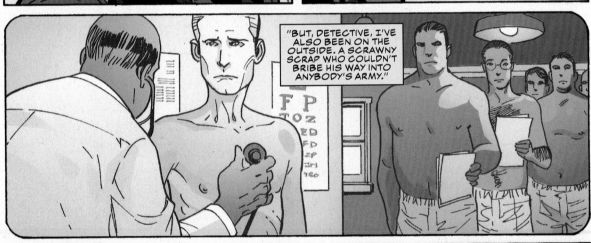

"BUT, DETECTIVE, I'VE ALSO BEEN ON THE OUTSIDE. A SCRAWNY SCRAP WHO COULDN'T BRIBE HIS WAY INTO ANYBODY'S ARMY."

IT WAS TERRIBLE. EVERY YOUNG MAN I KNEW WAS A JOE. AND I WAS THE GUY WHO COULDN'T CUT IT.

THE MAN WHO WASN'T.

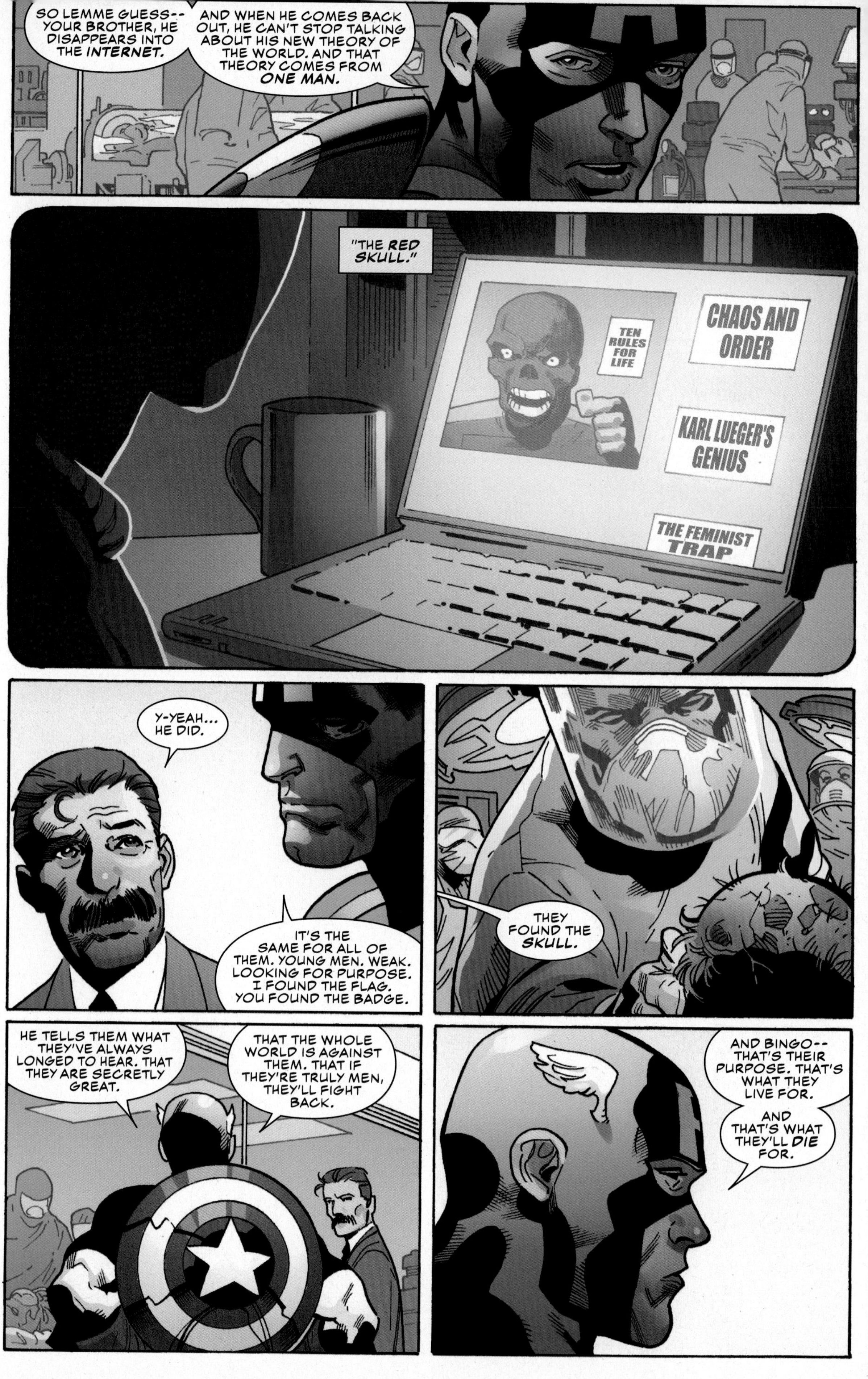
SO LEMME GUESS--YOUR BROTHER, HE DISAPPEARS INTO THE INTERNET.
AND WHEN HE COMES BACK OUT, HE CAN'T STOP TALKING ABOUT HIS NEW THEORY OF THE WORLD. AND THAT THEORY COMES FROM ONE MAN.
"THE RED SKULL."
TEN RULES FOR LIFE
CHAOS AND ORDER
KARL LUEGER'S GENIUS
THE FEMINIST TRAP
Y-YEAH... HE DID.
IT'S THE SAME FOR ALL OF THEM. YOUNG MEN. WEAK. LOOKING FOR PURPOSE. I FOUND THE FLAG. YOU FOUND THE BADGE.
THEY FOUND THE SKULL.
HE TELLS THEM WHAT THEY'VE ALWAYS LONGED TO HEAR. THAT THEY ARE SECRETLY GREAT.
THAT THE WHOLE WORLD IS AGAINST THEM. THAT IF THEY'RE TRULY MEN, THEY'LL FIGHT BACK.
AND BINGO--THAT'S THEIR PURPOSE. THAT'S WHAT THEY LIVE FOR.
AND THAT'S WHAT THEY'LL DIE FOR.

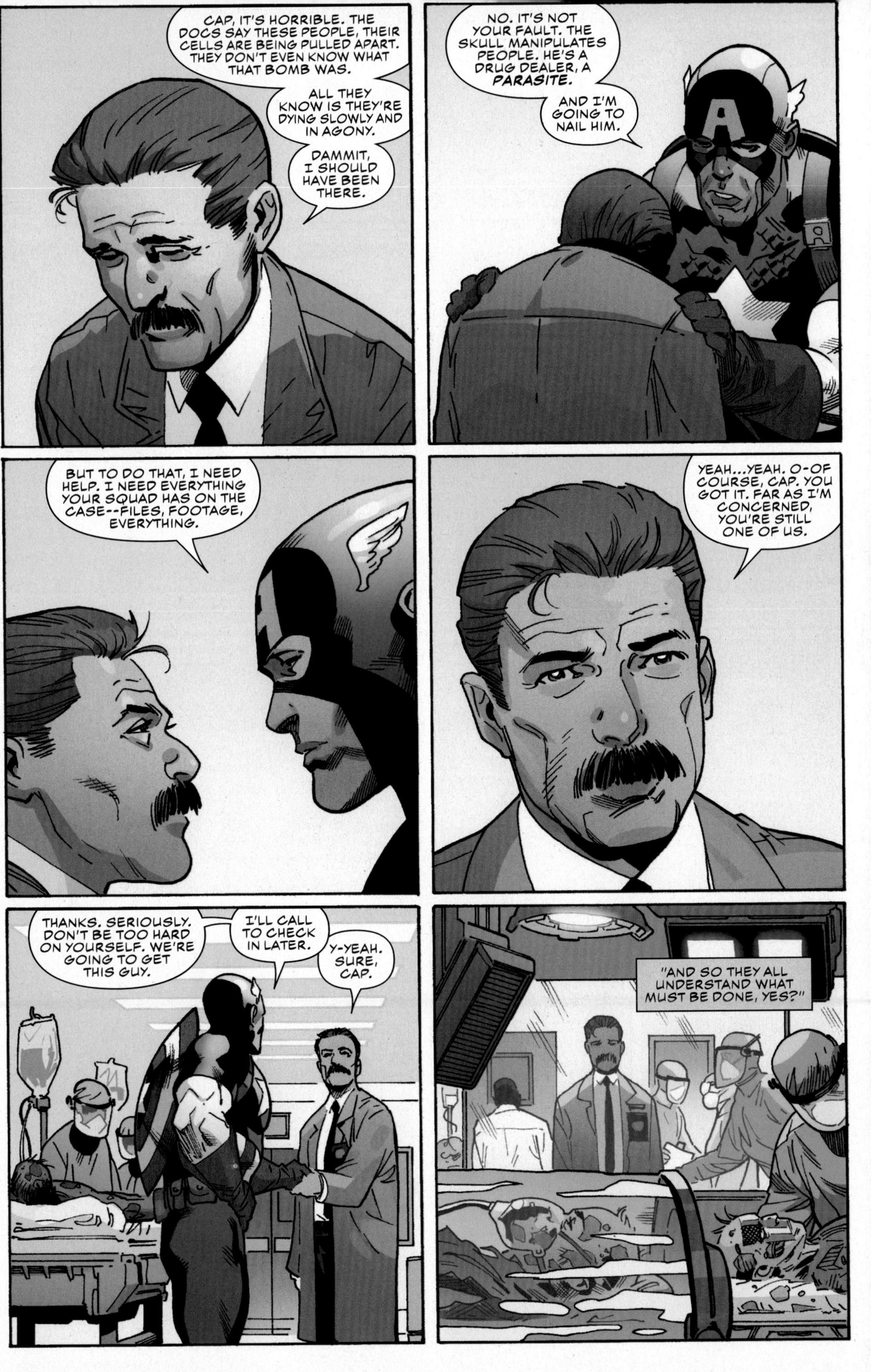
CAP, IT'S HORRIBLE. THE DOCS SAY THESE PEOPLE, THEIR CELLS ARE BEING PULLED APART. THEY DON'T EVEN KNOW WHAT THAT BOMB WAS.
ALL THEY KNOW IS THEY'RE DYING SLOWLY AND IN AGONY.
DAMMIT, I SHOULD HAVE BEEN THERE.
NO. IT'S NOT YOUR FAULT. THE SKULL MANIPULATES PEOPLE. HE'S A DRUG DEALER, A PARASITE.
AND I'M GOING TO NAIL HIM.
BUT TO DO THAT, I NEED HELP. I NEED EVERYTHING YOUR SQUAD HAS ON THE CASE--FILES, FOOTAGE, EVERYTHING.
YEAH...YEAH. O-OF COURSE, CAP. YOU GOT IT. FAR AS I'M CONCERNED, YOU'RE STILL ONE OF US.
THANKS. SERIOUSLY. DON'T BE TOO HARD ON YOURSELF. WE'RE GOING TO GET THIS GUY.
I'LL CALL TO CHECK IN LATER.
Y-YEAH. SURE, CAP.
"AND SO THEY ALL UNDERSTAND WHAT MUST BE DONE, YES?"

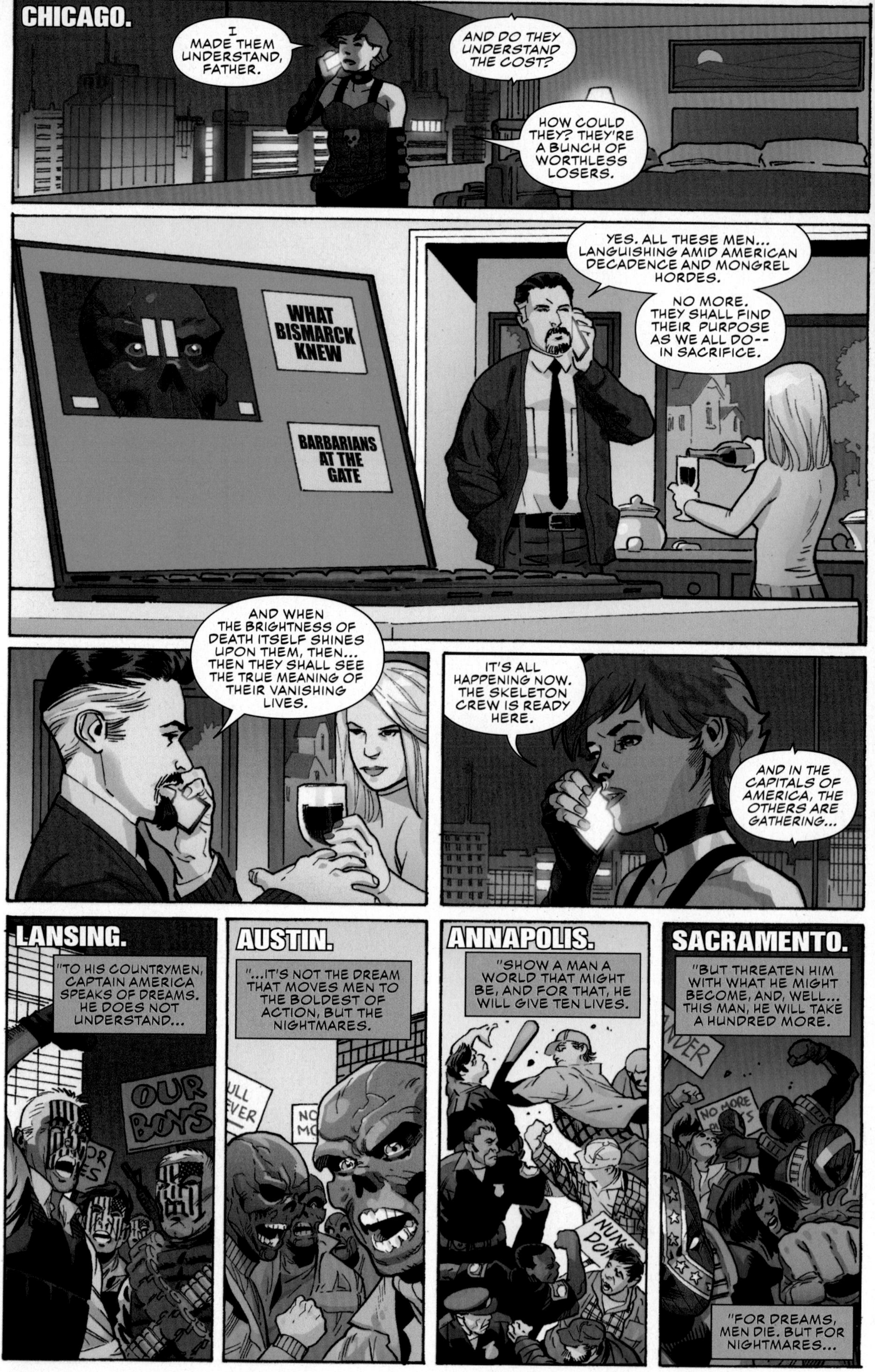
CHICAGO.
I MADE THEM UNDERSTAND, FATHER.
AND DO THEY UNDERSTAND THE COST?
HOW COULD THEY? THEY'RE A BUNCH OF WORTHLESS LOSERS.
WHAT BISMARCK KNEW
BARBARIANS AT THE GATE
YES. ALL THESE MEN... LANGUISHING AMID AMERICAN DECADENCE AND MONGREL HORDES.
NO MORE. THEY SHALL FIND THEIR PURPOSE AS WE ALL DO-- IN SACRIFICE.
AND WHEN THE BRIGHTNESS OF DEATH ITSELF SHINES UPON THEM, THEN... THEN THEY SHALL SEE THE TRUE MEANING OF THEIR VANISHING LIVES.
IT'S ALL HAPPENING NOW. THE SKELETON CREW IS READY HERE.
AND IN THE CAPITALS OF AMERICA, THE OTHERS ARE GATHERING...
LANSING.
"TO HIS COUNTRYMEN, CAPTAIN AMERICA SPEAKS OF DREAMS. HE DOES NOT UNDERSTAND...
OUR BOYS
AUSTIN.
"...IT'S NOT THE DREAM THAT MOVES MEN TO THE BOLDEST OF ACTION, BUT THE NIGHTMARES.
ANNAPOLIS.
"SHOW A MAN A WORLD THAT MIGHT BE, AND FOR THAT, HE WILL GIVE TEN LIVES.
SACRAMENTO.
"BUT THREATEN HIM WITH WHAT HE MIGHT BECOME, AND, WELL... THIS MAN, HE WILL TAKE A HUNDRED MORE.
NO MORE
"FOR DREAMS, MEN DIE. BUT FOR NIGHTMARES...

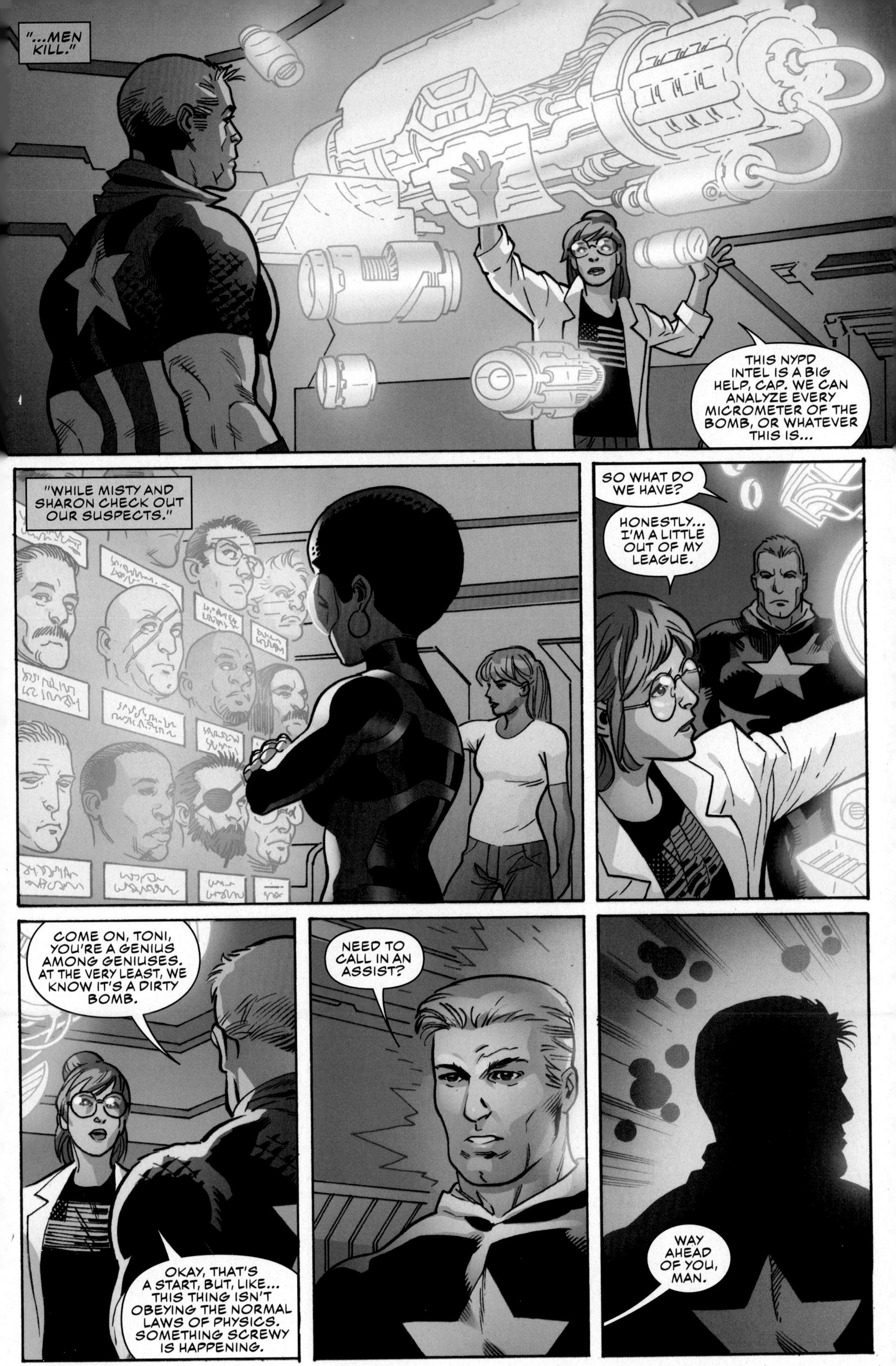
"...MEN KILL."
THIS NYPD INTEL IS A BIG HELP, CAP. WE CAN ANALYZE EVERY MICROMETER OF THE BOMB, OR WHATEVER THIS IS...
"WHILE MISTY AND SHARON CHECK OUT OUR SUSPECTS."
SO WHAT DO WE HAVE?
HONESTLY... I'M A LITTLE OUT OF MY LEAGUE.
COME ON, TONI, YOU'RE A GENIUS AMONG GENIUSES. AT THE VERY LEAST, WE KNOW IT'S A DIRTY BOMB.
OKAY, THAT'S A START, BUT, LIKE... THIS THING ISN'T OBEYING THE NORMAL LAWS OF PHYSICS. SOMETHING SCREWY IS HAPPENING.
NEED TO CALL IN AN ASSIST?
WAY AHEAD OF YOU, MAN.

AGATHA HARKNESS...

HELLO, STEVEN.

TONI.

FORGIVE THE RUSH, MY FRIENDS.

COVEN BUSINESS, YOU KNOW.

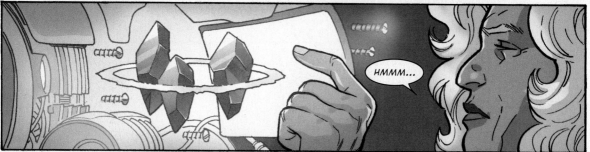

HMMM...

YOU SAID THIS DEVICE WENT OFF IN *CENTRAL PARK?*

YES. DO YOU RECOGNIZE IT?

I SHOULD THINK SO. I *CREATED* IT.

WHAT?

WELL...NOT *THIS* PARTICULAR VERSION. MINE WAS AN ENCHANTMENT, A KIND OF MORALE BOOST.

WHEN THE WILLS OF MEN FLAGGED, IT ALLOWED THE DAUGHTERS OF LIBERTY TO BE A BEACON OF HOPE.

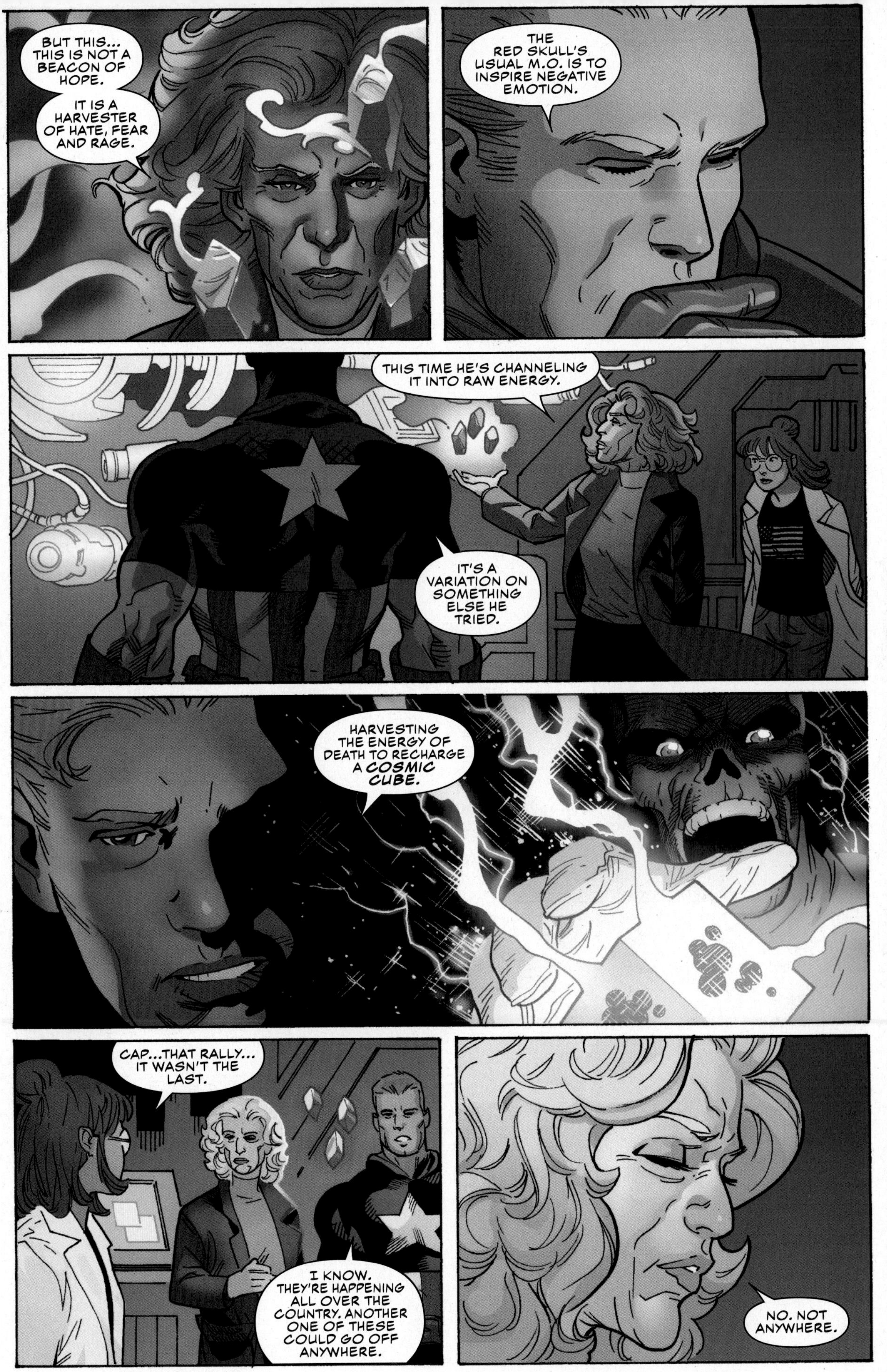
BUT THIS... THIS IS NOT A BEACON OF HOPE.
IT IS A HARVESTER OF HATE, FEAR AND RAGE.
THE RED SKULL'S USUAL M.O. IS TO INSPIRE NEGATIVE EMOTION.
THIS TIME HE'S CHANNELING IT INTO RAW ENERGY.
IT'S A VARIATION ON SOMETHING ELSE HE TRIED.
HARVESTING THE ENERGY OF DEATH TO RECHARGE A COSMIC CUBE.
CAP...THAT RALLY... IT WASN'T THE LAST.
I KNOW. THEY'RE HAPPENING ALL OVER THE COUNTRY. ANOTHER ONE OF THESE COULD GO OFF ANYWHERE.
NO. NOT ANYWHERE.

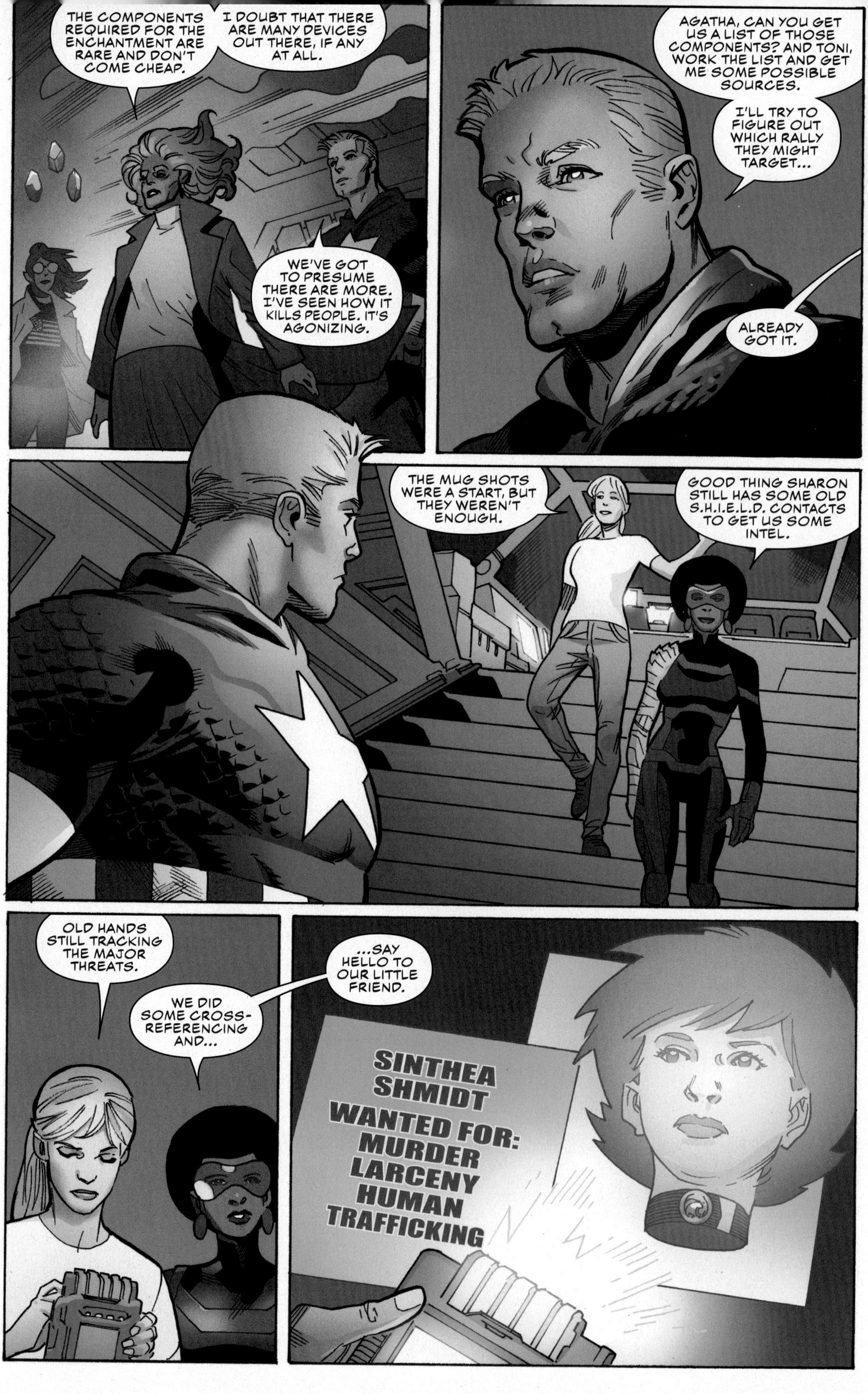
THE COMPONENTS REQUIRED FOR THE ENCHANTMENT ARE RARE AND DON'T COME CHEAP.
I DOUBT THAT THERE ARE MANY DEVICES OUT THERE, IF ANY AT ALL.
WE'VE GOT TO PRESUME THERE ARE MORE. I'VE SEEN HOW IT KILLS PEOPLE. IT'S AGONIZING.
AGATHA, CAN YOU GET US A LIST OF THOSE COMPONENTS? AND TONI, WORK THE LIST AND GET ME SOME POSSIBLE SOURCES.
I'LL TRY TO FIGURE OUT WHICH RALLY THEY MIGHT TARGET...
ALREADY GOT IT.
THE MUG SHOTS WERE A START, BUT THEY WEREN'T ENOUGH.
GOOD THING SHARON STILL HAS SOME OLD S.H.I.E.L.D. CONTACTS TO GET US SOME INTEL.
OLD HANDS STILL TRACKING THE MAJOR THREATS.
WE DID SOME CROSS-REFERENCING AND...
...SAY HELLO TO OUR LITTLE FRIEND.
SINTHEA SHMIDT
WANTED FOR: MURDER LARCENY HUMAN TRAFFICKING

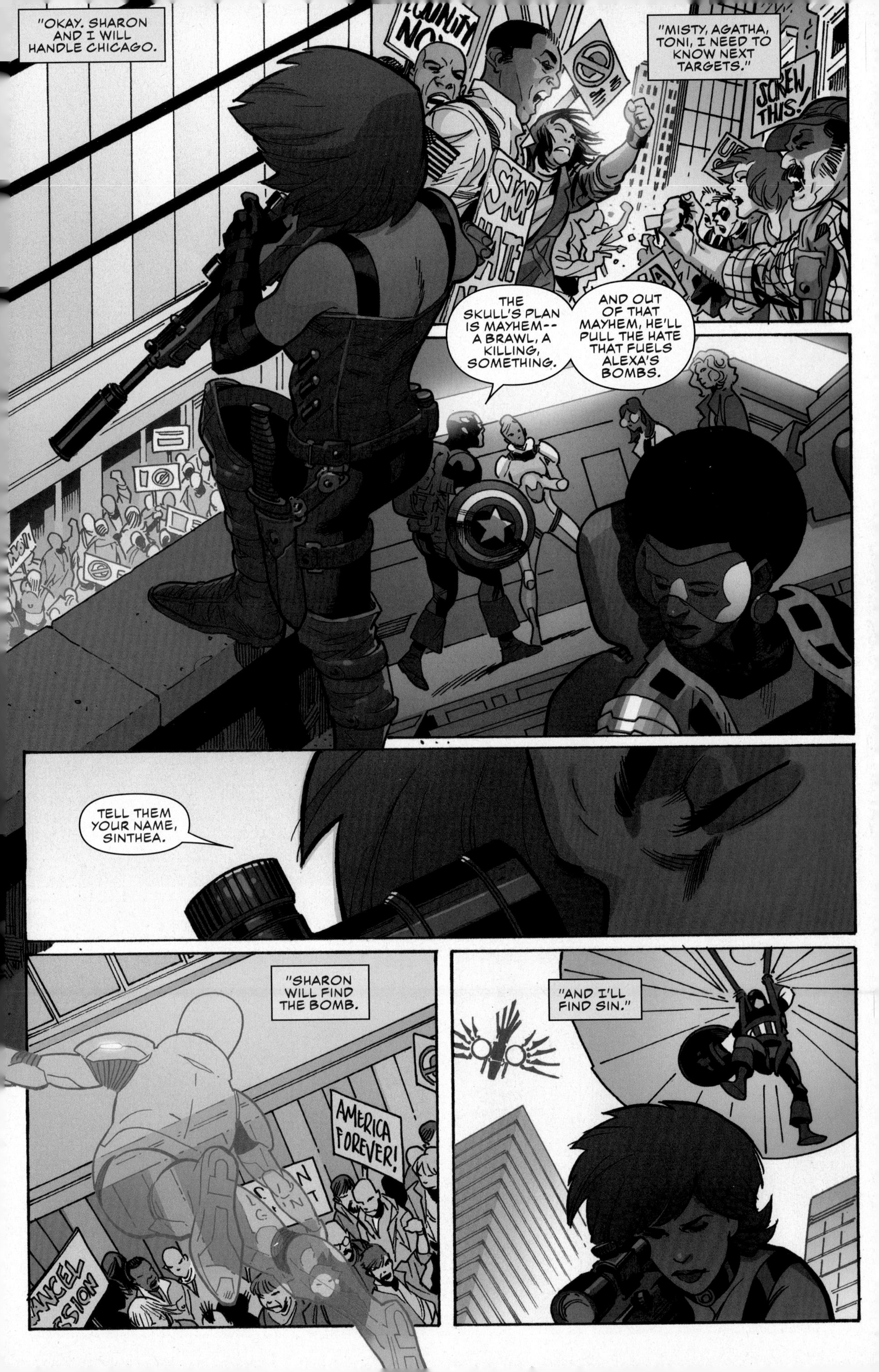
"OKAY. SHARON AND I WILL HANDLE CHICAGO.
EQUALITY NOW
"MISTY, AGATHA, TONI, I NEED TO KNOW NEXT TARGETS."
SCREW THIS!
STOP HATE
THE SKULL'S PLAN IS MAYHEM-- A BRAWL, A KILLING, SOMETHING.
AND OUT OF THAT MAYHEM, HE'LL PULL THE HATE THAT FUELS ALEXA'S BOMBS.
NO!
TELL THEM YOUR NAME, SINTHEA.
"SHARON WILL FIND THE BOMB.
AMERICA FOREVER!
"AND I'LL FIND SIN."

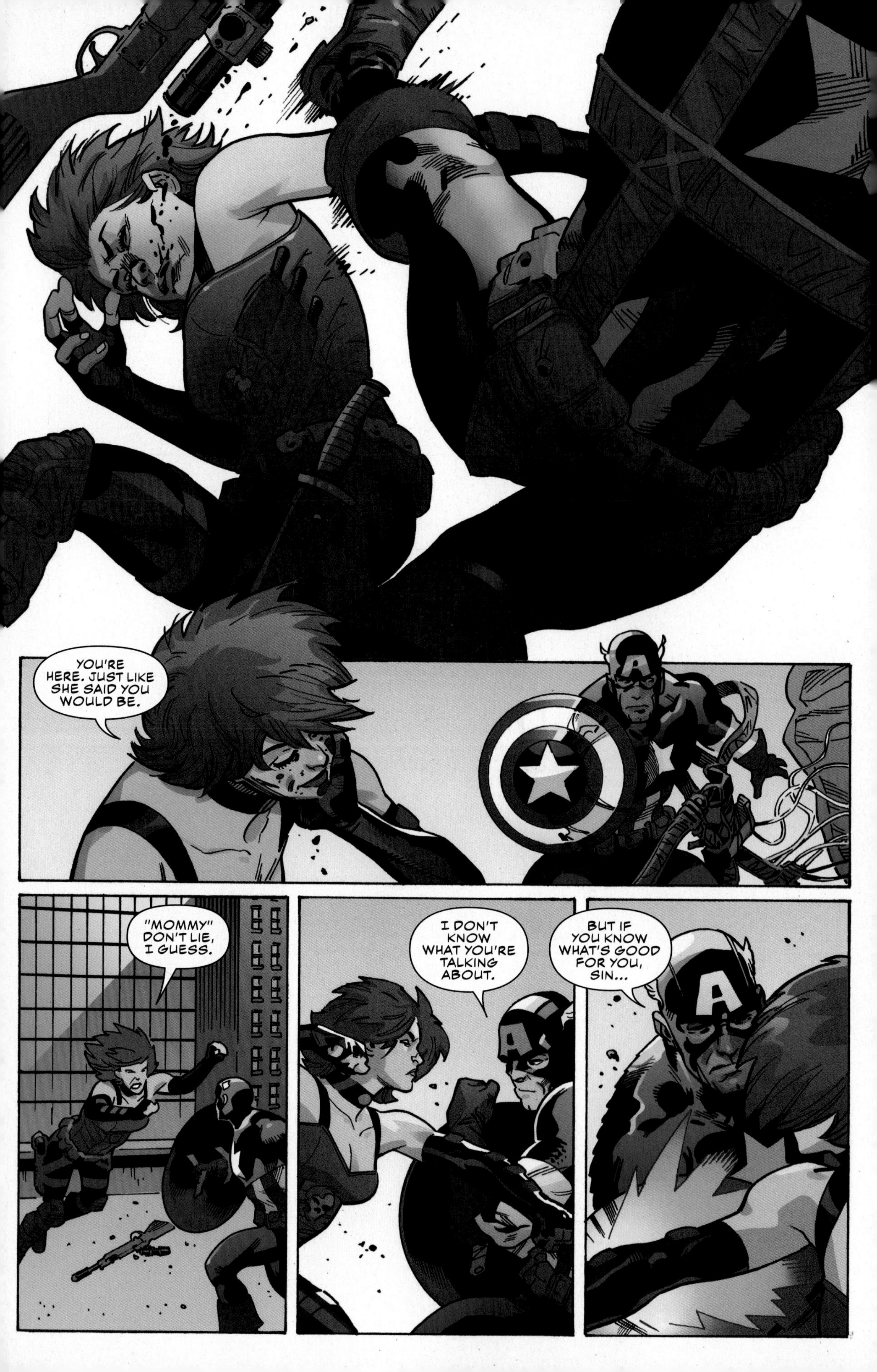
YOU'RE HERE. JUST LIKE SHE SAID YOU WOULD BE.
"MOMMY" DON'T LIE, I GUESS.
I DON'T KNOW WHAT YOU'RE TALKING ABOUT.
BUT IF YOU KNOW WHAT'S GOOD FOR YOU, SIN...

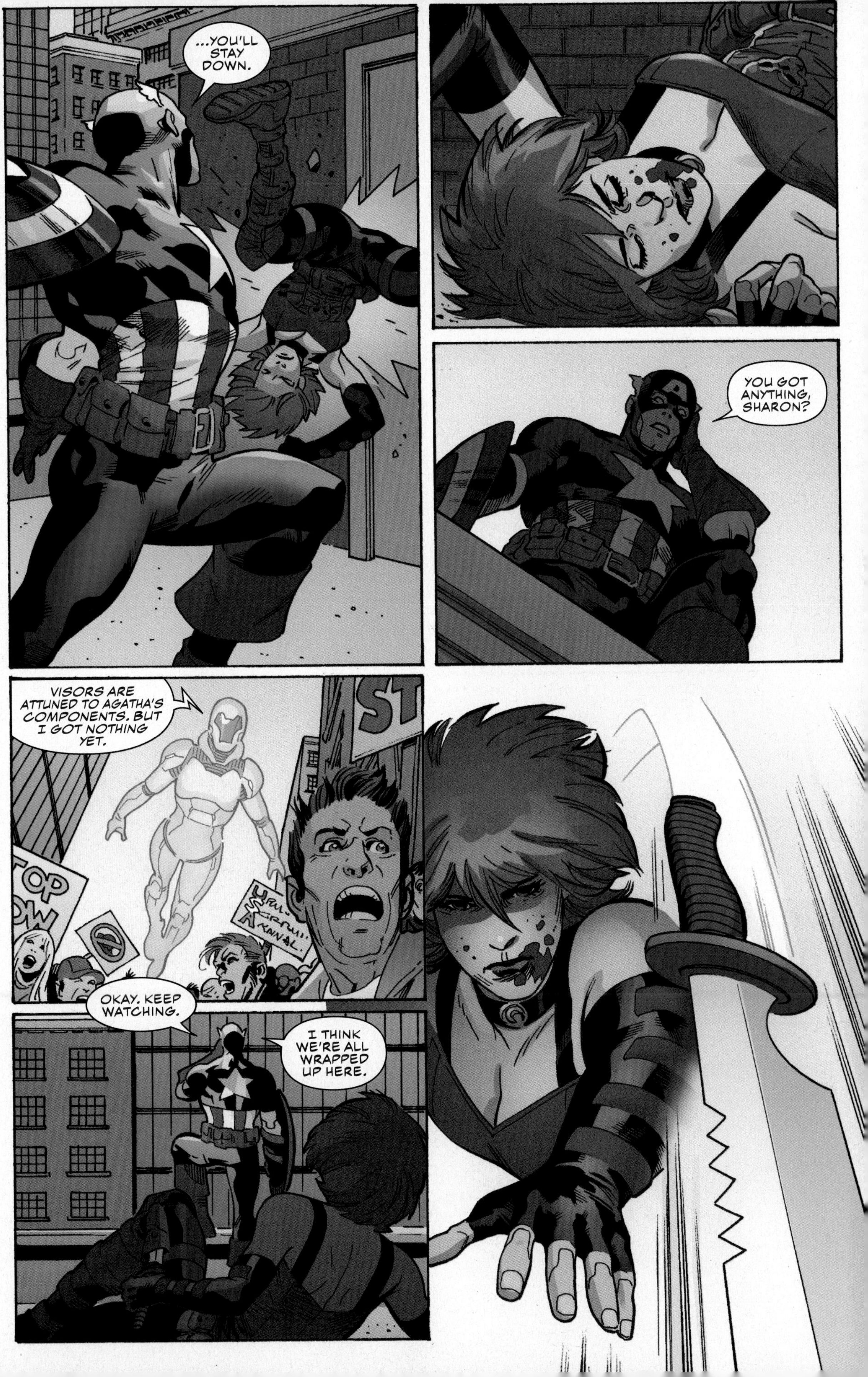
...YOU'LL STAY DOWN.
YOU GOT ANYTHING, SHARON?
VISORS ARE ATTUNED TO AGATHA'S COMPONENTS. BUT I GOT NOTHING YET.
OKAY. KEEP WATCHING.
I THINK WE'RE ALL WRAPPED UP HERE.

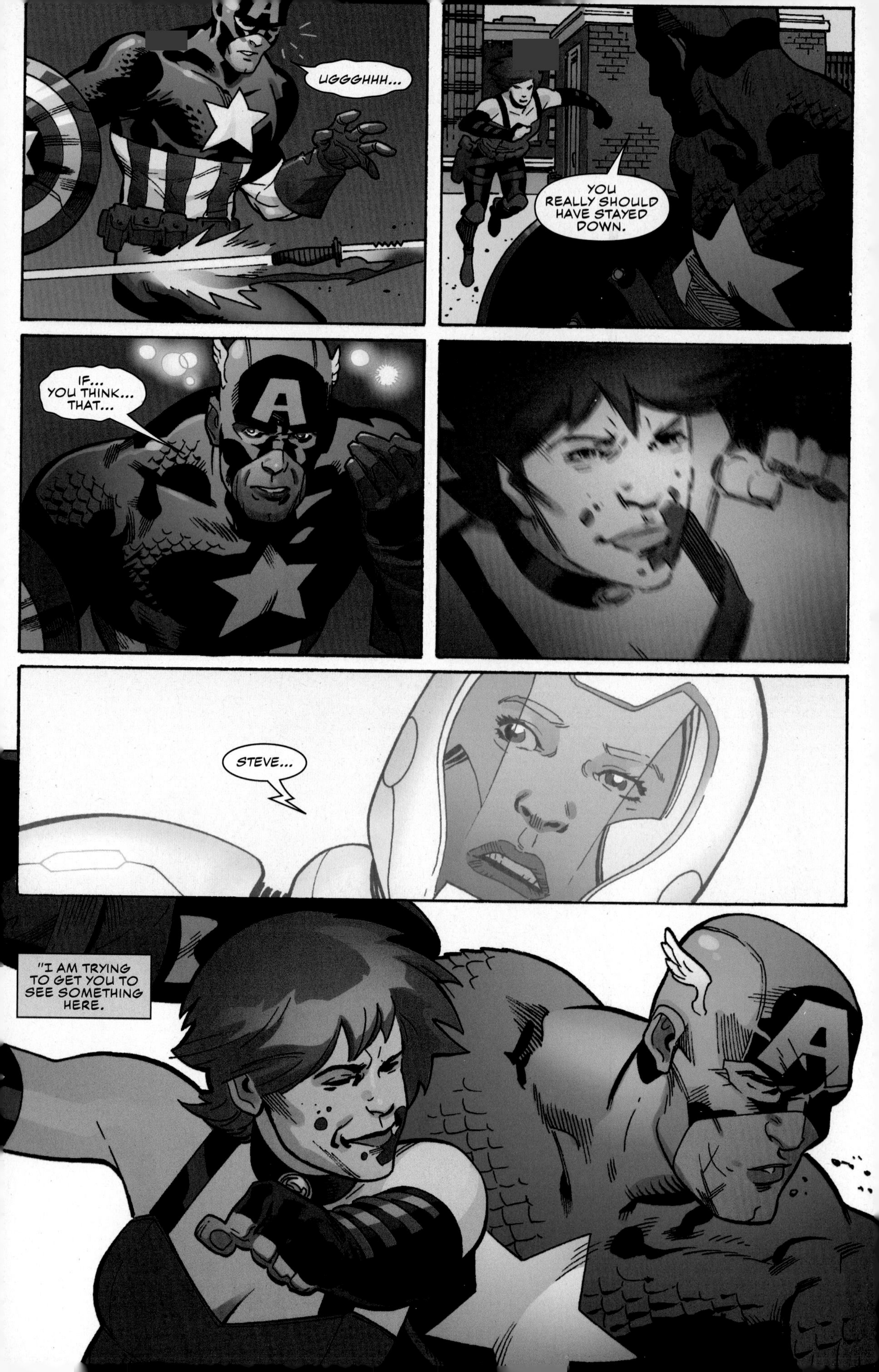
UGGGHHH...
YOU REALLY SHOULD HAVE STAYED DOWN.
IF... YOU THINK... THAT...
STEVE...
"I AM TRYING TO GET YOU TO SEE SOMETHING HERE.

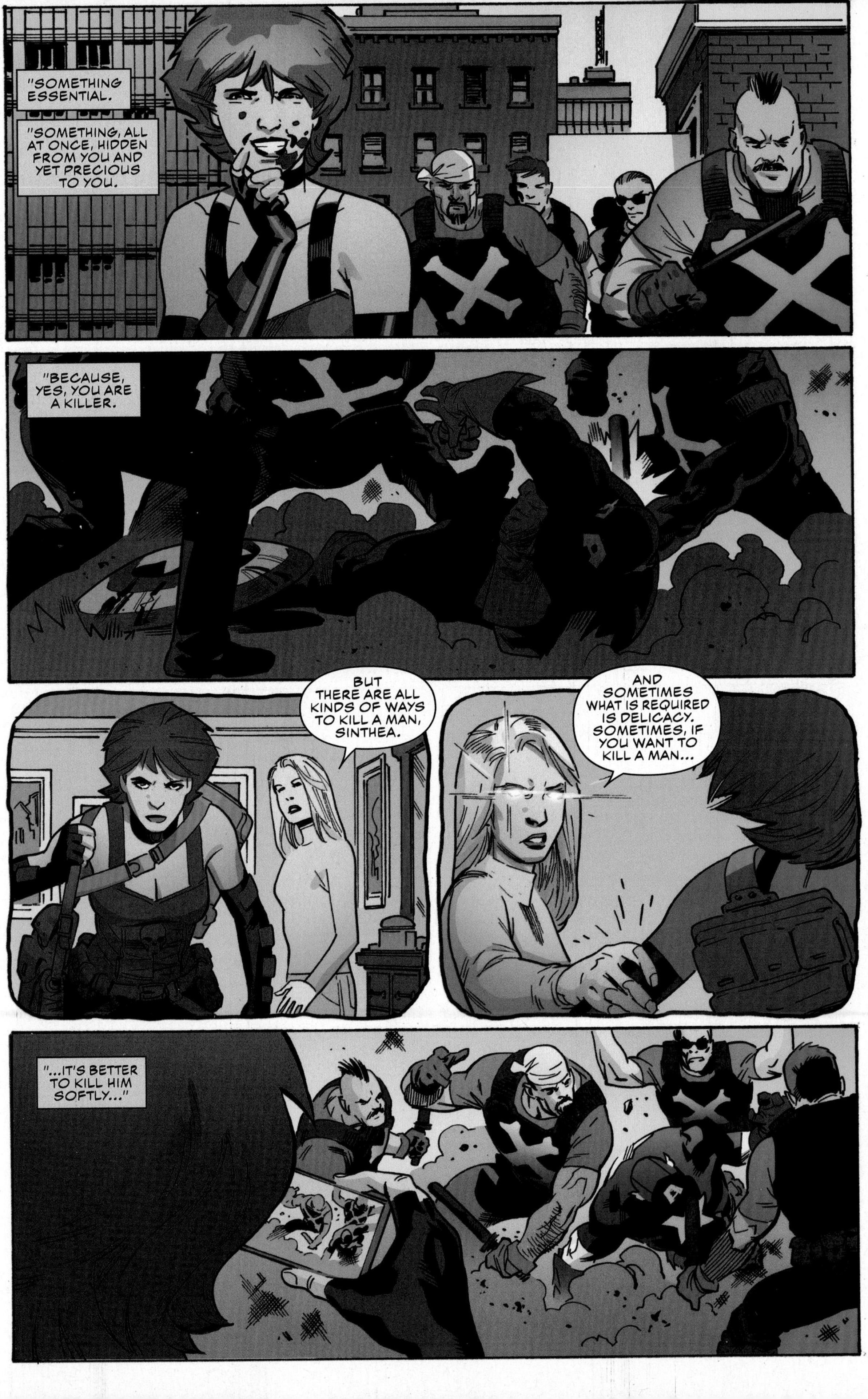
"SOMETHING ESSENTIAL.
"SOMETHING, ALL AT ONCE, HIDDEN FROM YOU AND YET PRECIOUS TO YOU.
"BECAUSE, YES, YOU ARE A KILLER.
BUT THERE ARE ALL KINDS OF WAYS TO KILL A MAN, SINTHEA.
AND SOMETIMES WHAT IS REQUIRED IS DELICACY. SOMETIMES, IF YOU WANT TO KILL A MAN...
"...IT'S BETTER TO KILL HIM SOFTLY..."

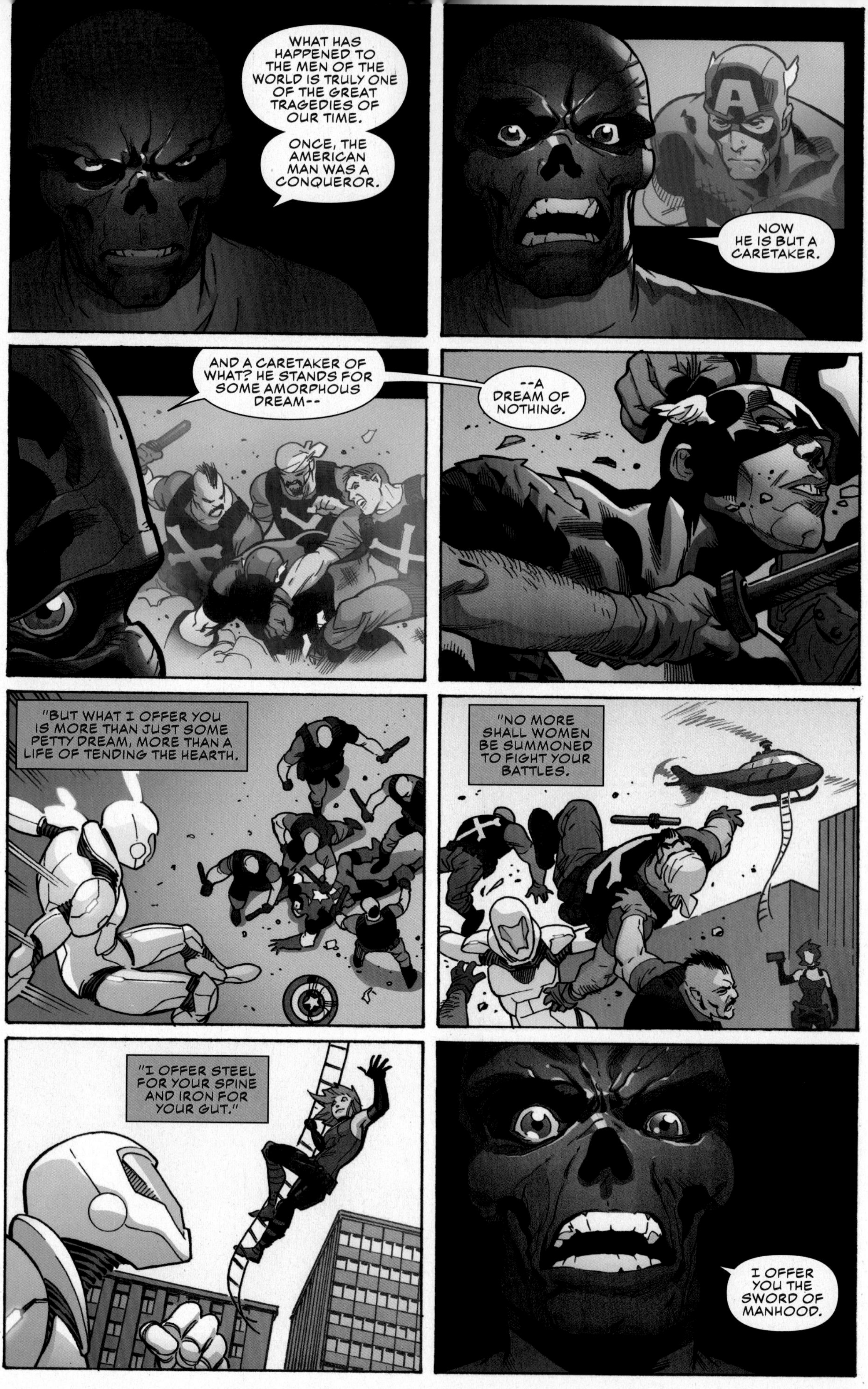
WHAT HAS HAPPENED TO THE MEN OF THE WORLD IS TRULY ONE OF THE GREAT TRAGEDIES OF OUR TIME.
ONCE, THE AMERICAN MAN WAS A CONQUEROR.
NOW HE IS BUT A CARETAKER.
AND A CARETAKER OF WHAT? HE STANDS FOR SOME AMORPHOUS DREAM--
--A DREAM OF NOTHING.
"BUT WHAT I OFFER YOU IS MORE THAN JUST SOME PETTY DREAM, MORE THAN A LIFE OF TENDING THE HEARTH.
"NO MORE SHALL WOMEN BE SUMMONED TO FIGHT YOUR BATTLES.
"I OFFER STEEL FOR YOUR SPINE AND IRON FOR YOUR GUT."
I OFFER YOU THE SWORD OF MANHOOD.

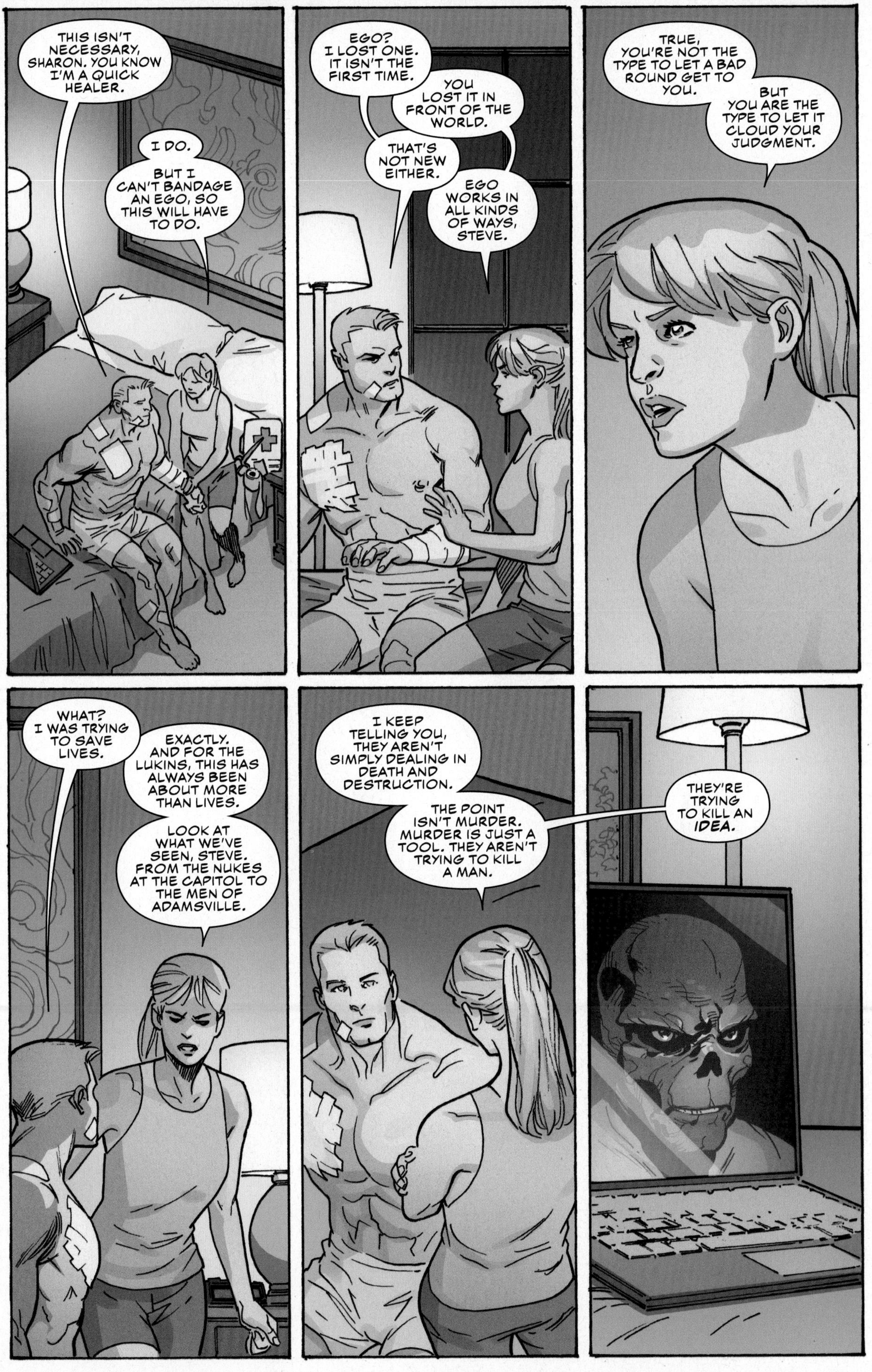
THIS ISN'T NECESSARY, SHARON. YOU KNOW I'M A QUICK HEALER.
I DO.
BUT I CAN'T BANDAGE AN EGO, SO THIS WILL HAVE TO DO.
EGO? I LOST ONE. IT ISN'T THE FIRST TIME.
YOU LOST IT IN FRONT OF THE WORLD.
THAT'S NOT NEW EITHER.
EGO WORKS IN ALL KINDS OF WAYS, STEVE.
TRUE, YOU'RE NOT THE TYPE TO LET A BAD ROUND GET TO YOU.
BUT YOU ARE THE TYPE TO LET IT CLOUD YOUR JUDGMENT.
WHAT? I WAS TRYING TO SAVE LIVES.
EXACTLY. AND FOR THE LUKINS, THIS HAS ALWAYS BEEN ABOUT MORE THAN LIVES.
LOOK AT WHAT WE'VE SEEN, STEVE. FROM THE NUKES AT THE CAPITOL TO THE MEN OF ADAMSVILLE.
I KEEP TELLING YOU, THEY AREN'T SIMPLY DEALING IN DEATH AND DESTRUCTION.
THE POINT ISN'T MURDER. MURDER IS JUST A TOOL. THEY AREN'T TRYING TO KILL A MAN.
THEY'RE TRYING TO KILL AN ***IDEA***.

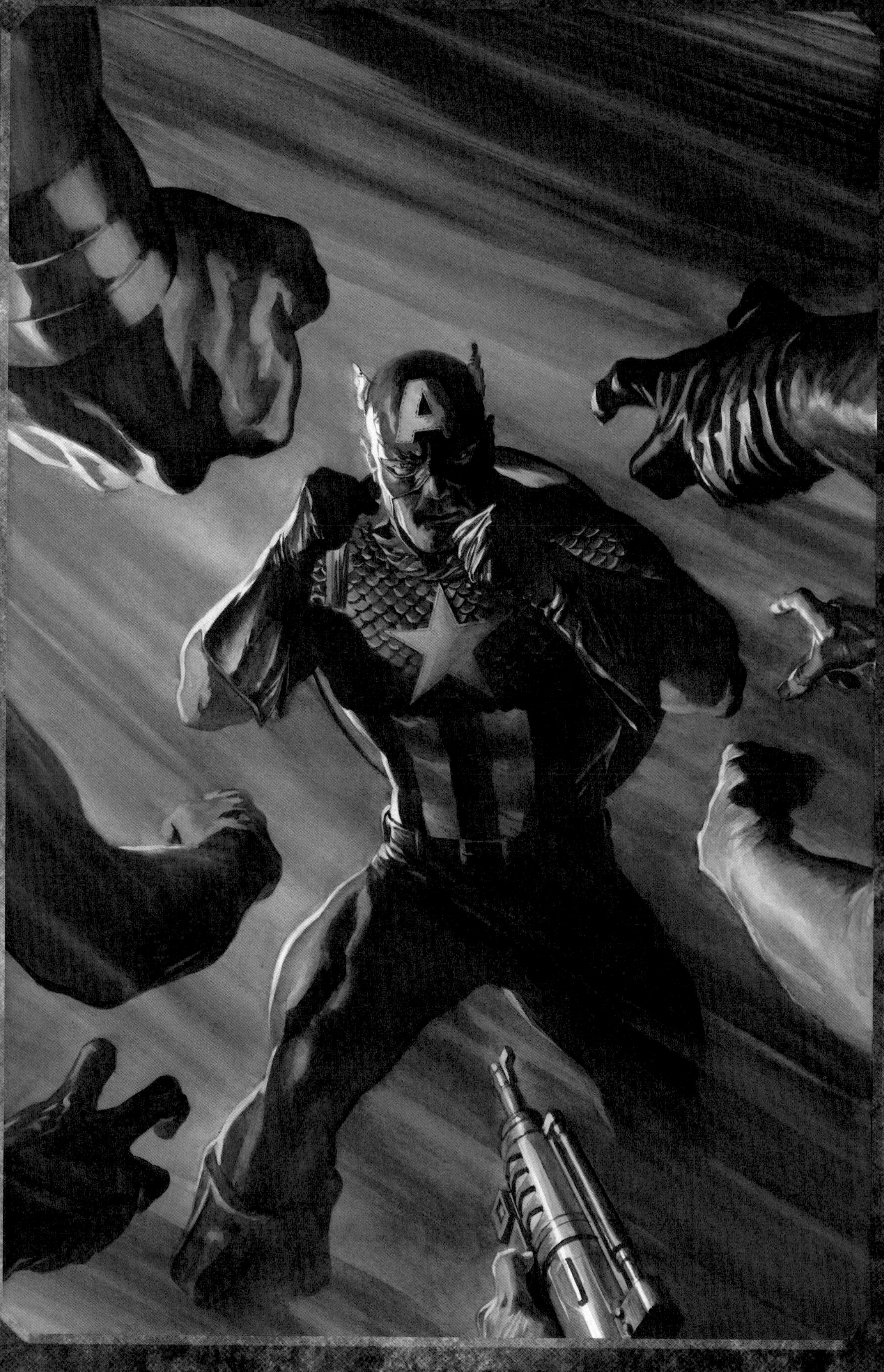

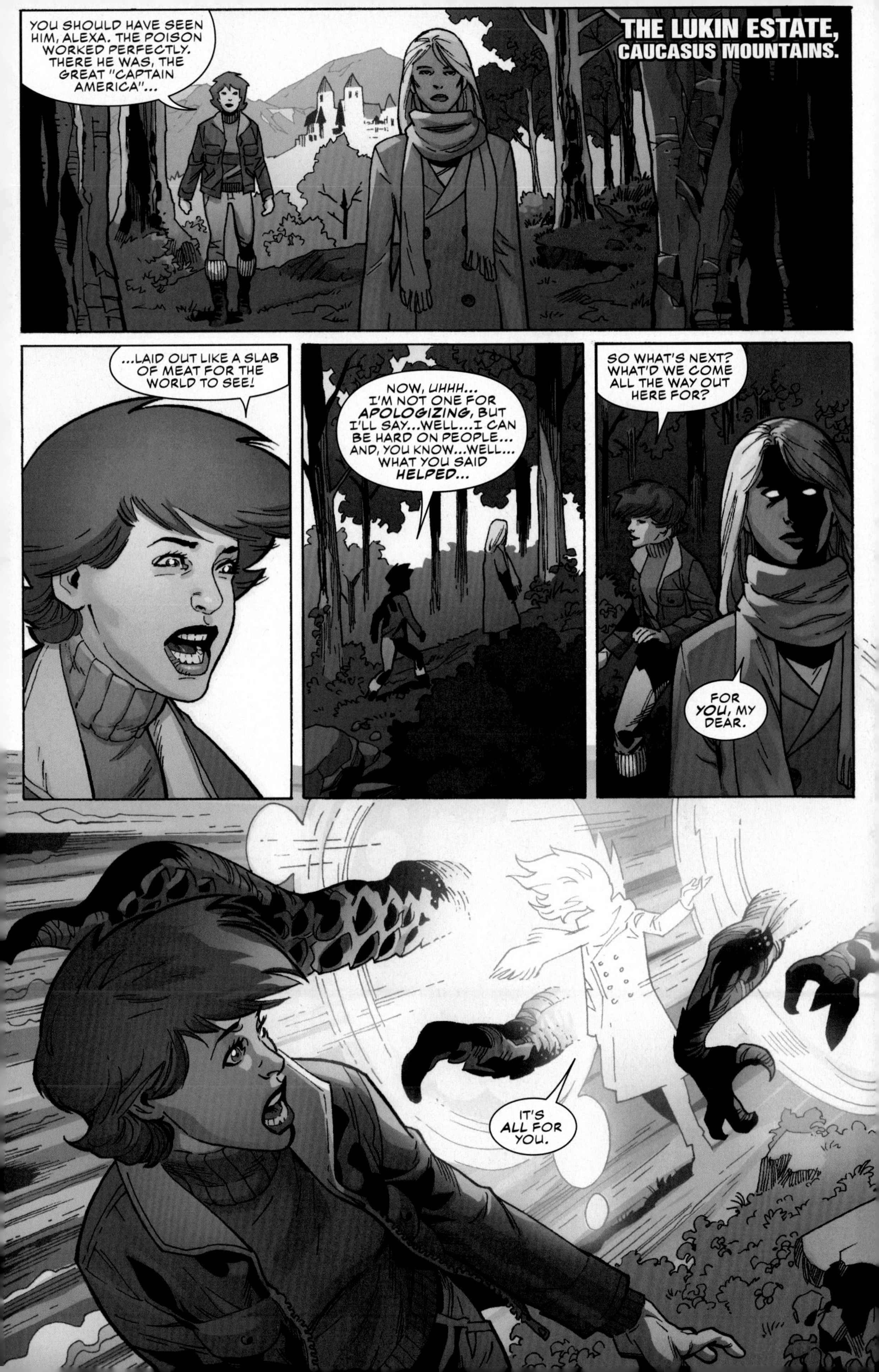
THE LUKIN ESTATE, CAUCASUS MOUNTAINS.
YOU SHOULD HAVE SEEN HIM, ALEXA. THE POISON WORKED PERFECTLY. THERE HE WAS, THE GREAT "CAPTAIN AMERICA"...
...LAID OUT LIKE A SLAB OF MEAT FOR THE WORLD TO SEE!
NOW, UHHH... I'M NOT ONE FOR APOLOGIZING, BUT I'LL SAY...WELL...I CAN BE HARD ON PEOPLE... AND, YOU KNOW...WELL... WHAT YOU SAID HELPED...
SO WHAT'S NEXT? WHAT'D WE COME ALL THE WAY OUT HERE FOR?
FOR YOU, MY DEAR.
IT'S ALL FOR YOU.

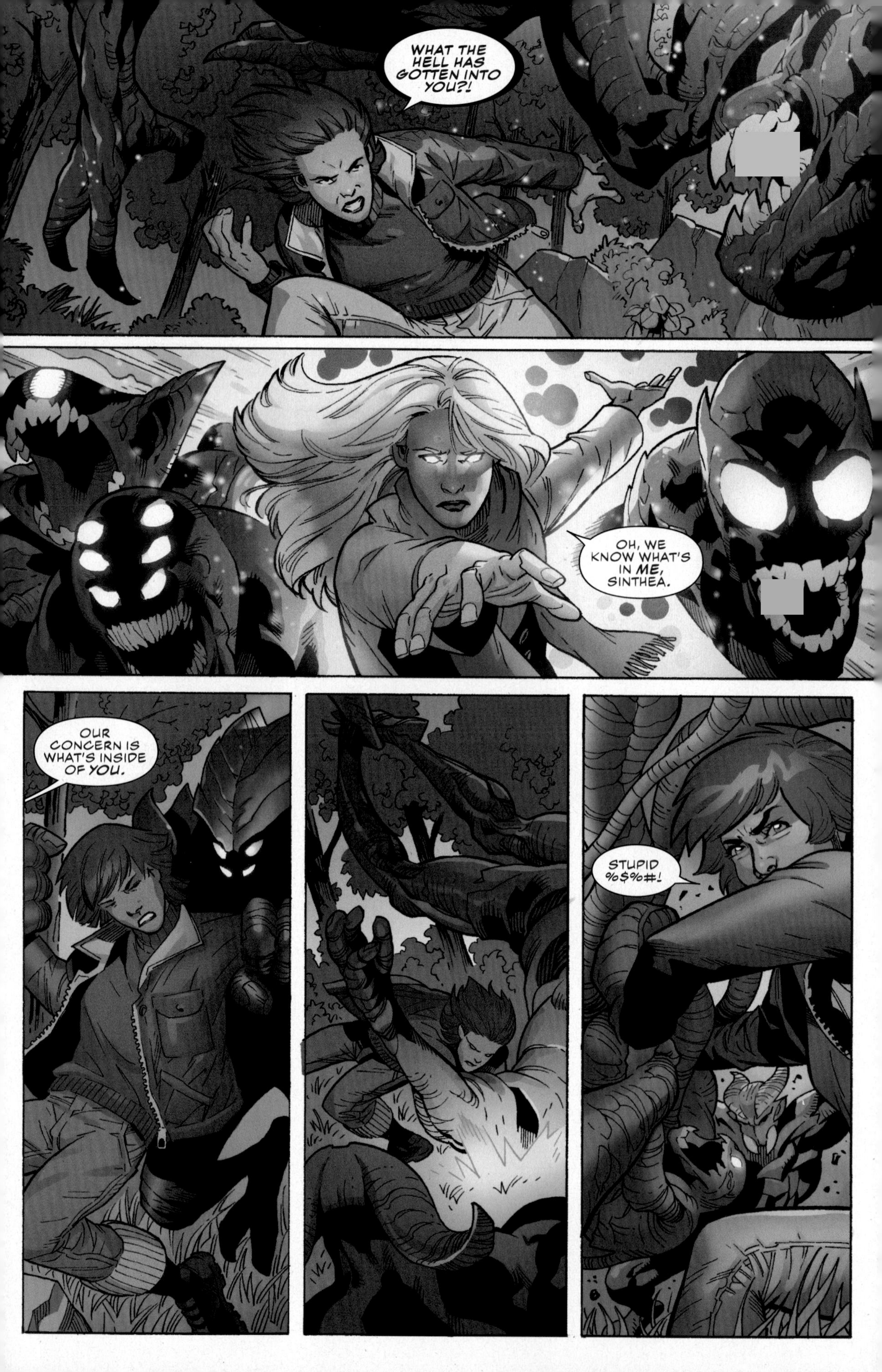
WHAT THE HELL HAS GOTTEN INTO YOU?!
OH, WE KNOW WHAT'S IN ME, SINTHEA.
OUR CONCERN IS WHAT'S INSIDE OF YOU.
STUPID %$%#!

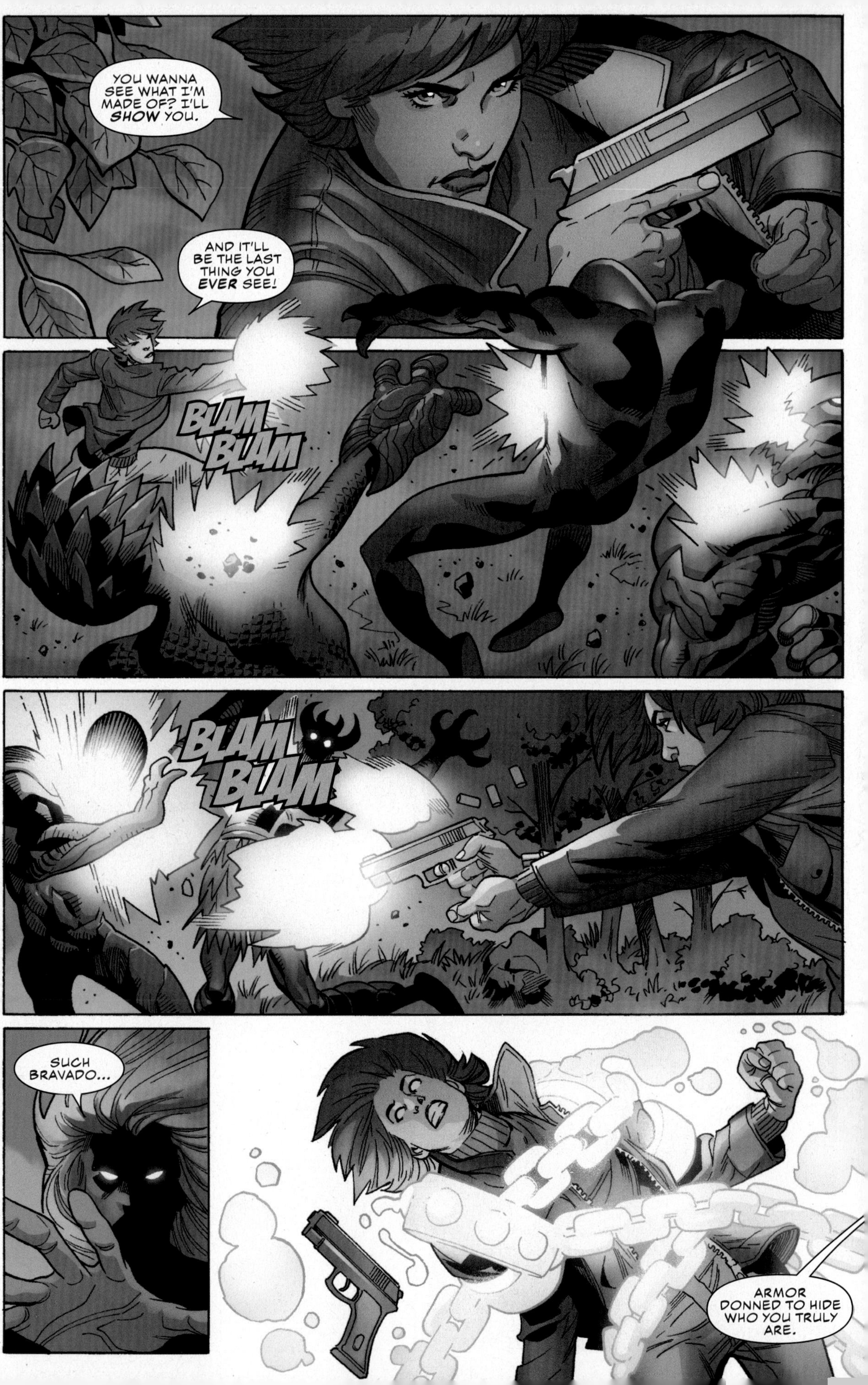
YOU WANNA SEE WHAT I'M MADE OF? I'LL SHOW YOU.
AND IT'LL BE THE LAST THING YOU EVER SEE!
BLAM BLAM
BLAM BLAM
SUCH BRAVADO...
ARMOR DONNED TO HIDE WHO YOU TRULY ARE.

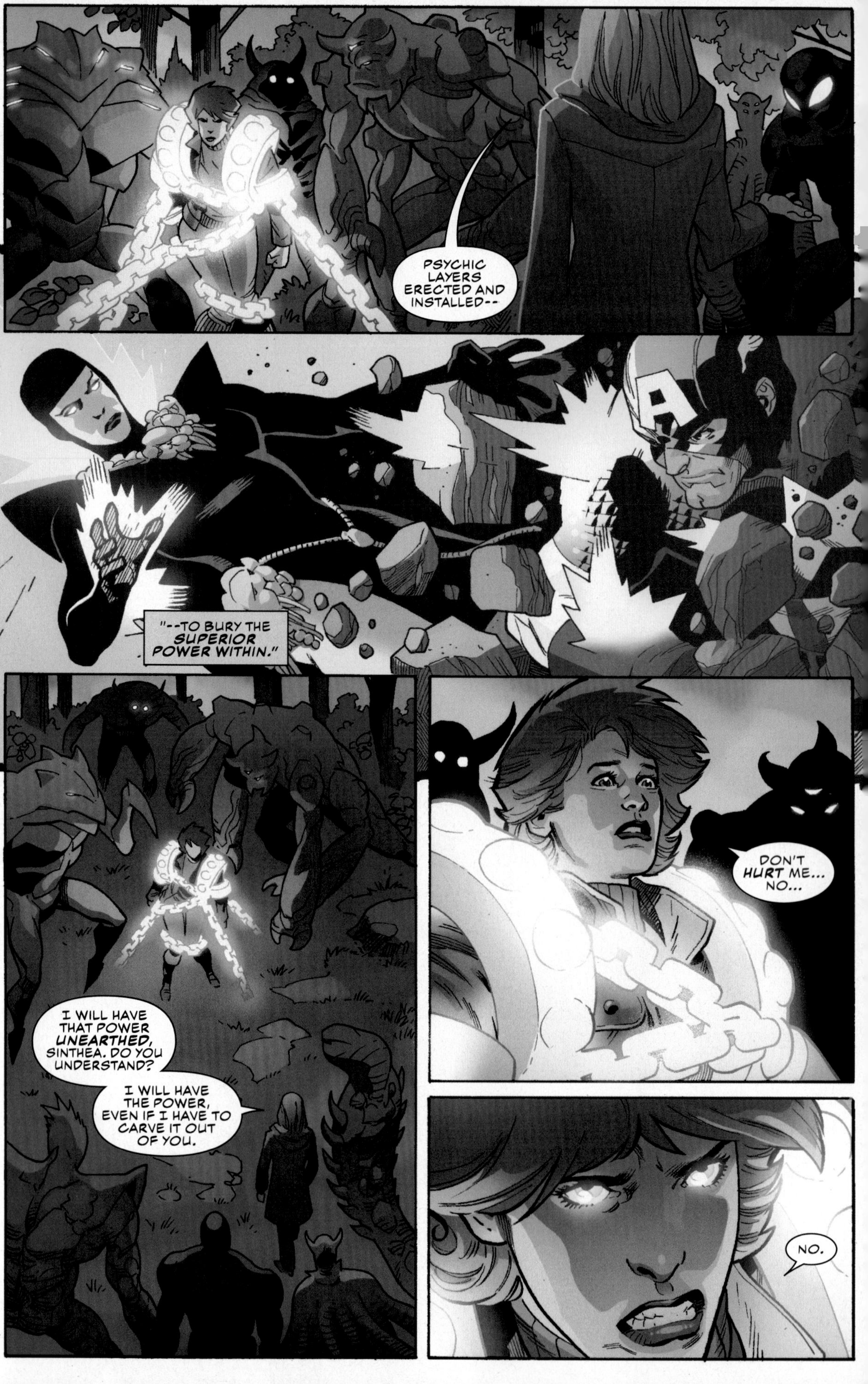
PSYCHIC LAYERS ERECTED AND INSTALLED--
"--TO BURY THE SUPERIOR POWER WITHIN."
DON'T HURT ME... NO...
I WILL HAVE THAT POWER UNEARTHED, SINTHEA. DO YOU UNDERSTAND?
I WILL HAVE THE POWER, EVEN IF I HAVE TO CARVE IT OUT OF YOU.
NO.

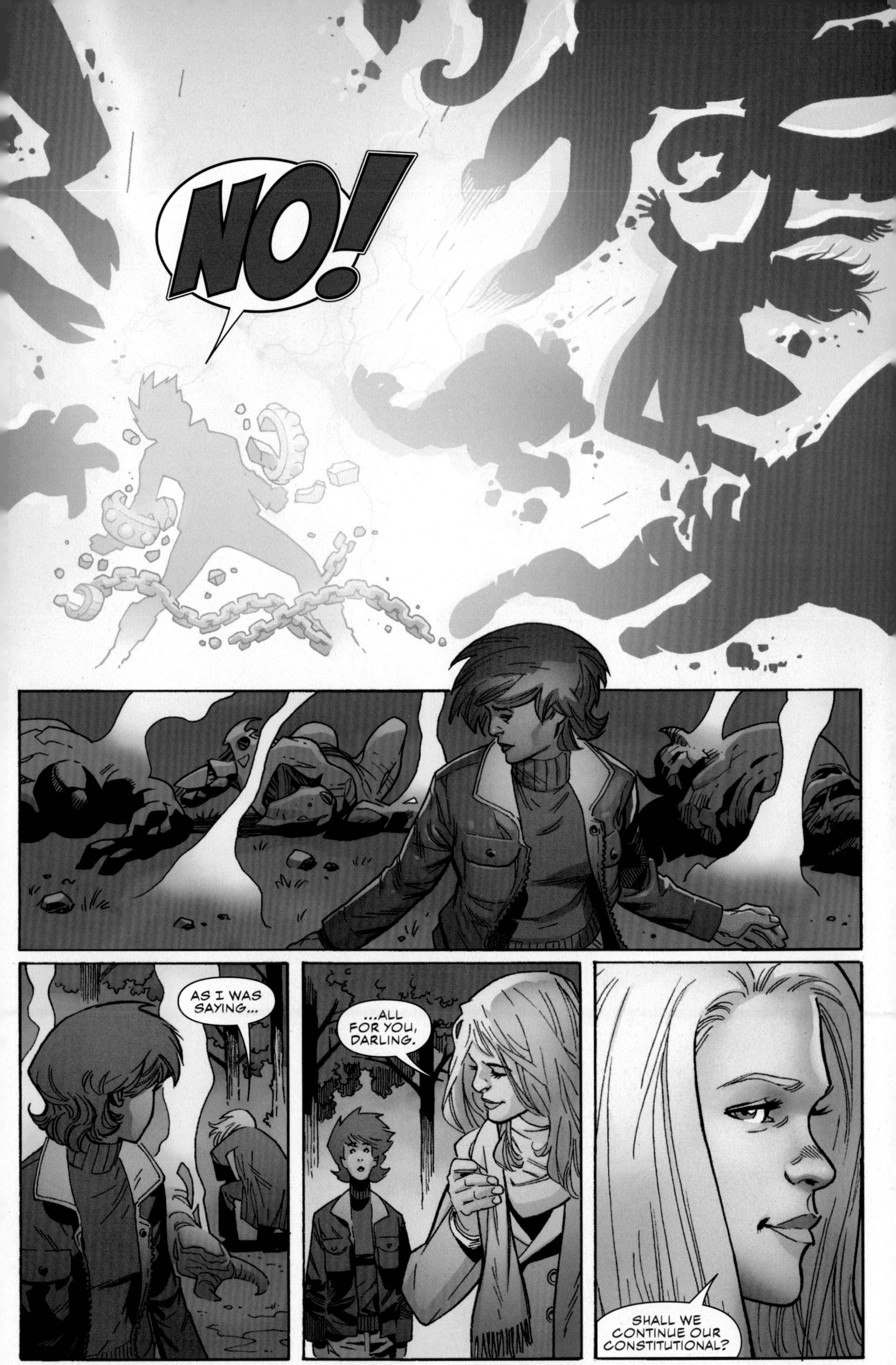
NO!
AS I WAS SAYING...
...ALL FOR YOU, DARLING.
SHALL WE CONTINUE OUR CONSTITUTIONAL?

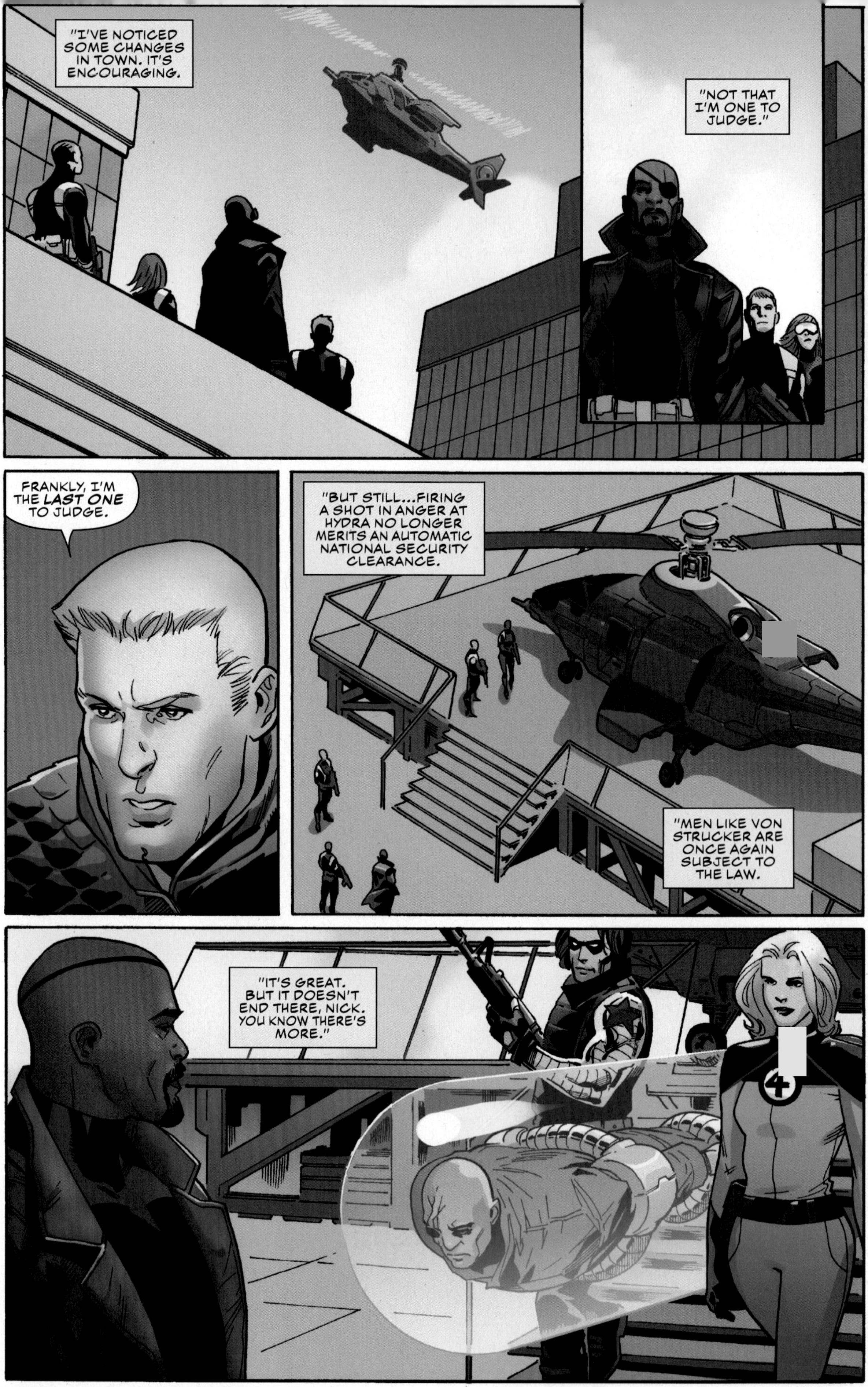
"I'VE NOTICED SOME CHANGES IN TOWN. IT'S ENCOURAGING.
"NOT THAT I'M ONE TO JUDGE."
FRANKLY, I'M THE *LAST ONE* TO JUDGE.
"BUT STILL...FIRING A SHOT IN ANGER AT HYDRA NO LONGER MERITS AN AUTOMATIC NATIONAL SECURITY CLEARANCE.
"MEN LIKE VON STRUCKER ARE ONCE AGAIN SUBJECT TO THE LAW.
"IT'S GREAT. BUT IT DOESN'T END THERE, NICK. YOU KNOW THERE'S MORE."

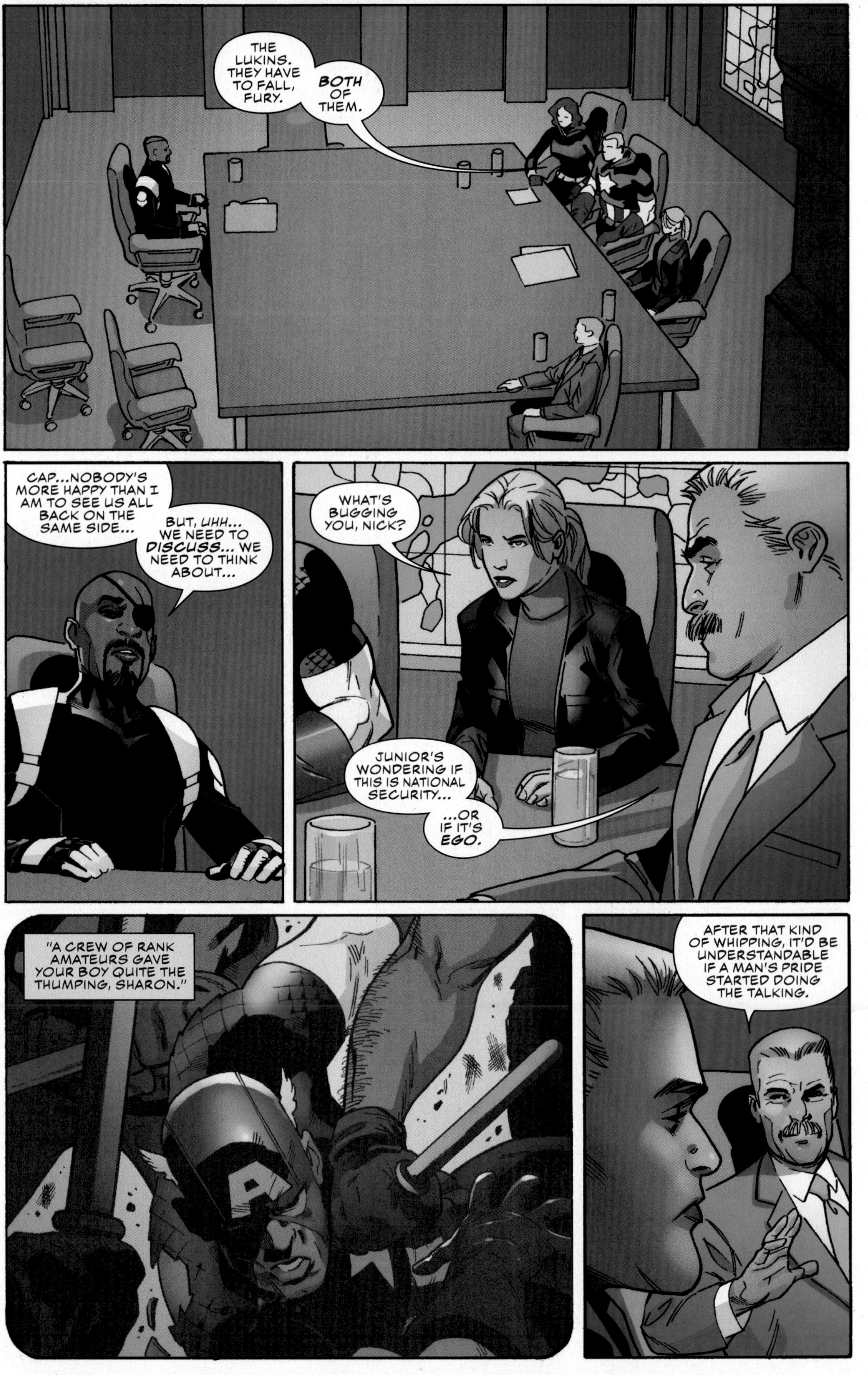
THE LUKINS. THEY HAVE TO FALL, FURY.
BOTH OF THEM.
CAP...NOBODY'S MORE HAPPY THAN I AM TO SEE US ALL BACK ON THE SAME SIDE...
BUT, UHH... WE NEED TO DISCUSS... WE NEED TO THINK ABOUT...
WHAT'S BUGGING YOU, NICK?
JUNIOR'S WONDERING IF THIS IS NATIONAL SECURITY...
...OR IF IT'S EGO.
"A CREW OF RANK AMATEURS GAVE YOUR BOY QUITE THE THUMPING, SHARON."
AFTER THAT KIND OF WHIPPING, IT'D BE UNDERSTANDABLE IF A MAN'S PRIDE STARTED DOING THE TALKING.

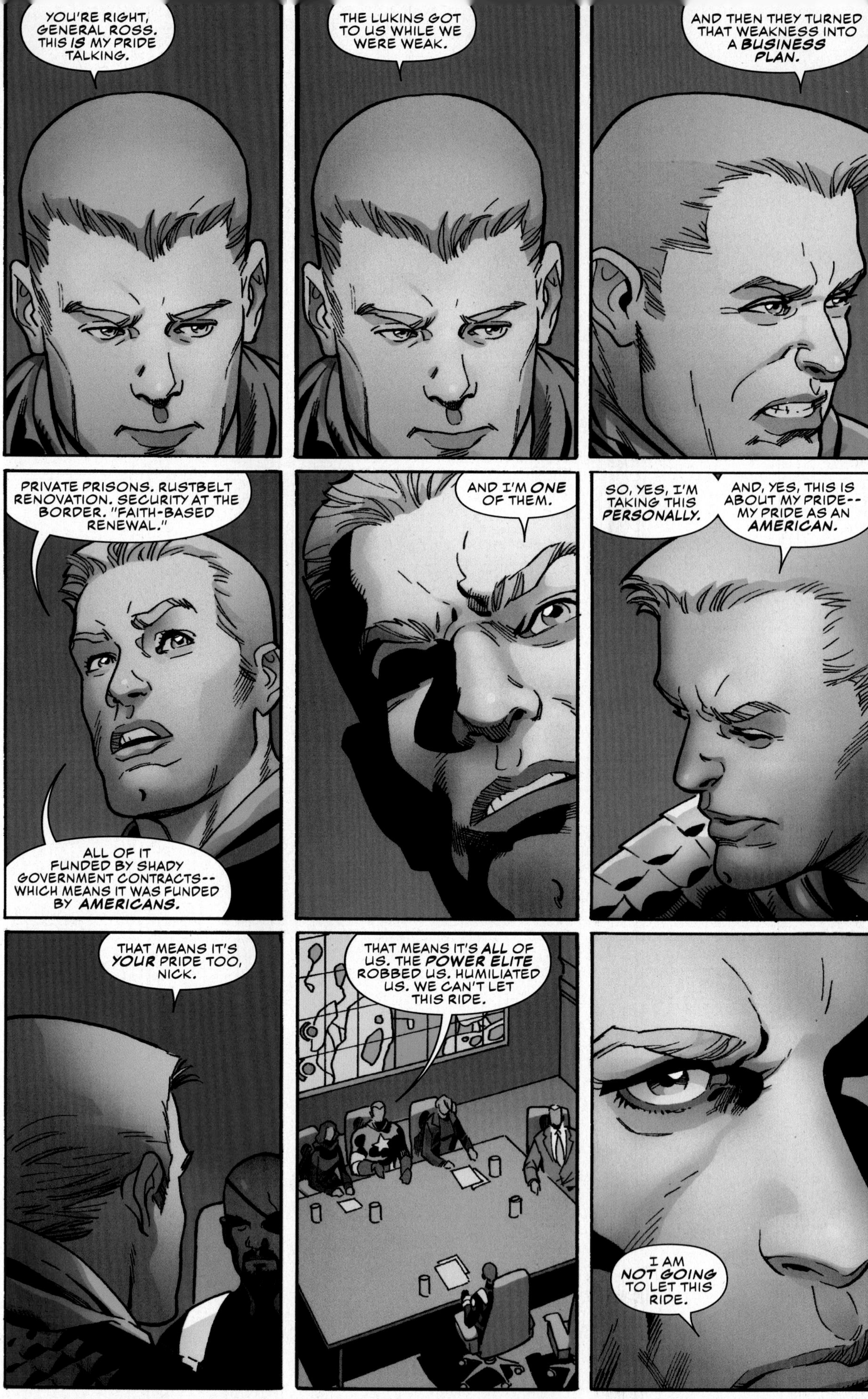
YOU'RE RIGHT, GENERAL ROSS. THIS IS MY PRIDE TALKING.
THE LUKINS GOT TO US WHILE WE WERE WEAK.
AND THEN THEY TURNED THAT WEAKNESS INTO A BUSINESS PLAN.
PRIVATE PRISONS. RUSTBELT RENOVATION. SECURITY AT THE BORDER. "FAITH-BASED RENEWAL."
ALL OF IT FUNDED BY SHADY GOVERNMENT CONTRACTS-- WHICH MEANS IT WAS FUNDED BY AMERICANS.
AND I'M ONE OF THEM.
SO, YES, I'M TAKING THIS PERSONALLY.
AND, YES, THIS IS ABOUT MY PRIDE-- MY PRIDE AS AN AMERICAN.
THAT MEANS IT'S YOUR PRIDE TOO, NICK.
THAT MEANS IT'S ALL OF US. THE POWER ELITE ROBBED US. HUMILIATED US. WE CAN'T LET THIS RIDE.
I AM NOT GOING TO LET THIS RIDE.

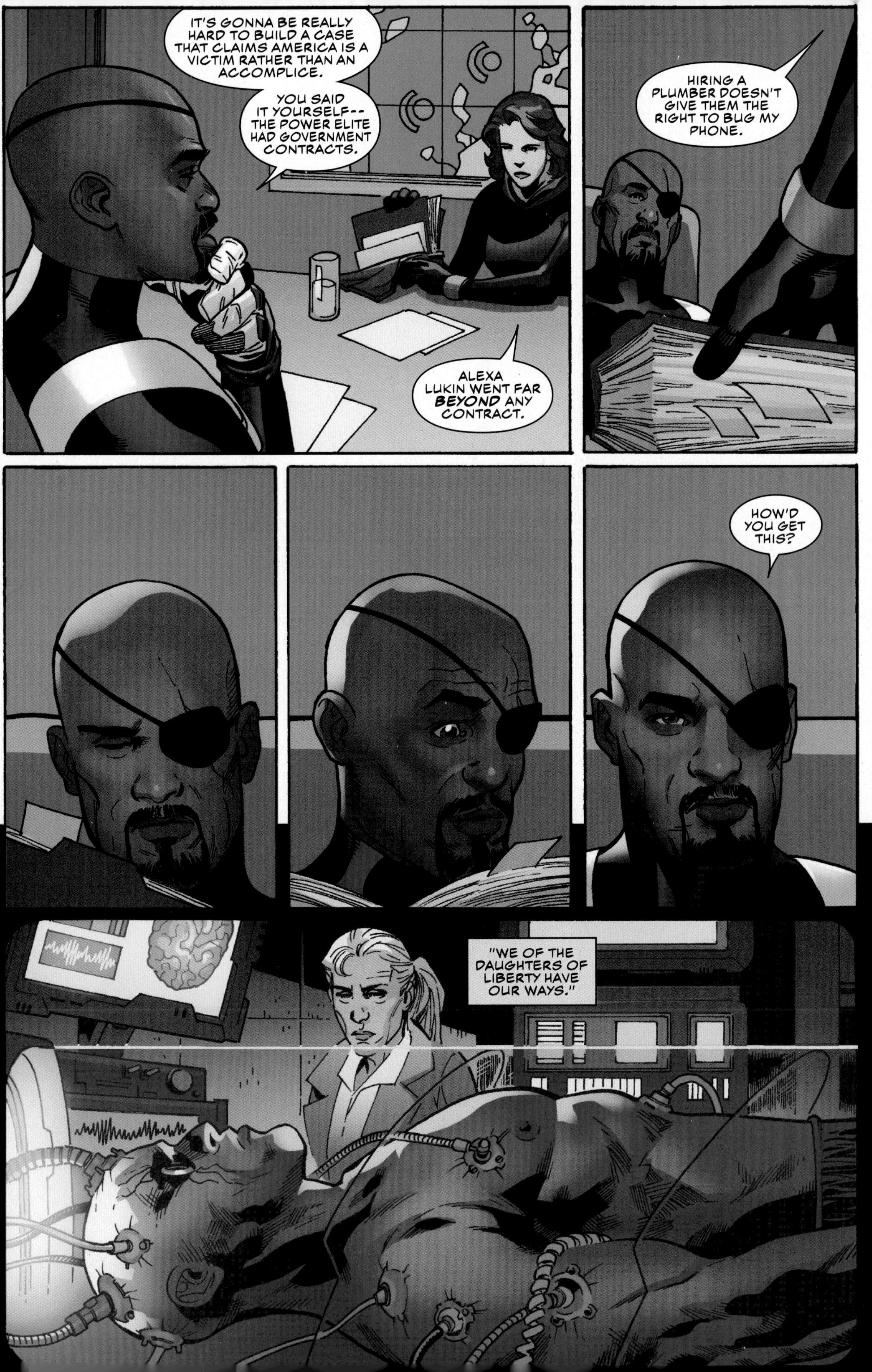
IT'S GONNA BE REALLY HARD TO BUILD A CASE THAT CLAIMS AMERICA IS A VICTIM RATHER THAN AN ACCOMPLICE.
YOU SAID IT YOURSELF-- THE POWER ELITE HAD GOVERNMENT CONTRACTS.
ALEXA LUKIN WENT FAR BEYOND ANY CONTRACT.
HIRING A PLUMBER DOESN'T GIVE THEM THE RIGHT TO BUG MY PHONE.
HOW'D YOU GET THIS?
"WE OF THE DAUGHTERS OF LIBERTY HAVE OUR WAYS."

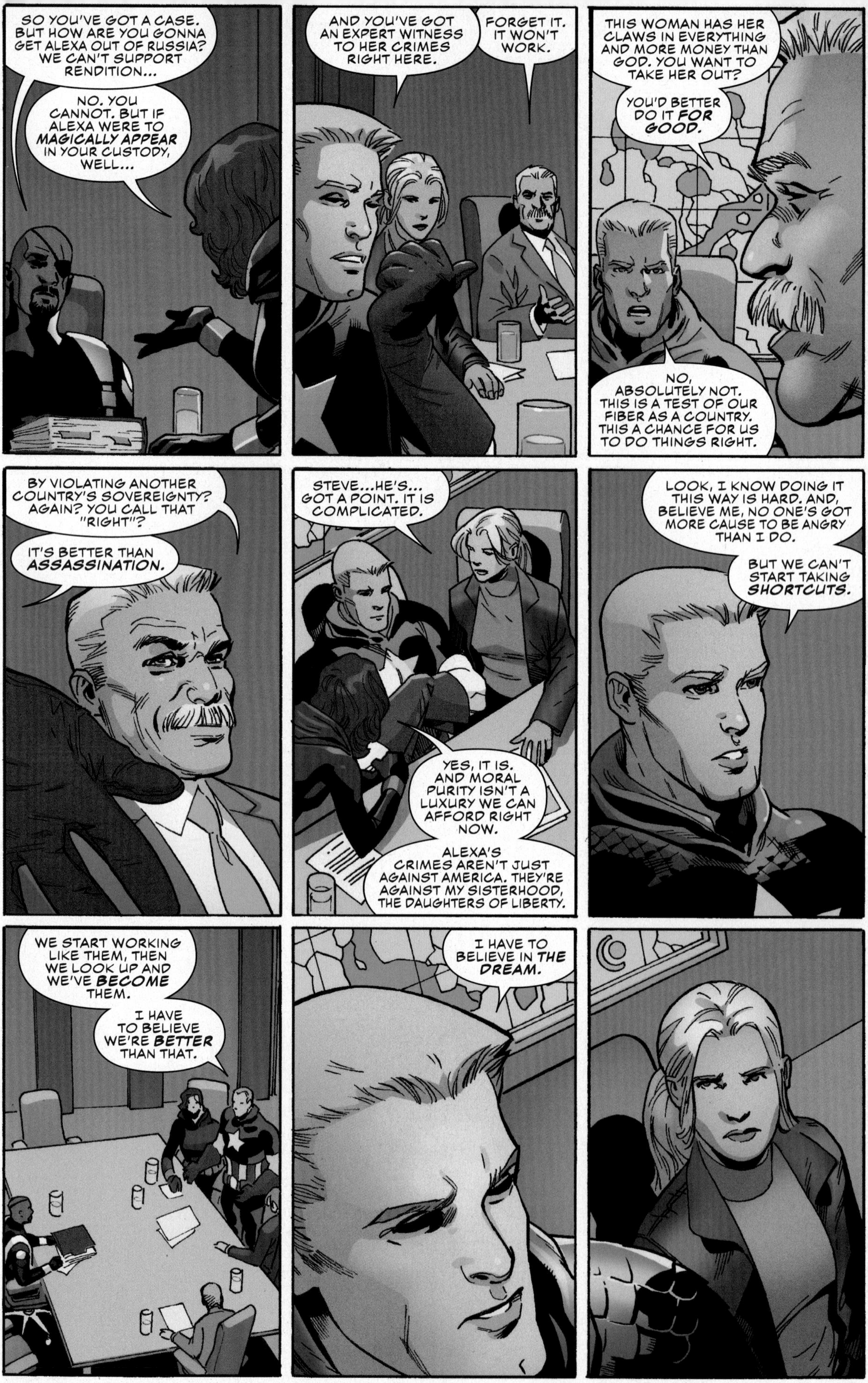
SO YOU'VE GOT A CASE. BUT HOW ARE YOU GONNA GET ALEXA OUT OF RUSSIA? WE CAN'T SUPPORT RENDITION...
NO. YOU CANNOT. BUT IF ALEXA WERE TO MAGICALLY APPEAR IN YOUR CUSTODY, WELL...
AND YOU'VE GOT AN EXPERT WITNESS TO HER CRIMES RIGHT HERE.
FORGET IT. IT WON'T WORK.
THIS WOMAN HAS HER CLAWS IN EVERYTHING AND MORE MONEY THAN GOD. YOU WANT TO TAKE HER OUT?
YOU'D BETTER DO IT FOR GOOD.
NO, ABSOLUTELY NOT. THIS IS A TEST OF OUR FIBER AS A COUNTRY. THIS A CHANCE FOR US TO DO THINGS RIGHT.
BY VIOLATING ANOTHER COUNTRY'S SOVEREIGNTY? AGAIN? YOU CALL THAT "RIGHT"?
IT'S BETTER THAN ASSASSINATION.
STEVE...HE'S... GOT A POINT. IT IS COMPLICATED.
YES, IT IS. AND MORAL PURITY ISN'T A LUXURY WE CAN AFFORD RIGHT NOW.
ALEXA'S CRIMES AREN'T JUST AGAINST AMERICA. THEY'RE AGAINST MY SISTERHOOD, THE DAUGHTERS OF LIBERTY.
LOOK, I KNOW DOING IT THIS WAY IS HARD. AND, BELIEVE ME, NO ONE'S GOT MORE CAUSE TO BE ANGRY THAN I DO.
BUT WE CAN'T START TAKING SHORTCUTS.
WE START WORKING LIKE THEM, THEN WE LOOK UP AND WE'VE BECOME THEM.
I HAVE TO BELIEVE WE'RE BETTER THAN THAT.
I HAVE TO BELIEVE IN THE DREAM.

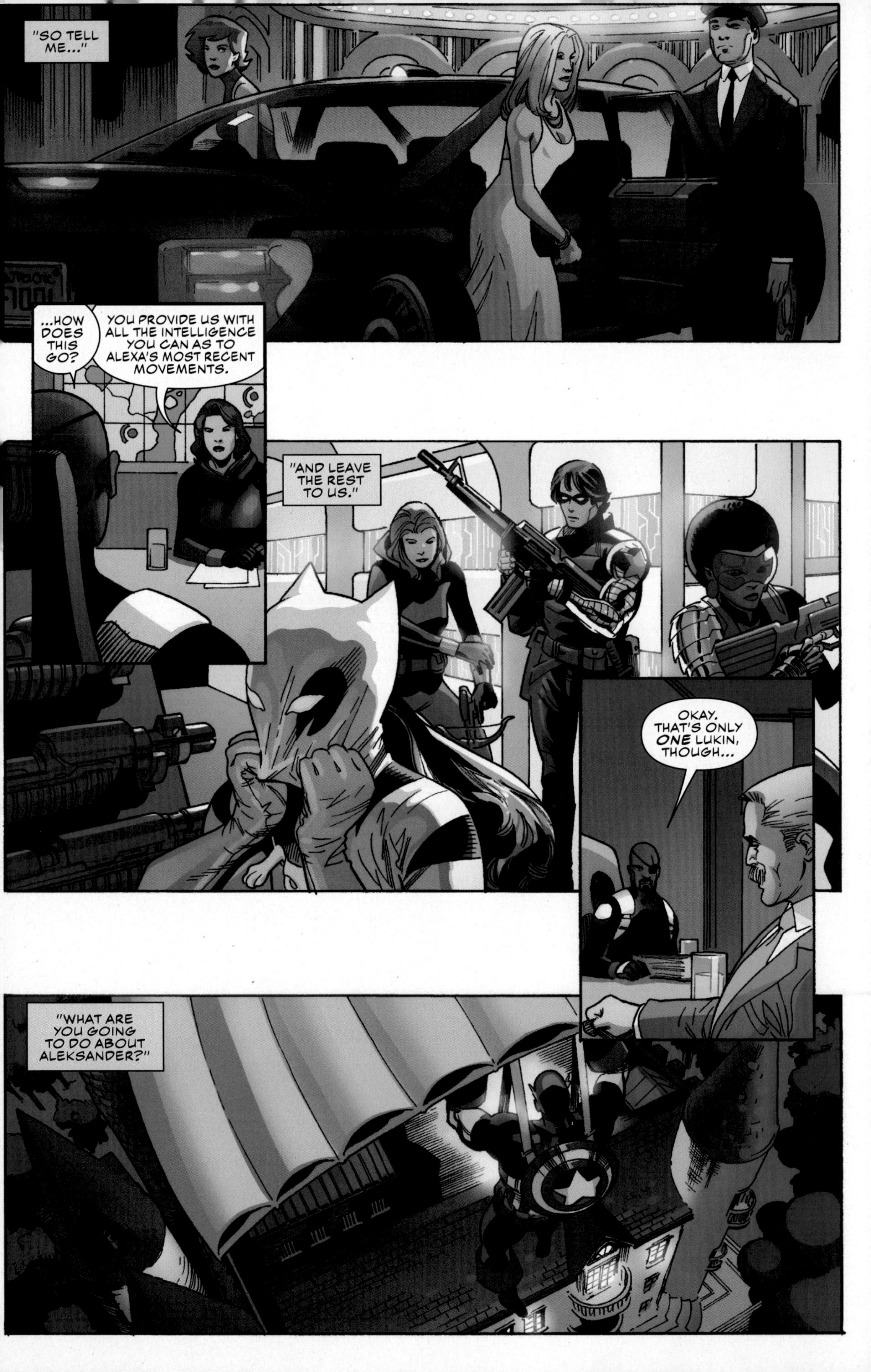
"SO TELL ME..."
...HOW DOES THIS GO?
YOU PROVIDE US WITH ALL THE INTELLIGENCE YOU CAN AS TO ALEXA'S MOST RECENT MOVEMENTS.
"AND LEAVE THE REST TO US."
OKAY. THAT'S ONLY *ONE* LUKIN, THOUGH...
"WHAT ARE YOU GOING TO DO ABOUT ALEKSANDER?"

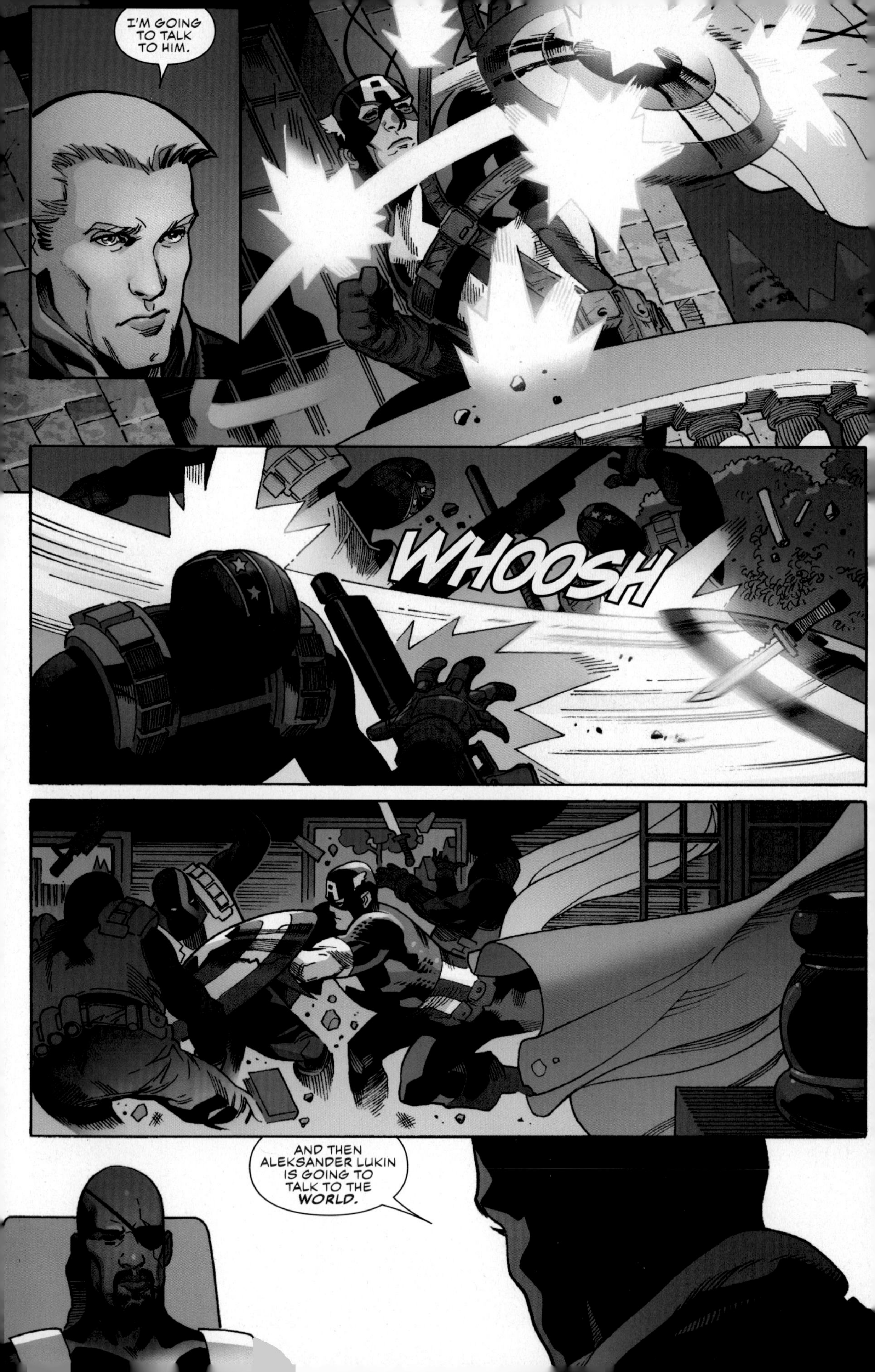

I'M GOING TO TALK TO HIM.
WHOOSH
AND THEN ALEKSANDER LUKIN IS GOING TO TALK TO THE WORLD.

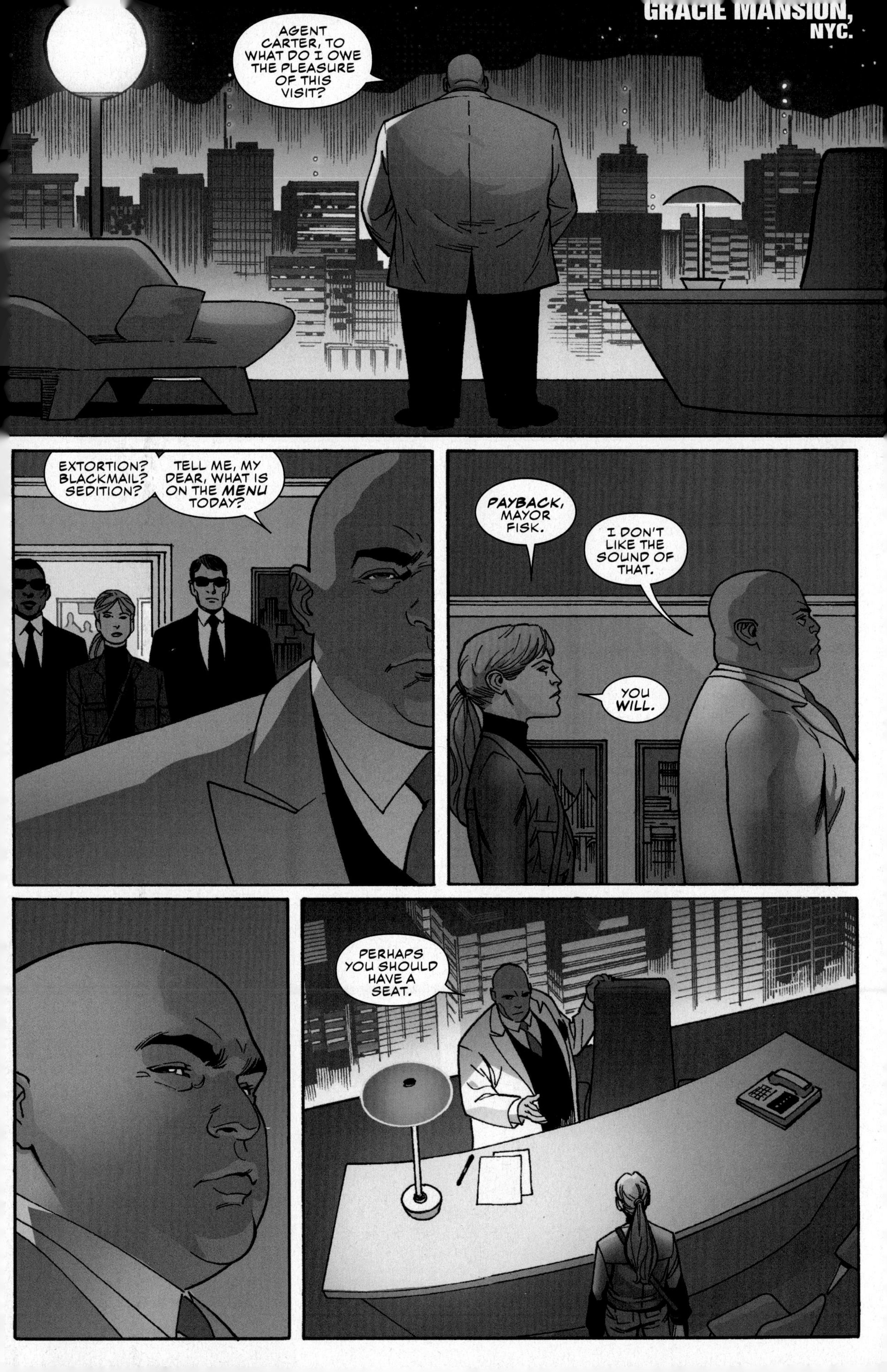
GRACIE MANSION, NYC.
AGENT CARTER, TO WHAT DO I OWE THE PLEASURE OF THIS VISIT?
EXTORTION? BLACKMAIL? SEDITION?
TELL ME, MY DEAR, WHAT IS ON THE MENU TODAY?
PAYBACK, MAYOR FISK.
I DON'T LIKE THE SOUND OF THAT.
YOU WILL.
PERHAPS YOU SHOULD HAVE A SEAT.

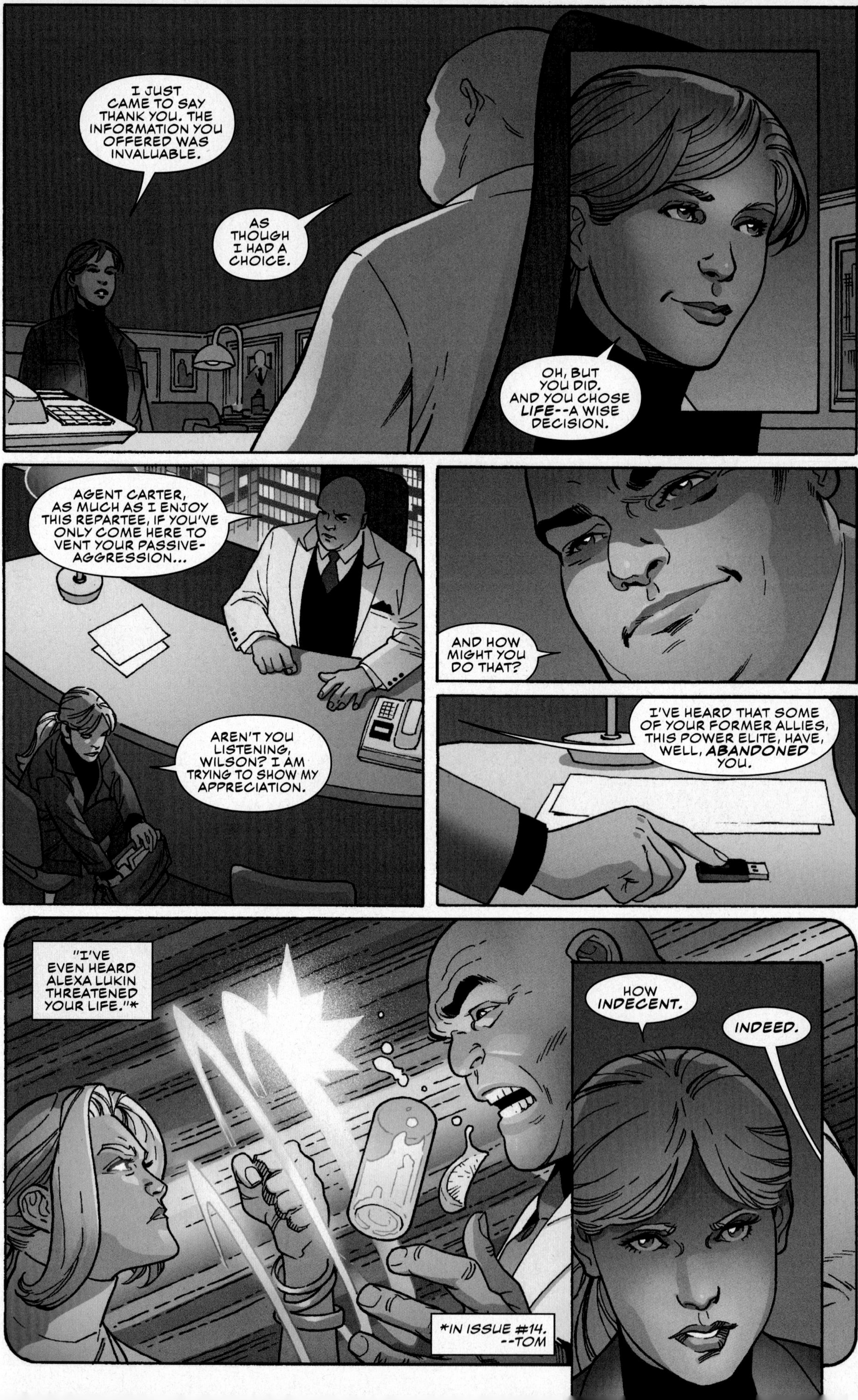
I JUST CAME TO SAY THANK YOU. THE INFORMATION YOU OFFERED WAS INVALUABLE.
AS THOUGH I HAD A CHOICE.
OH, BUT YOU DID. AND YOU CHOSE LIFE--A WISE DECISION.
AGENT CARTER, AS MUCH AS I ENJOY THIS REPARTEE, IF YOU'VE ONLY COME HERE TO VENT YOUR PASSIVE-AGGRESSION...
AREN'T YOU LISTENING, WILSON? I AM TRYING TO SHOW MY APPRECIATION.
AND HOW MIGHT YOU DO THAT?
I'VE HEARD THAT SOME OF YOUR FORMER ALLIES, THIS POWER ELITE, HAVE, WELL, ABANDONED YOU.
"I'VE EVEN HEARD ALEXA LUKIN THREATENED YOUR LIFE."*
HOW INDECENT.
INDEED.
*IN ISSUE #14. --TOM

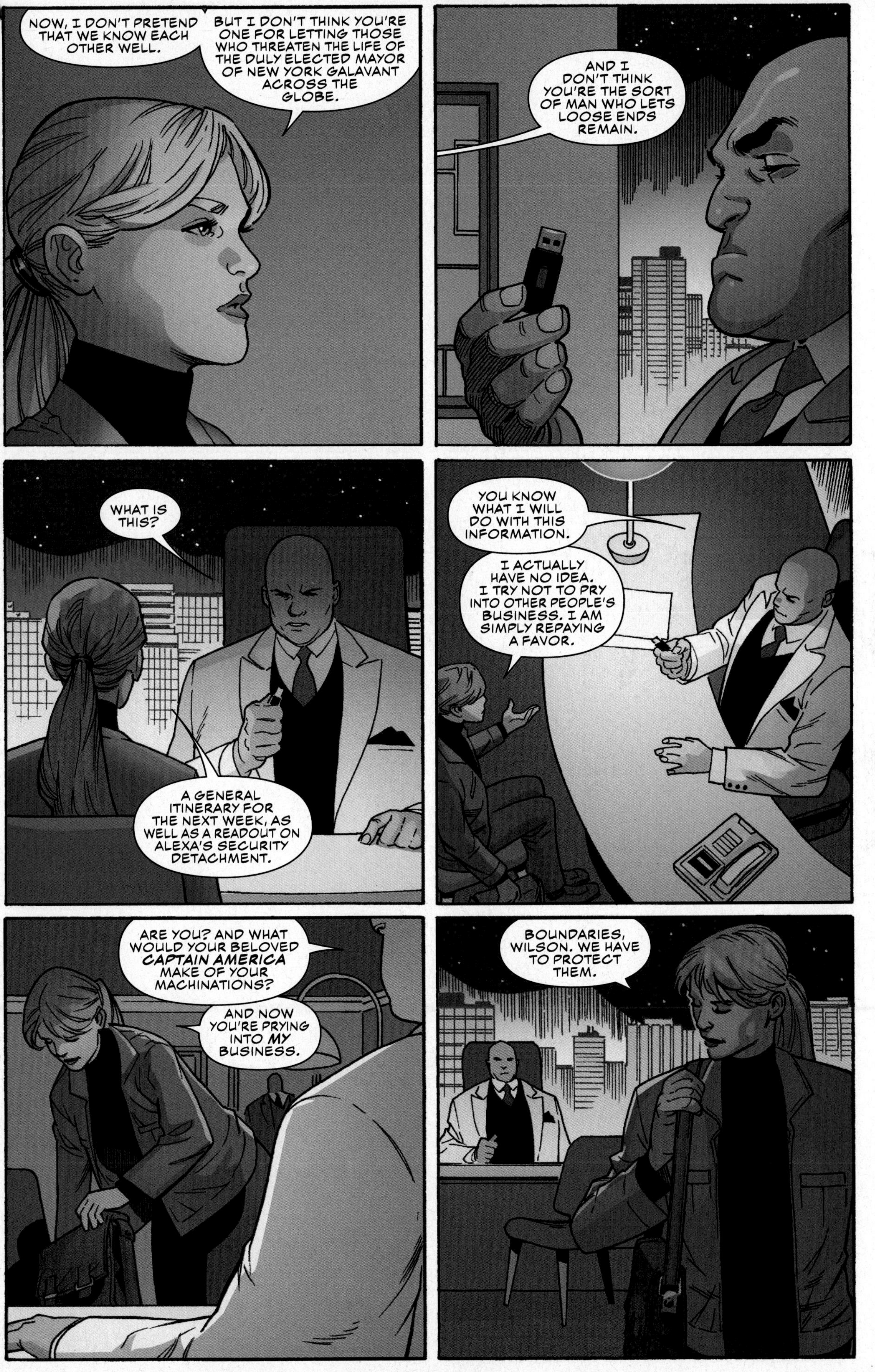
NOW, I DON'T PRETEND THAT WE KNOW EACH OTHER WELL.
BUT I DON'T THINK YOU'RE ONE FOR LETTING THOSE WHO THREATEN THE LIFE OF THE DULY ELECTED MAYOR OF NEW YORK GALAVANT ACROSS THE GLOBE.
AND I DON'T THINK YOU'RE THE SORT OF MAN WHO LETS LOOSE ENDS REMAIN.
WHAT IS THIS?
A GENERAL ITINERARY FOR THE NEXT WEEK, AS WELL AS A READOUT ON ALEXA'S SECURITY DETACHMENT.
YOU KNOW WHAT I WILL DO WITH THIS INFORMATION.
I ACTUALLY HAVE NO IDEA. I TRY NOT TO PRY INTO OTHER PEOPLE'S BUSINESS. I AM SIMPLY REPAYING A FAVOR.
ARE YOU? AND WHAT WOULD YOUR BELOVED *CAPTAIN AMERICA* MAKE OF YOUR MACHINATIONS?
AND NOW YOU'RE PRYING INTO *MY* BUSINESS.
BOUNDARIES, WILSON. WE HAVE TO PROTECT THEM.

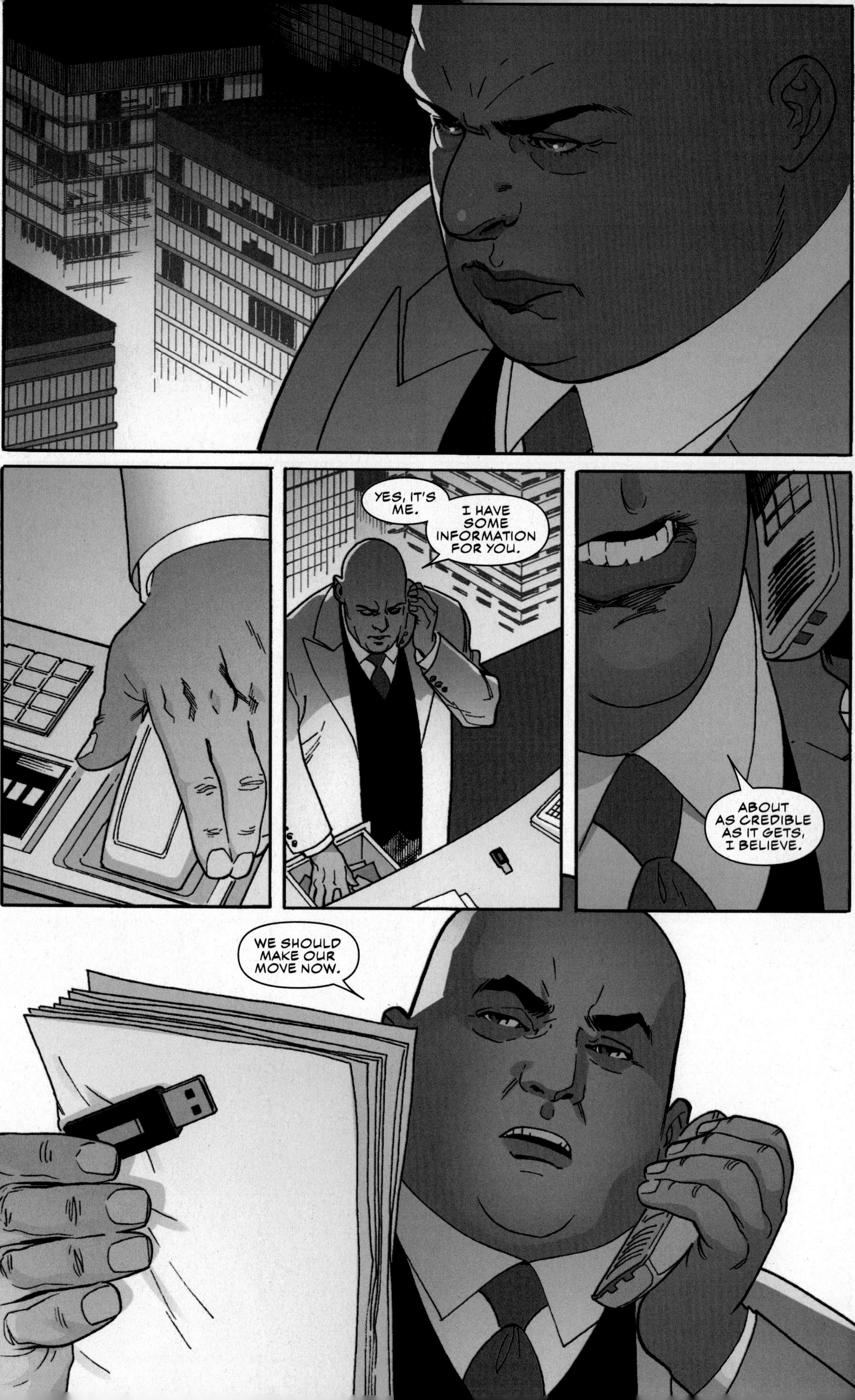
YES, IT'S ME.
I HAVE SOME INFORMATION FOR YOU.
ABOUT AS CREDIBLE AS IT GETS, I BELIEVE.
WE SHOULD MAKE OUR MOVE NOW.

"OKAY. IT'S THEM. ALEXA, SIN AND A FEW OF THEIR THUGS."

AVA AND I ARE READY DOWN HERE. LET'S TAKE 'EM.

ROGER THAT, BUCKY.

INCOMING.

ALEXA!

NAH.

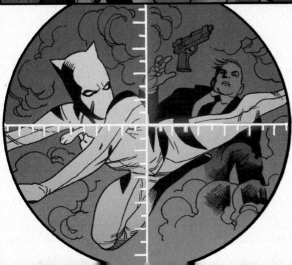

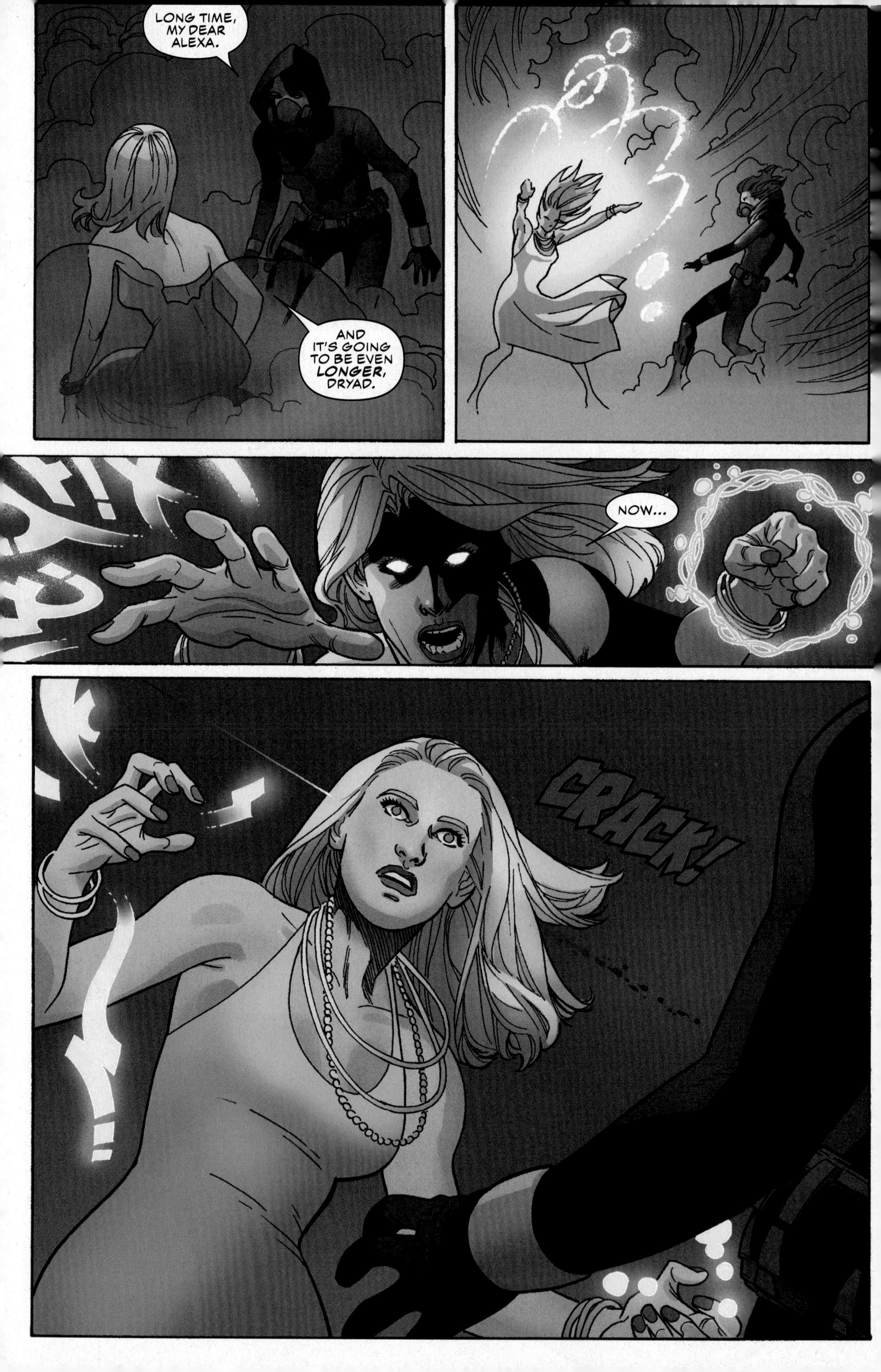
LONG TIME, MY DEAR ALEXA.
AND IT'S GOING TO BE EVEN LONGER, DRYAD.
NOW...
CRACK!

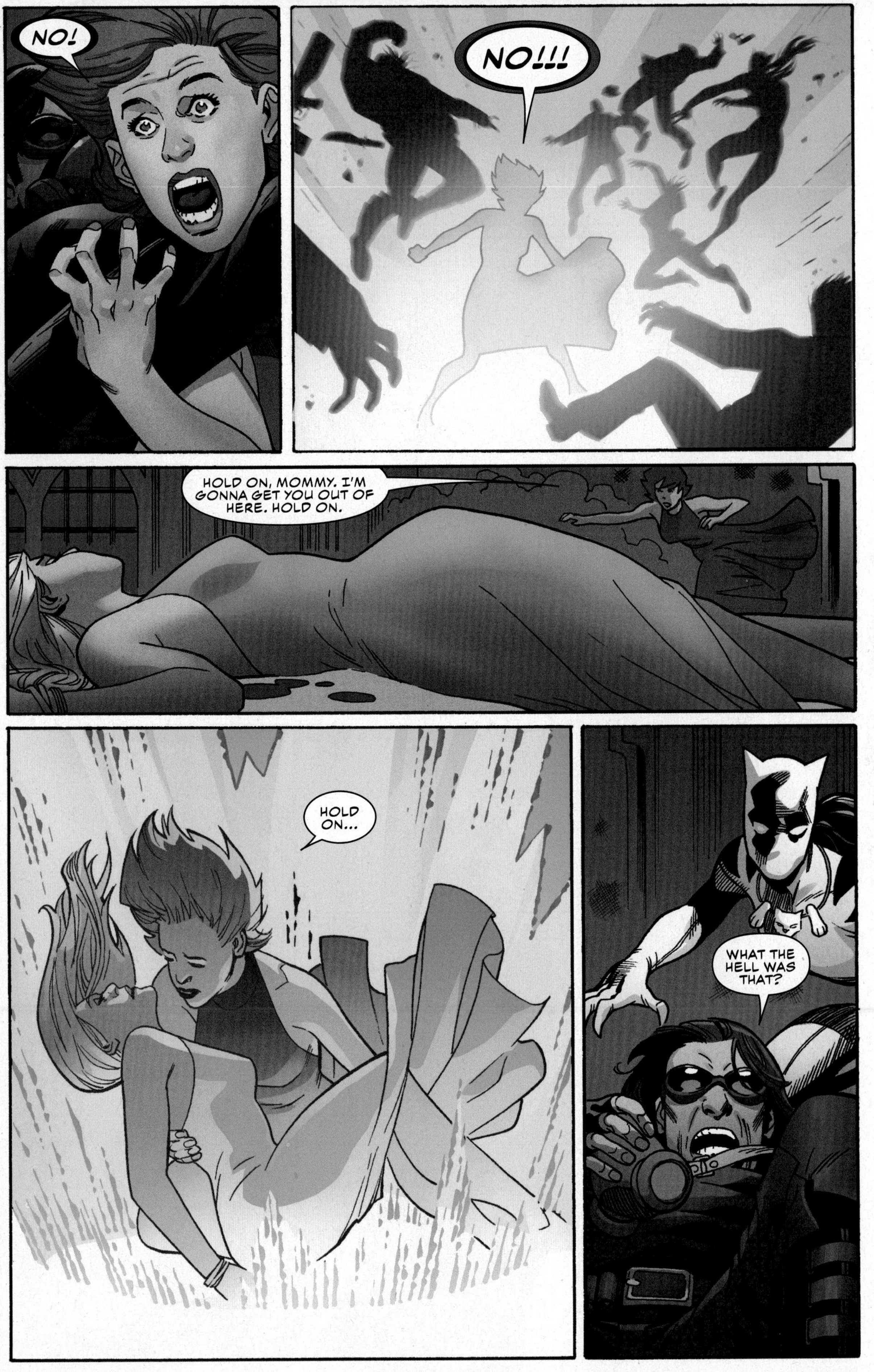
NO!
NO!!!
HOLD ON, MOMMY. I'M GONNA GET YOU OUT OF HERE. HOLD ON.
HOLD ON...
WHAT THE HELL WAS THAT?

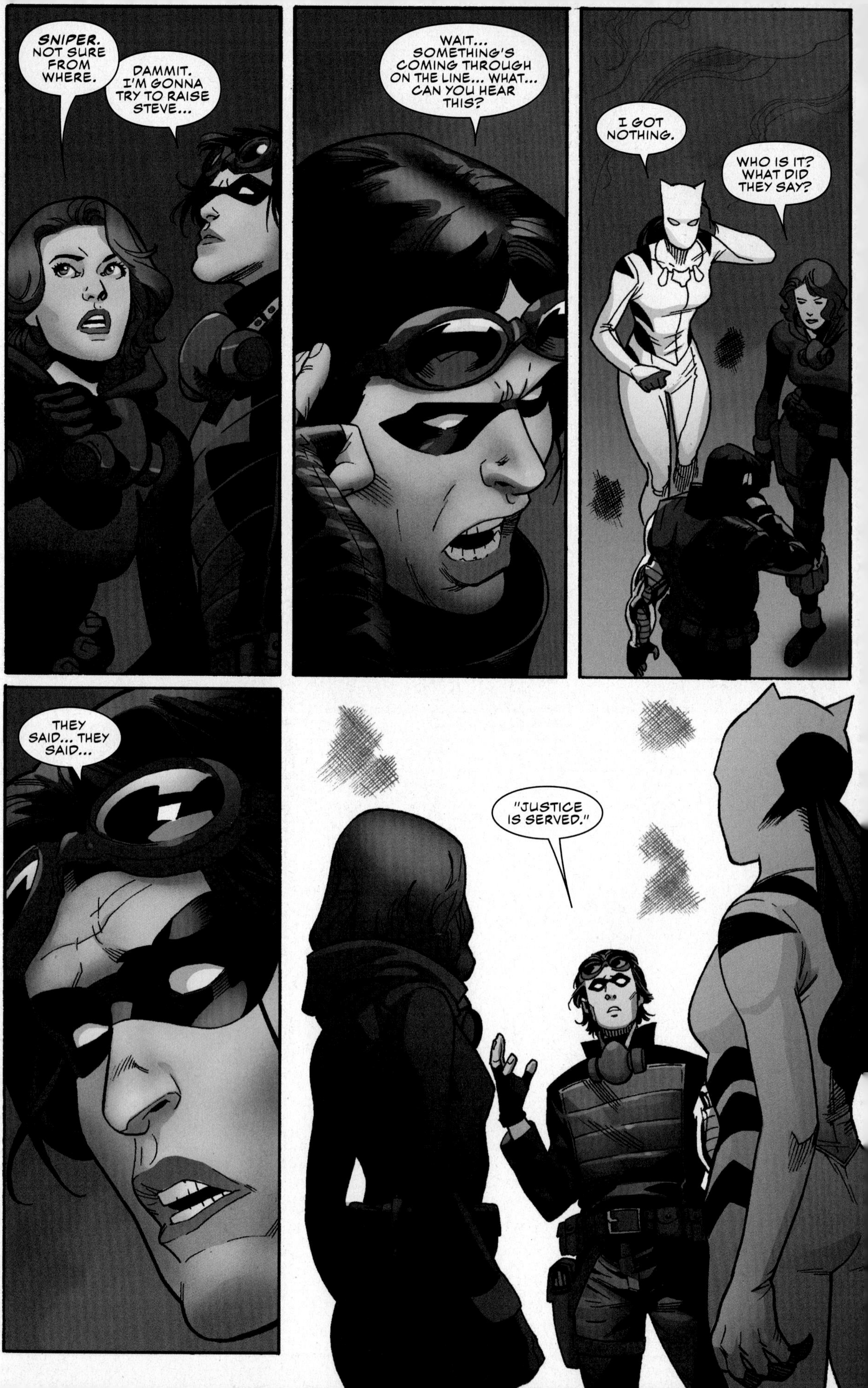
SNIPER. NOT SURE FROM WHERE.
DAMMIT. I'M GONNA TRY TO RAISE STEVE...
WAIT... SOMETHING'S COMING THROUGH ON THE LINE... WHAT... CAN YOU HEAR THIS?
I GOT NOTHING.
WHO IS IT? WHAT DID THEY SAY?
THEY SAID... THEY SAID...
"JUSTICE IS SERVED."

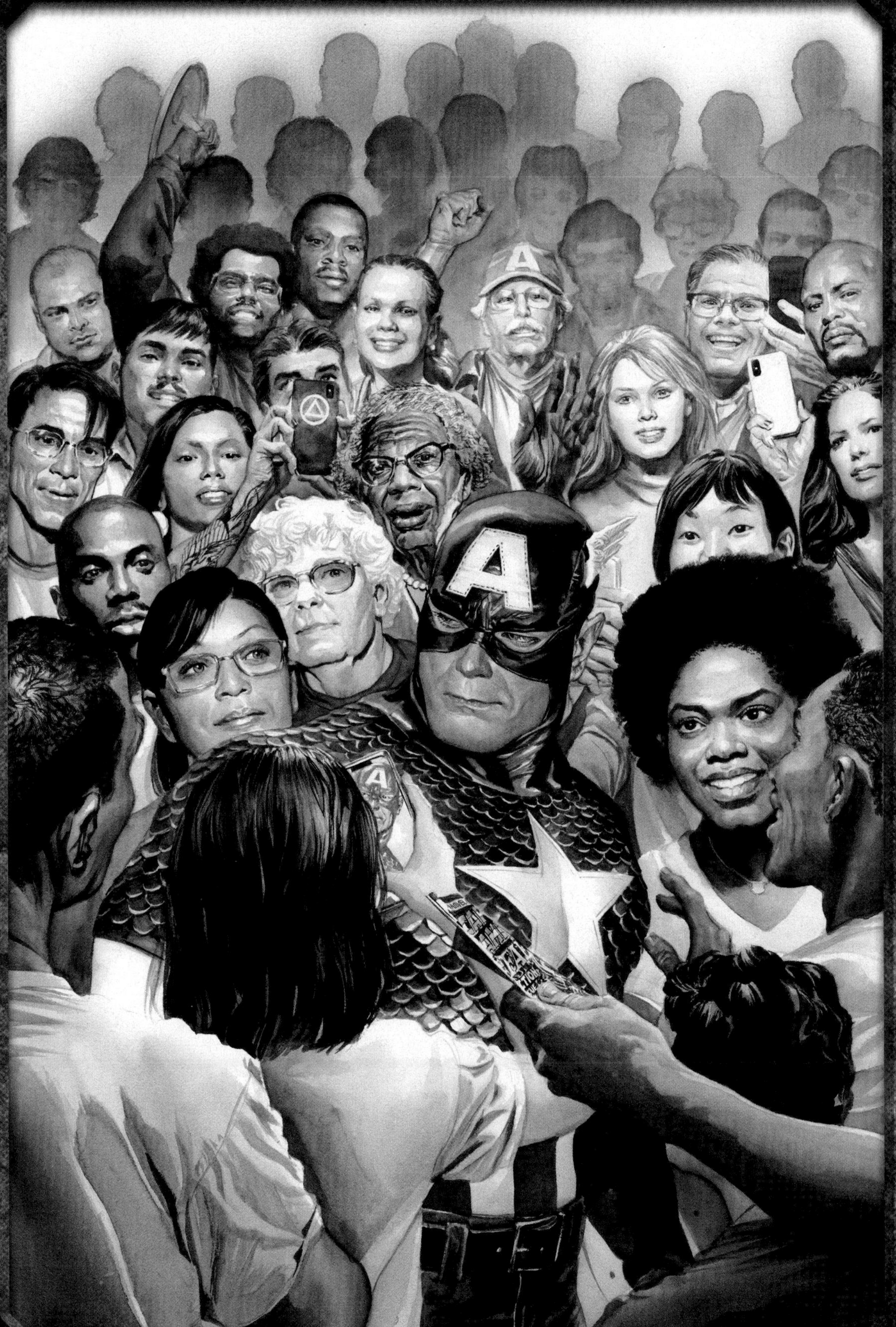

30

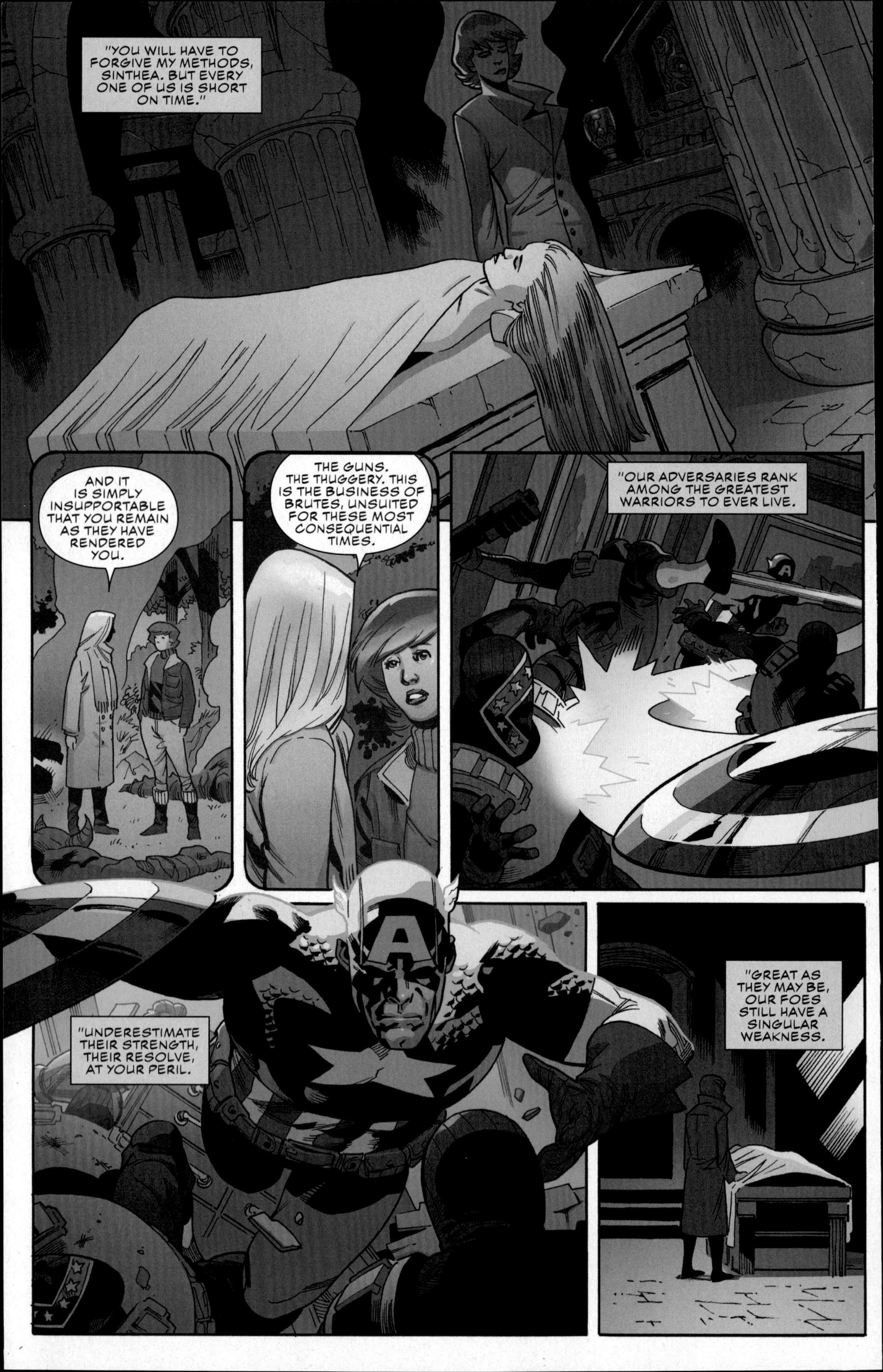
"YOU WILL HAVE TO FORGIVE MY METHODS, SINTHEA. BUT EVERY ONE OF US IS SHORT ON TIME."
AND IT IS SIMPLY INSUPPORTABLE THAT YOU REMAIN AS THEY HAVE RENDERED YOU.
THE GUNS. THE THUGGERY. THIS IS THE BUSINESS OF BRUTES, UNSUITED FOR THESE MOST CONSEQUENTIAL TIMES.
"OUR ADVERSARIES RANK AMONG THE GREATEST WARRIORS TO EVER LIVE.
"UNDERESTIMATE THEIR STRENGTH, THEIR RESOLVE, AT YOUR PERIL.
"GREAT AS THEY MAY BE, OUR FOES STILL HAVE A SINGULAR WEAKNESS.

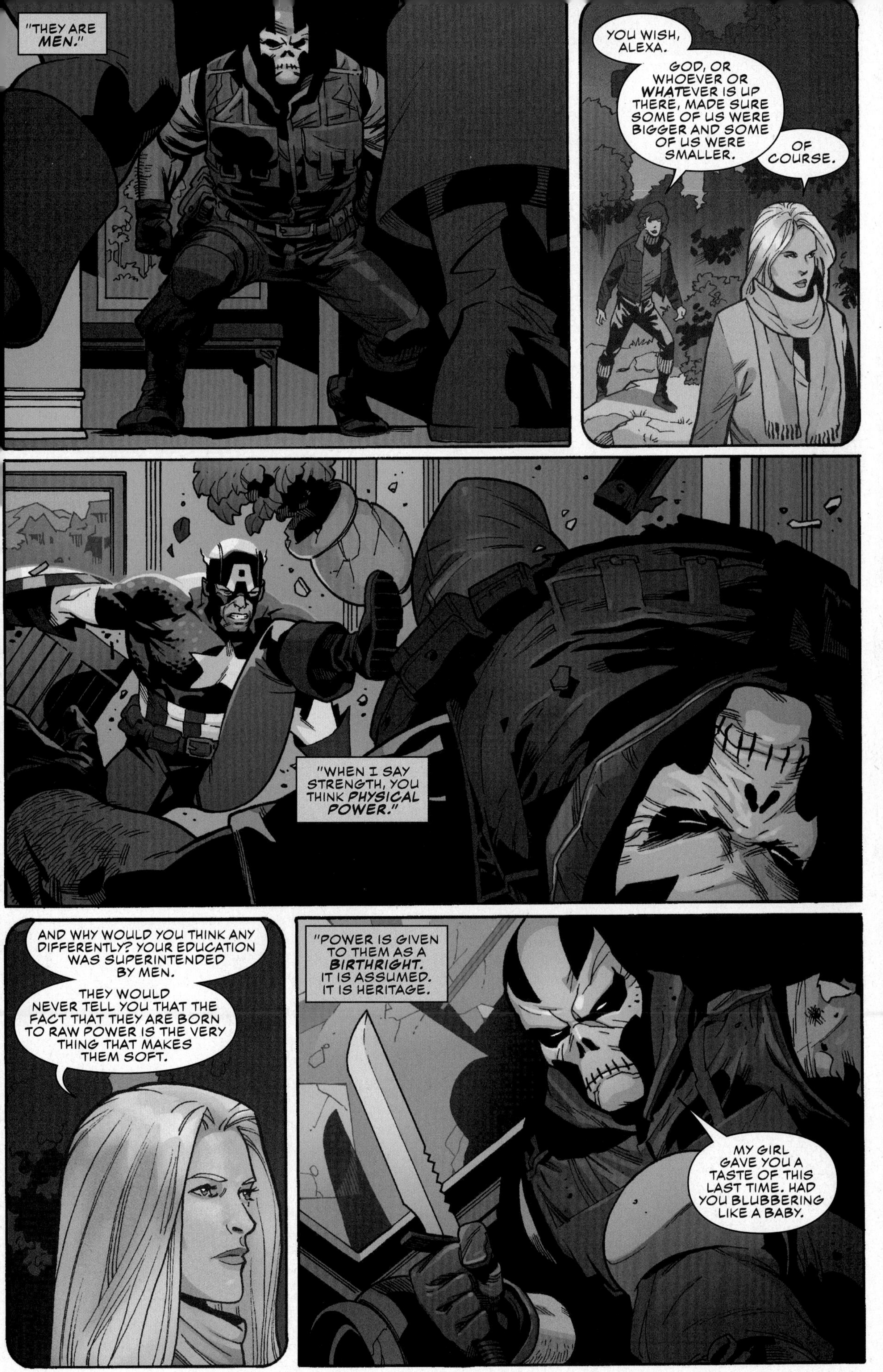
"THEY ARE MEN."
YOU WISH, ALEXA.
GOD, OR WHOEVER OR WHATEVER IS UP THERE, MADE SURE SOME OF US WERE BIGGER AND SOME OF US WERE SMALLER.
OF COURSE.
"WHEN I SAY STRENGTH, YOU THINK PHYSICAL POWER."
AND WHY WOULD YOU THINK ANY DIFFERENTLY? YOUR EDUCATION WAS SUPERINTENDED BY MEN.
THEY WOULD NEVER TELL YOU THAT THE FACT THAT THEY ARE BORN TO RAW POWER IS THE VERY THING THAT MAKES THEM SOFT.
"POWER IS GIVEN TO THEM AS A BIRTHRIGHT. IT IS ASSUMED. IT IS HERITAGE.
MY GIRL GAVE YOU A TASTE OF THIS LAST TIME. HAD YOU BLUBBERING LIKE A BABY.

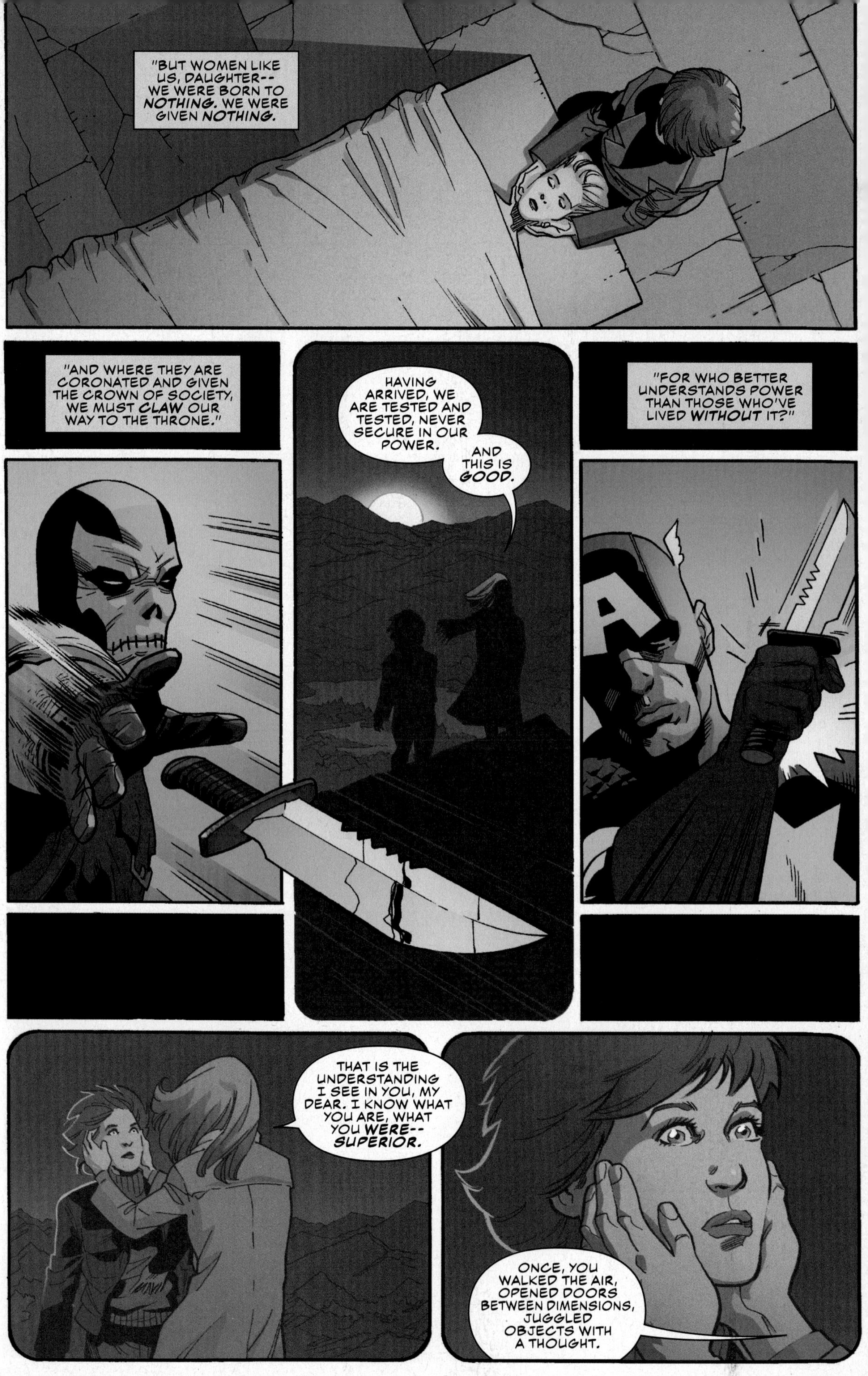
"BUT WOMEN LIKE US, DAUGHTER-- WE WERE BORN TO NOTHING. WE WERE GIVEN NOTHING.
"AND WHERE THEY ARE CORONATED AND GIVEN THE CROWN OF SOCIETY, WE MUST CLAW OUR WAY TO THE THRONE."
HAVING ARRIVED, WE ARE TESTED AND TESTED, NEVER SECURE IN OUR POWER.
AND THIS IS GOOD.
"FOR WHO BETTER UNDERSTANDS POWER THAN THOSE WHO'VE LIVED WITHOUT IT?"
THAT IS THE UNDERSTANDING I SEE IN YOU, MY DEAR. I KNOW WHAT YOU ARE, WHAT YOU WERE-- SUPERIOR.
ONCE, YOU WALKED THE AIR, OPENED DOORS BETWEEN DIMENSIONS, JUGGLED OBJECTS WITH A THOUGHT.

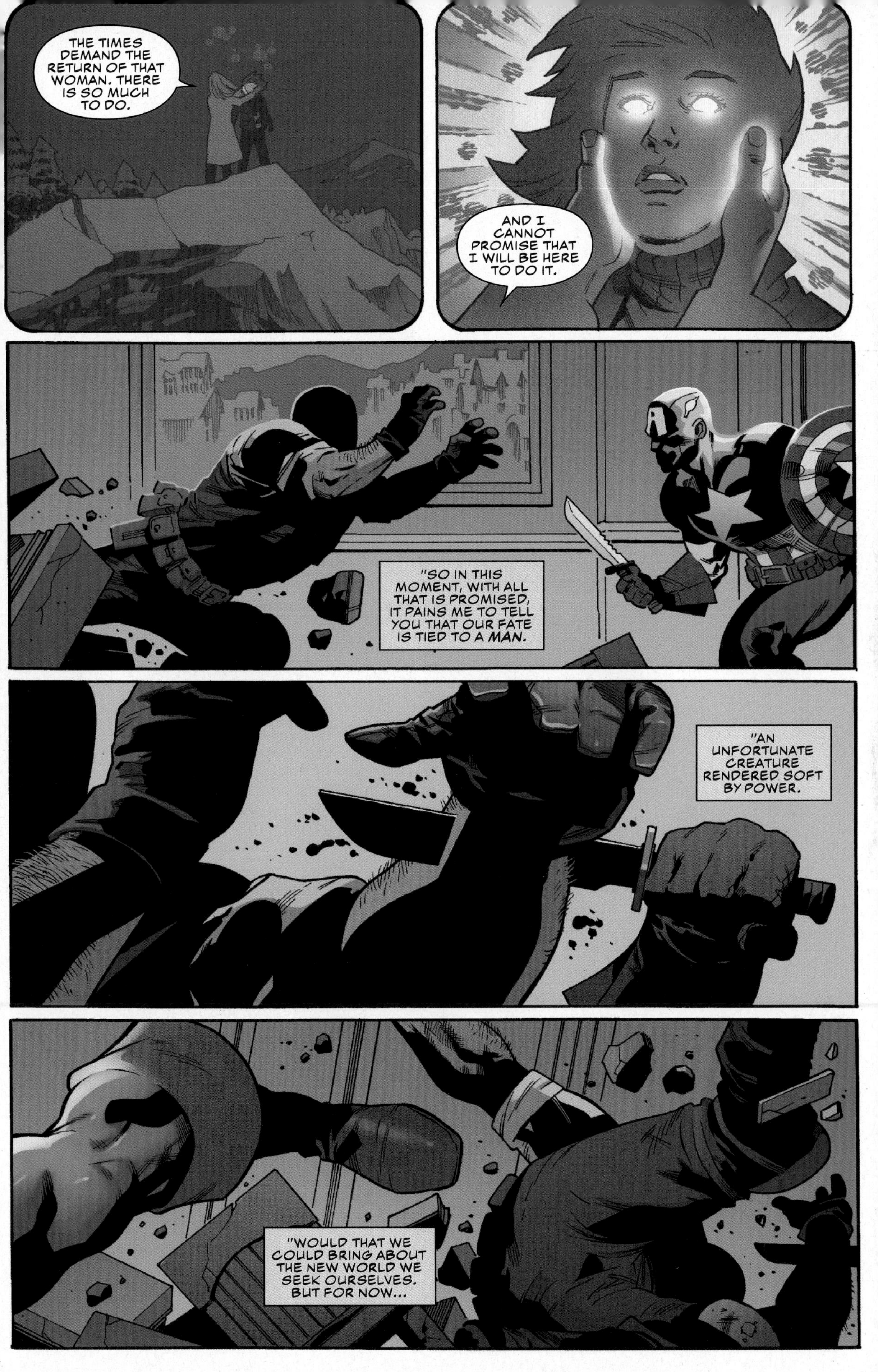
THE TIMES DEMAND THE RETURN OF THAT WOMAN. THERE IS SO MUCH TO DO.
AND I CANNOT PROMISE THAT I WILL BE HERE TO DO IT.
"SO IN THIS MOMENT, WITH ALL THAT IS PROMISED, IT PAINS ME TO TELL YOU THAT OUR FATE IS TIED TO A *MAN.*
"AN UNFORTUNATE CREATURE RENDERED SOFT BY POWER.
"WOULD THAT WE COULD BRING ABOUT THE NEW WORLD WE SEEK OURSELVES. BUT FOR NOW...

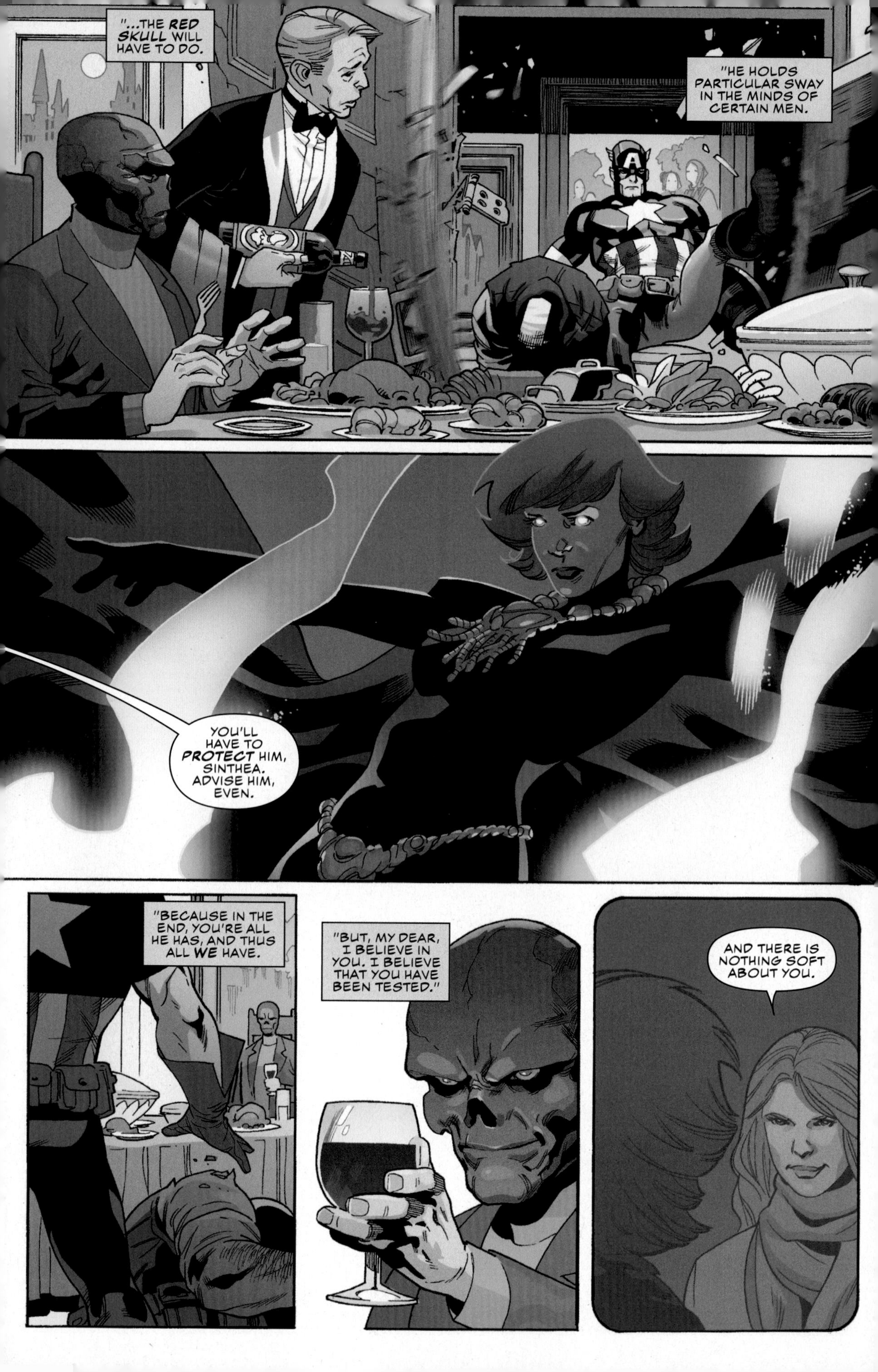
"...THE RED SKULL WILL HAVE TO DO.
"HE HOLDS PARTICULAR SWAY IN THE MINDS OF CERTAIN MEN.
YOU'LL HAVE TO PROTECT HIM, SINTHEA. ADVISE HIM, EVEN.
"BECAUSE IN THE END, YOU'RE ALL HE HAS, AND THUS ALL WE HAVE.
"BUT, MY DEAR, I BELIEVE IN YOU. I BELIEVE THAT YOU HAVE BEEN TESTED."
AND THERE IS NOTHING SOFT ABOUT YOU.

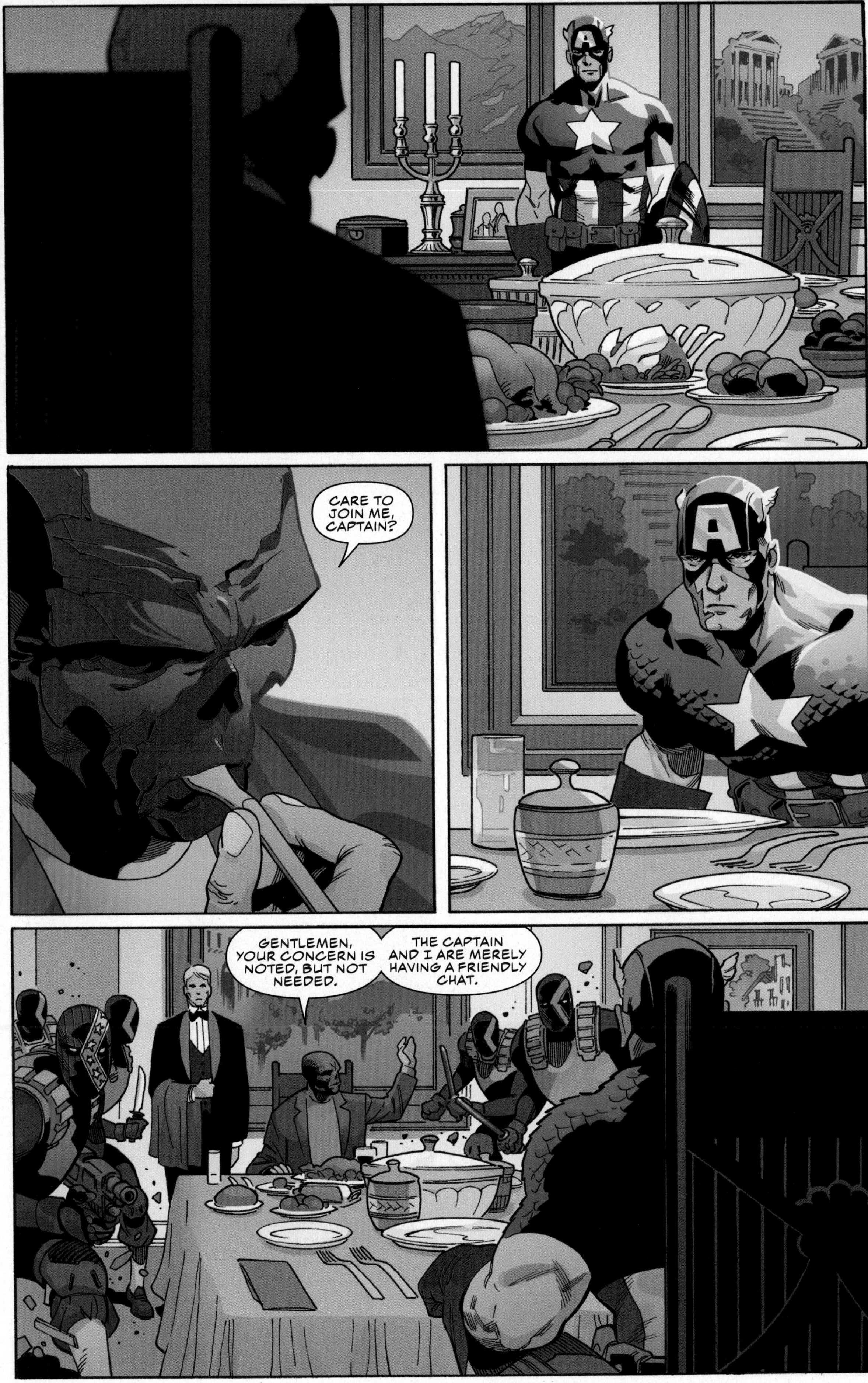
CARE TO JOIN ME, CAPTAIN?
GENTLEMEN, YOUR CONCERN IS NOTED, BUT NOT NEEDED.
THE CAPTAIN AND I ARE MERELY HAVING A FRIENDLY CHAT.

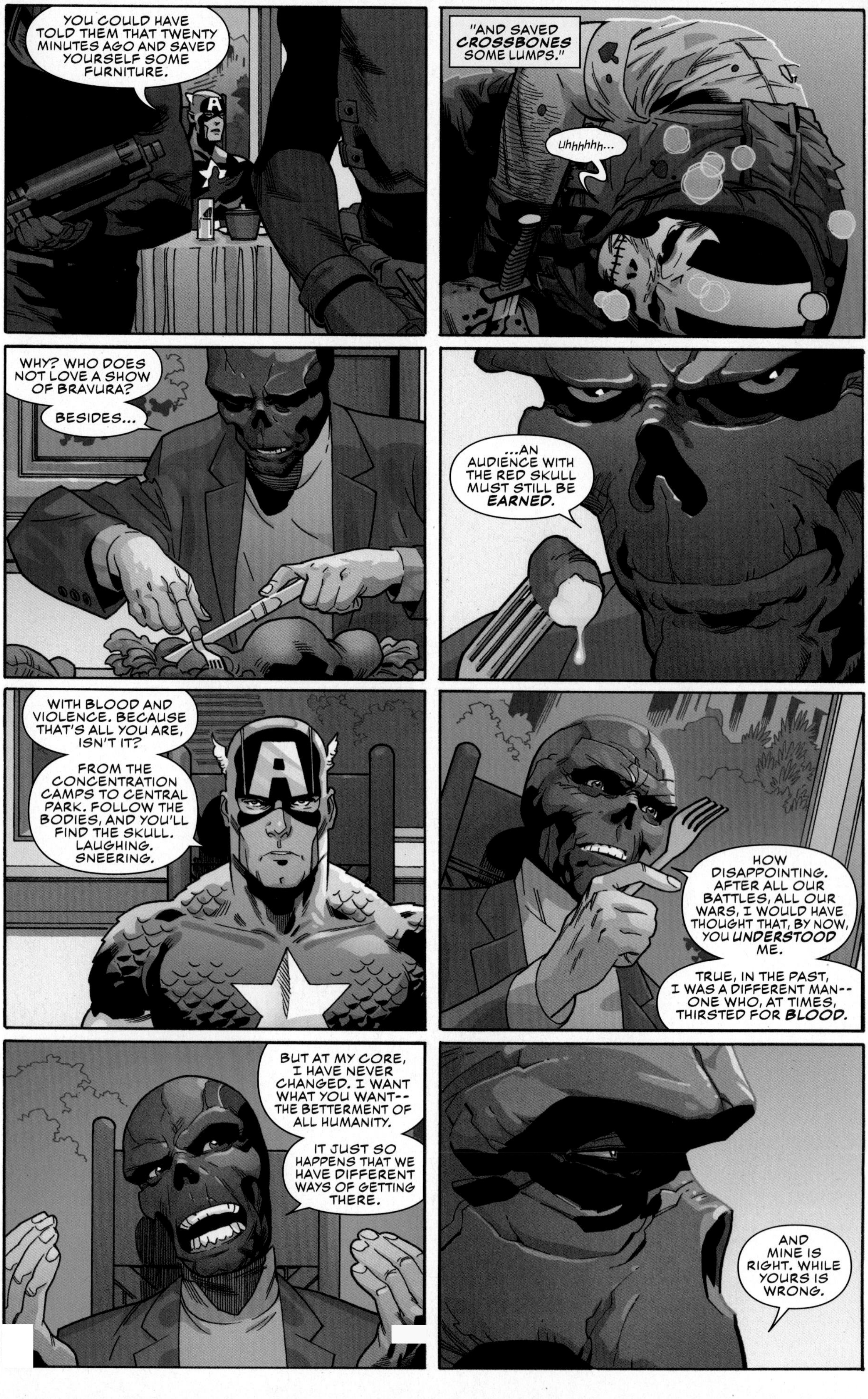
YOU COULD HAVE TOLD THEM THAT TWENTY MINUTES AGO AND SAVED YOURSELF SOME FURNITURE.
"AND SAVED CROSSBONES SOME LUMPS."
Uhhhhhh...
WHY? WHO DOES NOT LOVE A SHOW OF BRAVURA?
BESIDES...
...AN AUDIENCE WITH THE RED SKULL MUST STILL BE EARNED.
WITH BLOOD AND VIOLENCE. BECAUSE THAT'S ALL YOU ARE, ISN'T IT?
FROM THE CONCENTRATION CAMPS TO CENTRAL PARK. FOLLOW THE BODIES, AND YOU'LL FIND THE SKULL. LAUGHING. SNEERING.
HOW DISAPPOINTING. AFTER ALL OUR BATTLES, ALL OUR WARS, I WOULD HAVE THOUGHT THAT, BY NOW, YOU UNDERSTOOD ME.
TRUE, IN THE PAST, I WAS A DIFFERENT MAN-- ONE WHO, AT TIMES, THIRSTED FOR BLOOD.
BUT AT MY CORE, I HAVE NEVER CHANGED. I WANT WHAT YOU WANT-- THE BETTERMENT OF ALL HUMANITY.
IT JUST SO HAPPENS THAT WE HAVE DIFFERENT WAYS OF GETTING THERE.
AND MINE IS RIGHT. WHILE YOURS IS WRONG.

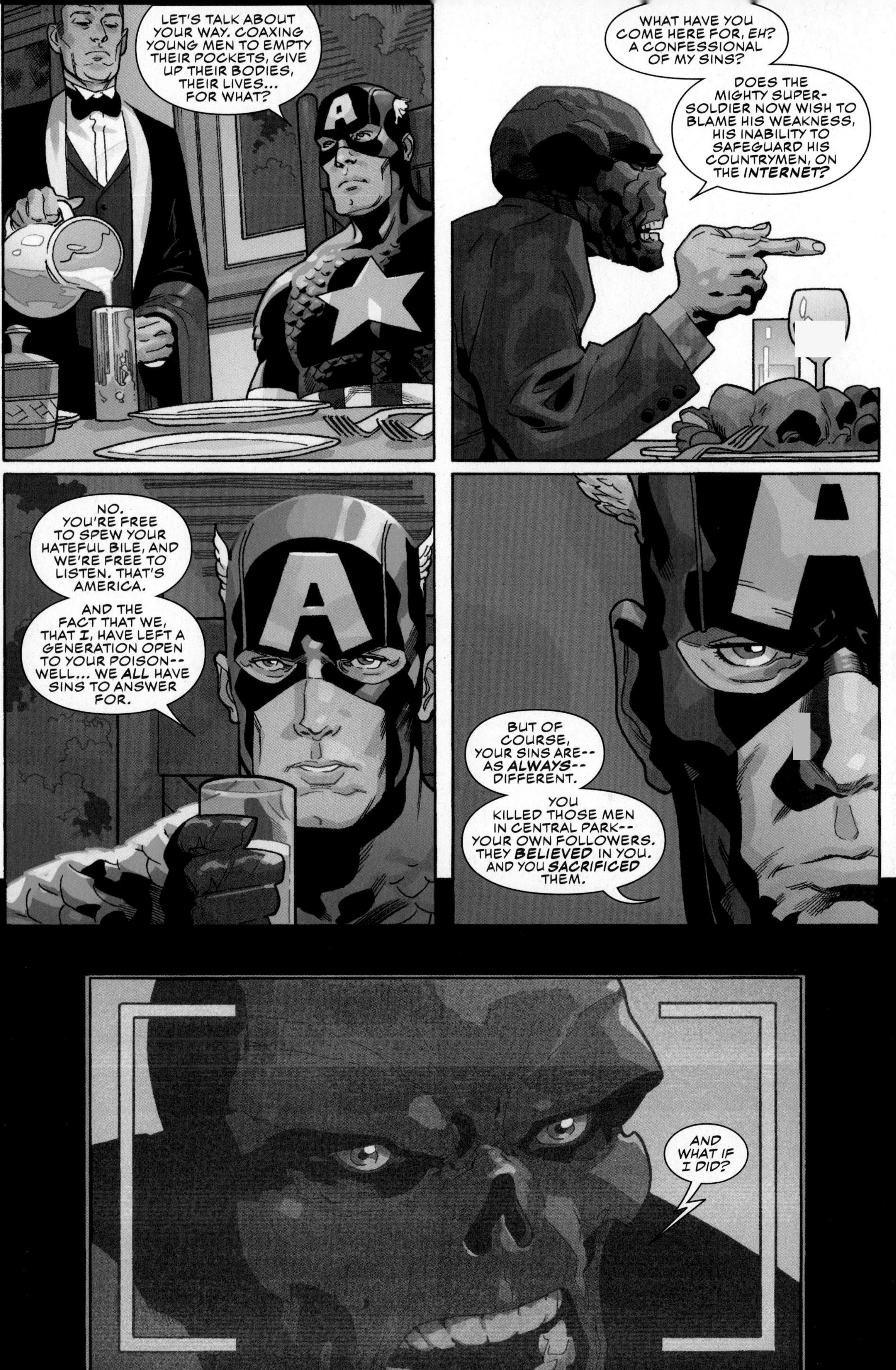
LET'S TALK ABOUT YOUR WAY. COAXING YOUNG MEN TO EMPTY THEIR POCKETS, GIVE UP THEIR BODIES, THEIR LIVES... FOR WHAT?
WHAT HAVE YOU COME HERE FOR, EH? A CONFESSIONAL OF MY SINS?
DOES THE MIGHTY SUPER-SOLDIER NOW WISH TO BLAME HIS WEAKNESS, HIS INABILITY TO SAFEGUARD HIS COUNTRYMEN, ON THE INTERNET?
NO. YOU'RE FREE TO SPEW YOUR HATEFUL BILE, AND WE'RE FREE TO LISTEN. THAT'S AMERICA.
AND THE FACT THAT WE, THAT I, HAVE LEFT A GENERATION OPEN TO YOUR POISON-- WELL... WE ALL HAVE SINS TO ANSWER FOR.
BUT OF COURSE, YOUR SINS ARE-- AS ALWAYS-- DIFFERENT.
YOU KILLED THOSE MEN IN CENTRAL PARK-- YOUR OWN FOLLOWERS. THEY BELIEVED IN YOU. AND YOU SACRIFICED THEM.
AND WHAT IF I DID?

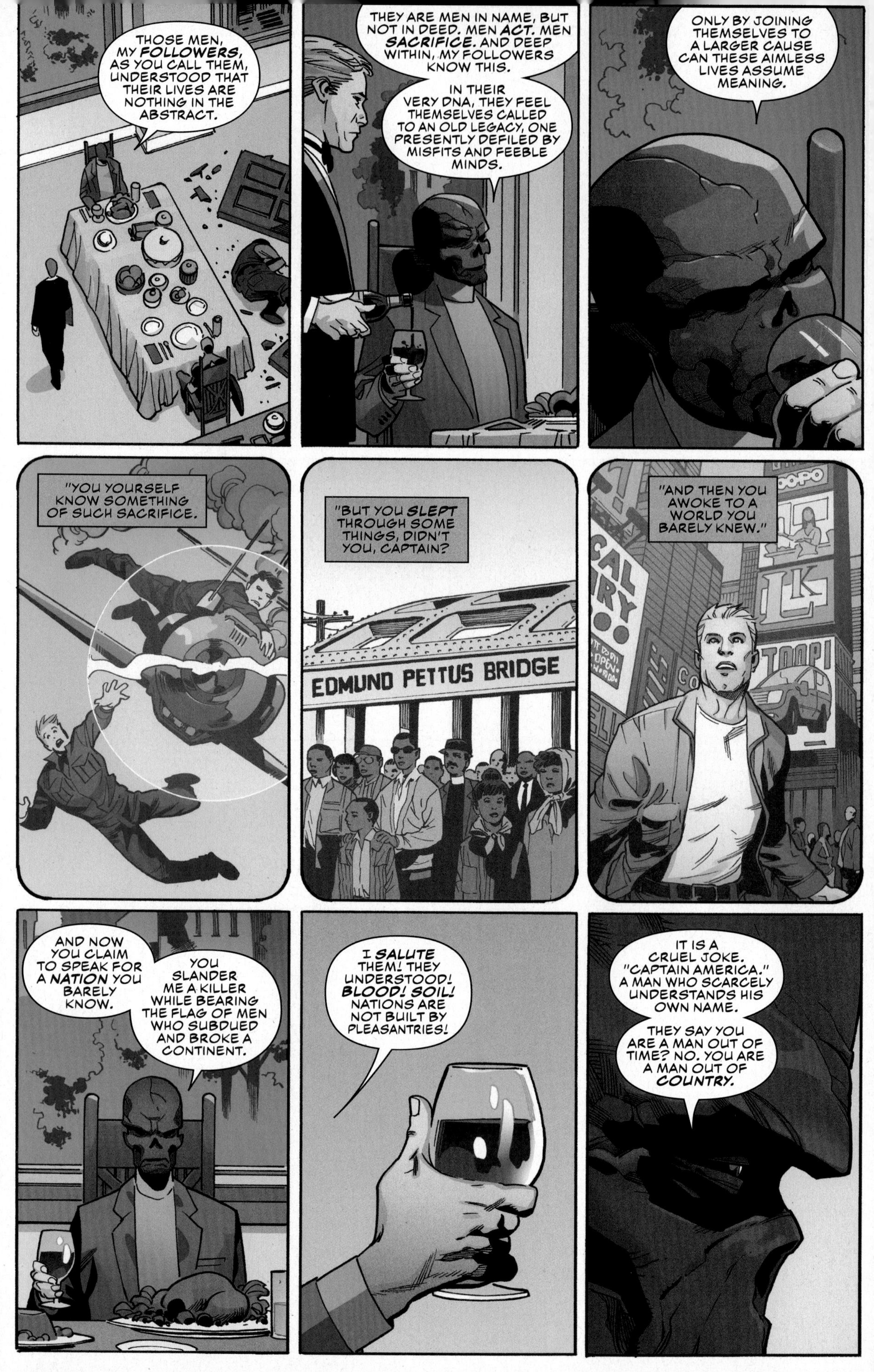

THOSE MEN, MY FOLLOWERS, AS YOU CALL THEM, UNDERSTOOD THAT THEIR LIVES ARE NOTHING IN THE ABSTRACT.
THEY ARE MEN IN NAME, BUT NOT IN DEED. MEN ACT. MEN SACRIFICE. AND DEEP WITHIN, MY FOLLOWERS KNOW THIS.
IN THEIR VERY DNA, THEY FEEL THEMSELVES CALLED TO AN OLD LEGACY, ONE PRESENTLY DEFILED BY MISFITS AND FEEBLE MINDS.
ONLY BY JOINING THEMSELVES TO A LARGER CAUSE CAN THESE AIMLESS LIVES ASSUME MEANING.
"YOU YOURSELF KNOW SOMETHING OF SUCH SACRIFICE.
"BUT YOU SLEPT THROUGH SOME THINGS, DIDN'T YOU, CAPTAIN?
EDMUND PETTUS BRIDGE
"AND THEN YOU AWOKE TO A WORLD YOU BARELY KNEW."
AND NOW YOU CLAIM TO SPEAK FOR A NATION YOU BARELY KNOW.
YOU SLANDER ME A KILLER WHILE BEARING THE FLAG OF MEN WHO SUBDUED AND BROKE A CONTINENT.
I SALUTE THEM! THEY UNDERSTOOD! BLOOD! SOIL! NATIONS ARE NOT BUILT BY PLEASANTRIES!
IT IS A CRUEL JOKE. "CAPTAIN AMERICA." A MAN WHO SCARCELY UNDERSTANDS HIS OWN NAME.
THEY SAY YOU ARE A MAN OUT OF TIME? NO. YOU ARE A MAN OUT OF COUNTRY.

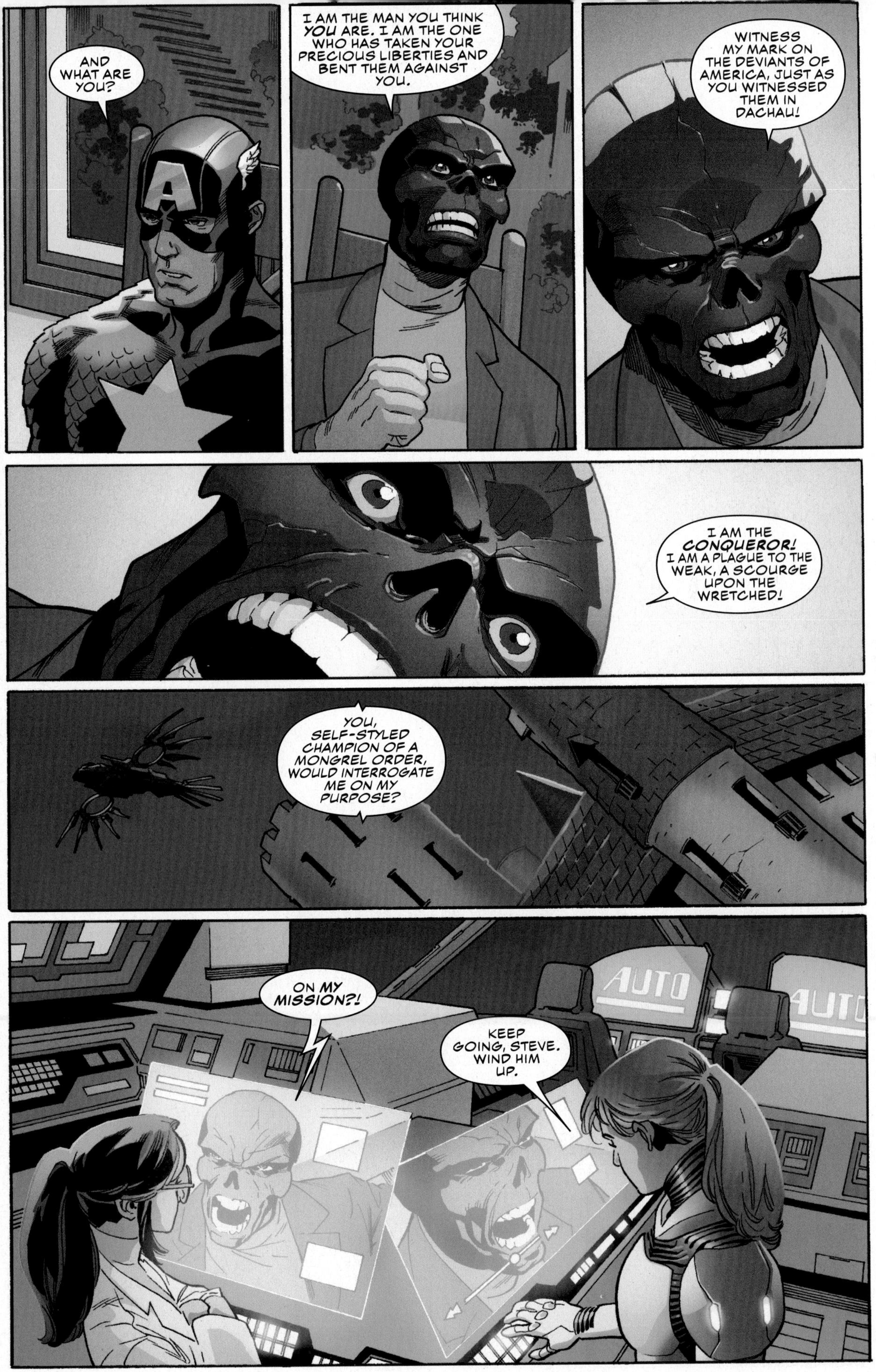
AND WHAT ARE YOU?
I AM THE MAN YOU THINK YOU ARE. I AM THE ONE WHO HAS TAKEN YOUR PRECIOUS LIBERTIES AND BENT THEM AGAINST YOU.
WITNESS MY MARK ON THE DEVIANTS OF AMERICA, JUST AS YOU WITNESSED THEM IN DACHAU!
I AM THE CONQUEROR! I AM A PLAGUE TO THE WEAK, A SCOURGE UPON THE WRETCHED!
YOU, SELF-STYLED CHAMPION OF A MONGREL ORDER, WOULD INTERROGATE ME ON MY PURPOSE?
ON MY MISSION?!
AUTO
AUTO
KEEP GOING, STEVE. WIND HIM UP.

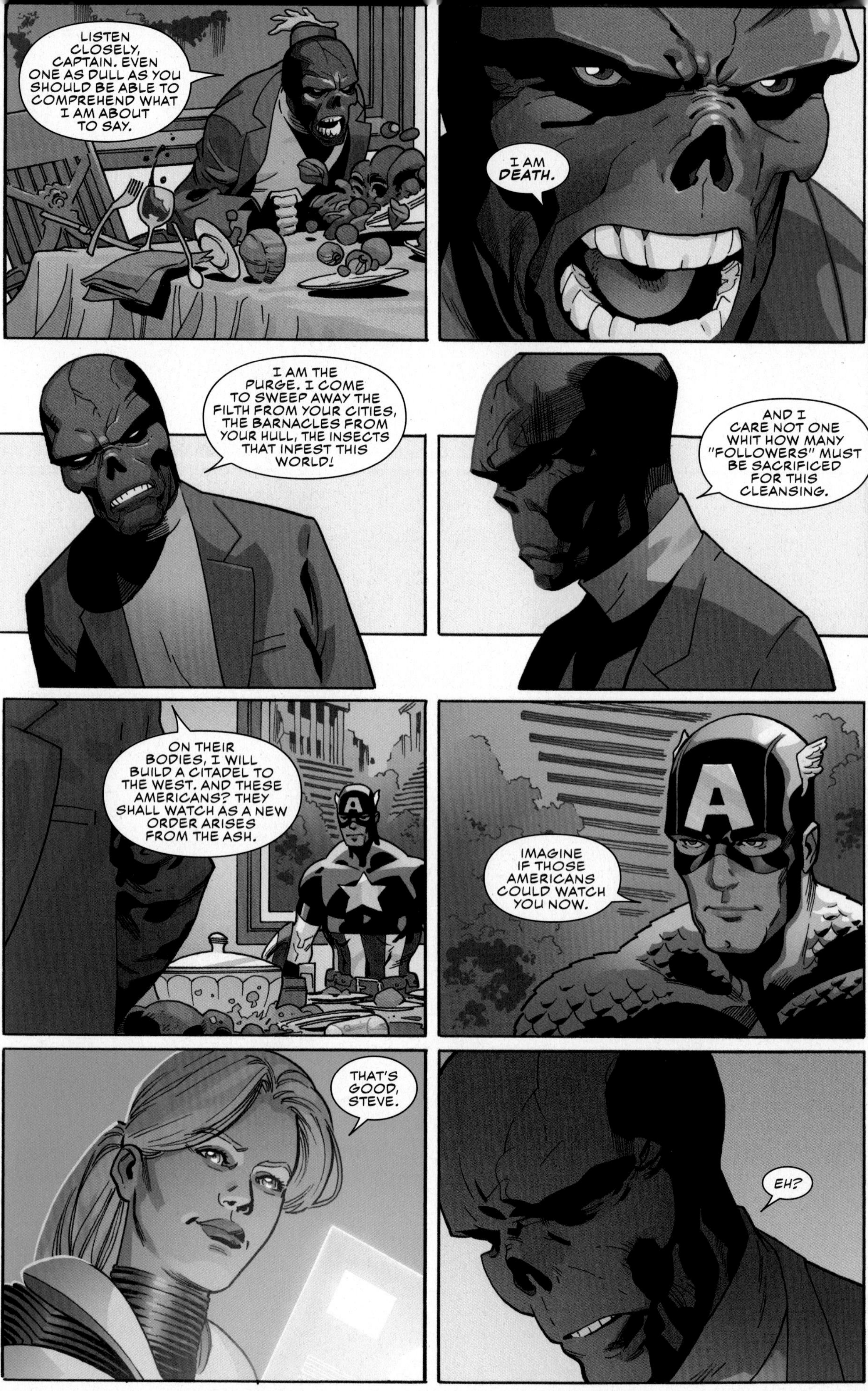
LISTEN CLOSELY, CAPTAIN. EVEN ONE AS DULL AS YOU SHOULD BE ABLE TO COMPREHEND WHAT I AM ABOUT TO SAY.
I AM *DEATH.*
I AM THE PURGE. I COME TO SWEEP AWAY THE FILTH FROM YOUR CITIES, THE BARNACLES FROM YOUR HULL, THE INSECTS THAT INFEST THIS WORLD!
AND I CARE NOT ONE WHIT HOW MANY "FOLLOWERS" MUST BE SACRIFICED FOR THIS CLEANSING.
ON THEIR BODIES, I WILL BUILD A CITADEL TO THE WEST. AND THESE AMERICANS? THEY SHALL WATCH AS A NEW ORDER ARISES FROM THE ASH.
IMAGINE IF THOSE AMERICANS COULD WATCH YOU NOW.
THAT'S GOOD, STEVE.
EH?

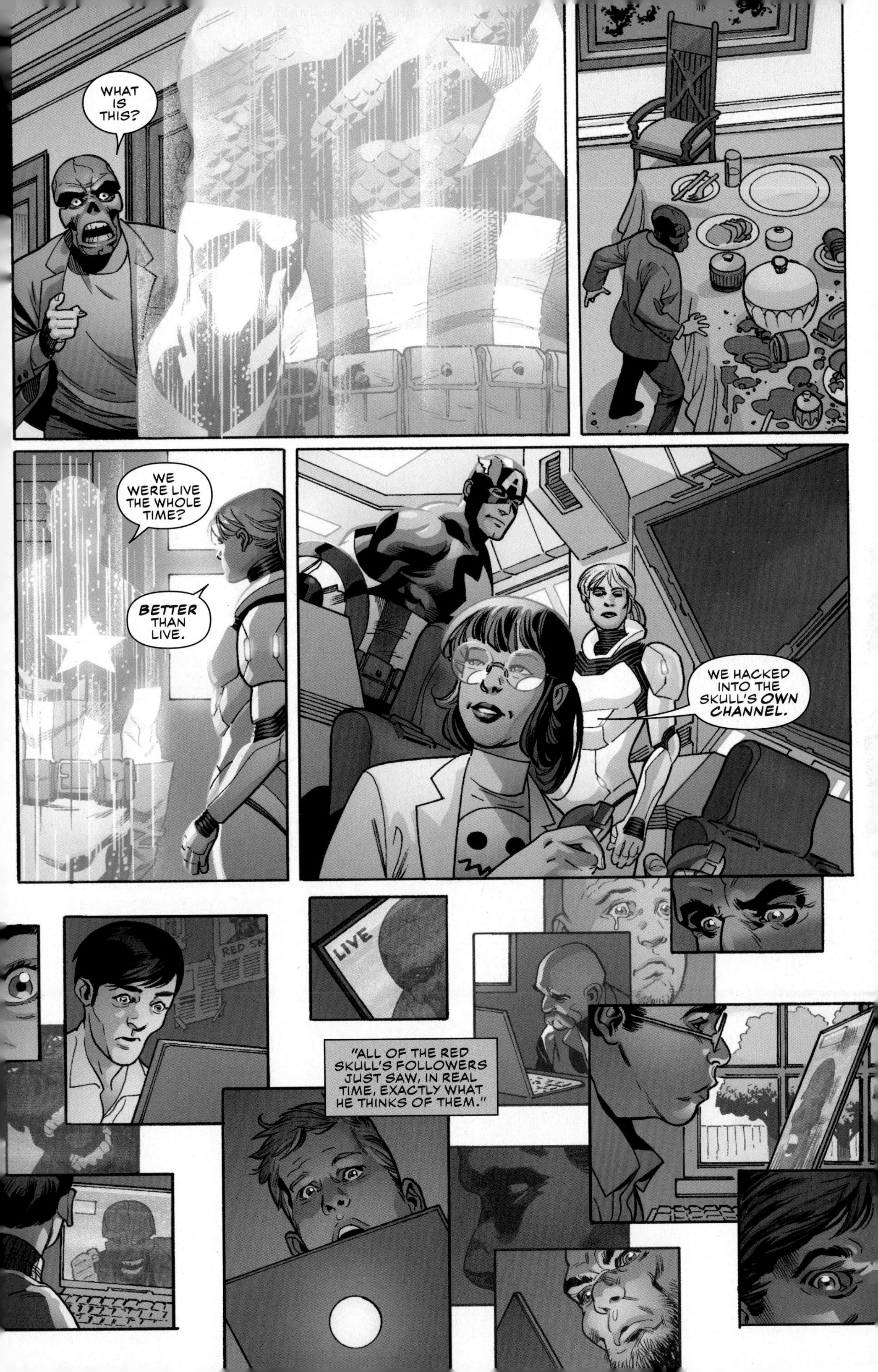
WHAT IS THIS?
WE WERE LIVE THE WHOLE TIME?
BETTER THAN LIVE.
WE HACKED INTO THE SKULL'S OWN CHANNEL.
LIVE
"ALL OF THE RED SKULL'S FOLLOWERS JUST SAW, IN REAL TIME, EXACTLY WHAT HE THINKS OF THEM."

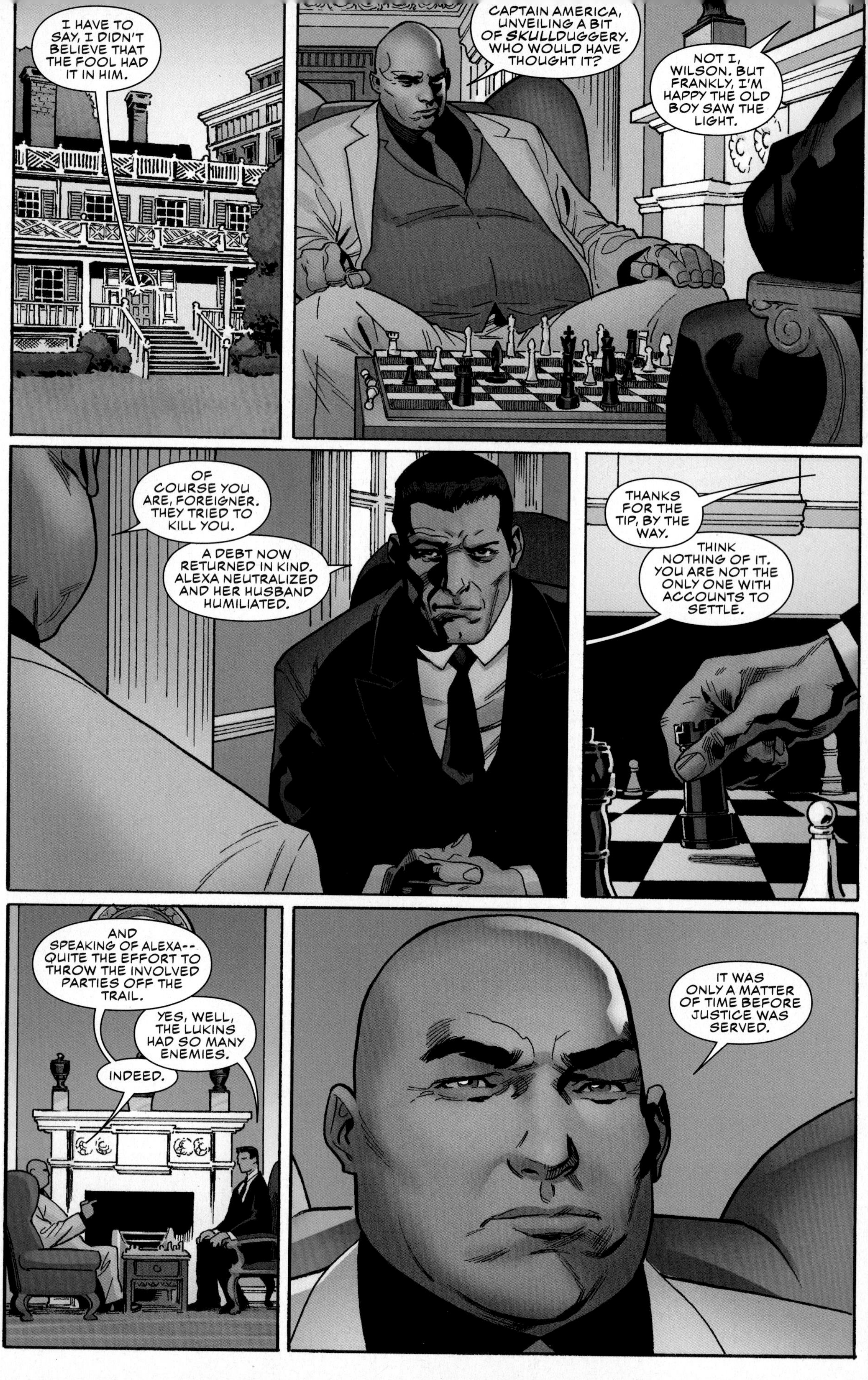
I HAVE TO SAY, I DIDN'T BELIEVE THAT THE FOOL HAD IT IN HIM.
CAPTAIN AMERICA, UNVEILING A BIT OF SKULLDUGGERY. WHO WOULD HAVE THOUGHT IT?
NOT I, WILSON. BUT FRANKLY, I'M HAPPY THE OLD BOY SAW THE LIGHT.
OF COURSE YOU ARE, FOREIGNER. THEY TRIED TO KILL YOU.
A DEBT NOW RETURNED IN KIND. ALEXA NEUTRALIZED AND HER HUSBAND HUMILIATED.
THANKS FOR THE TIP, BY THE WAY.
THINK NOTHING OF IT. YOU ARE NOT THE ONLY ONE WITH ACCOUNTS TO SETTLE.
AND SPEAKING OF ALEXA-- QUITE THE EFFORT TO THROW THE INVOLVED PARTIES OFF THE TRAIL.
YES, WELL, THE LUKINS HAD SO MANY ENEMIES.
INDEED.
IT WAS ONLY A MATTER OF TIME BEFORE JUSTICE WAS SERVED.

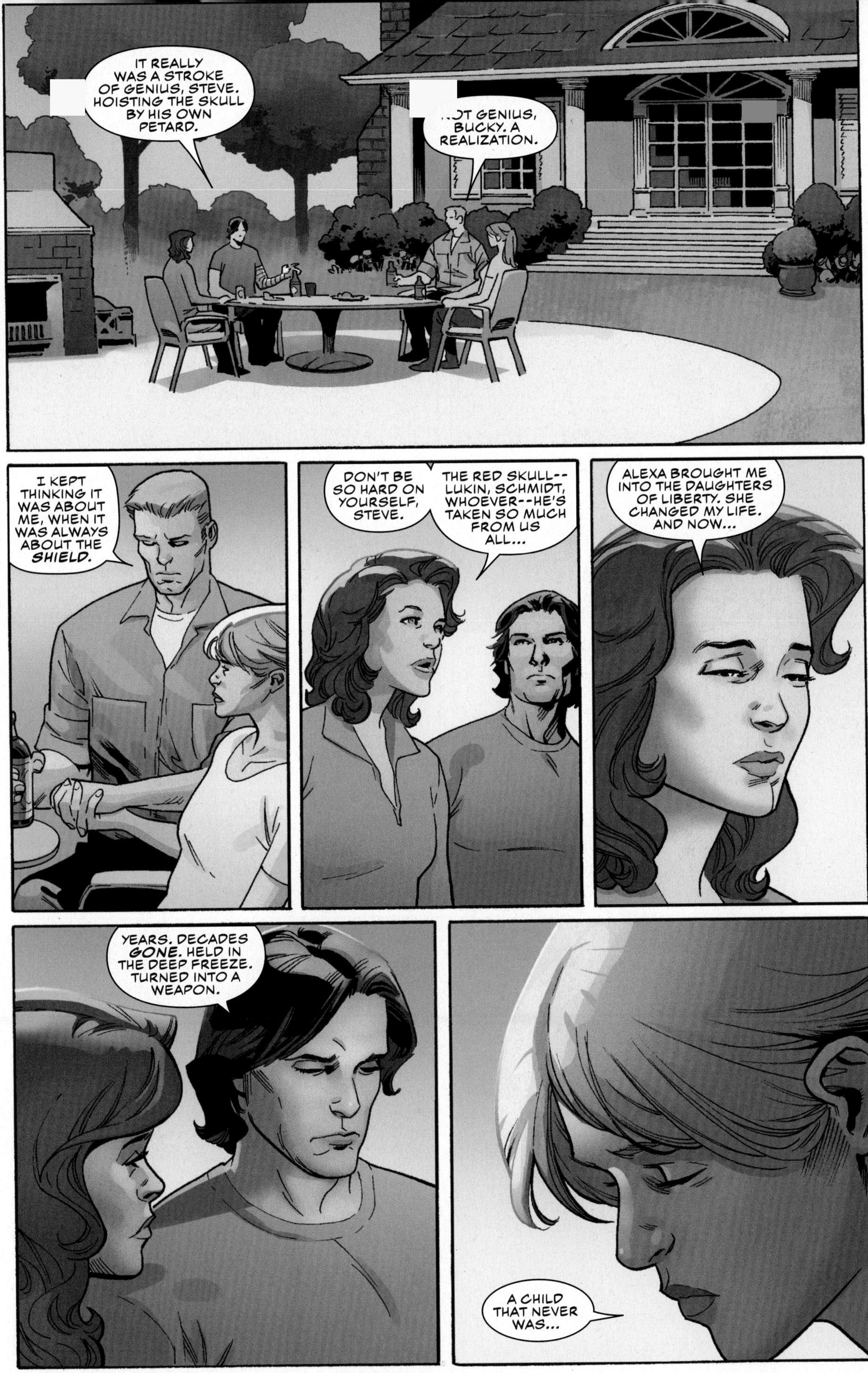

IT REALLY WAS A STROKE OF GENIUS, STEVE. HOISTING THE SKULL BY HIS OWN PETARD.
NOT GENIUS, BUCKY. A REALIZATION.
I KEPT THINKING IT WAS ABOUT ME, WHEN IT WAS ALWAYS ABOUT THE SHIELD.
DON'T BE SO HARD ON YOURSELF, STEVE.
THE RED SKULL--LUKIN, SCHMIDT, WHOEVER--HE'S TAKEN SO MUCH FROM US ALL...
ALEXA BROUGHT ME INTO THE DAUGHTERS OF LIBERTY. SHE CHANGED MY LIFE. AND NOW...
YEARS. DECADES GONE. HELD IN THE DEEP FREEZE. TURNED INTO A WEAPON.
A CHILD THAT NEVER WAS...

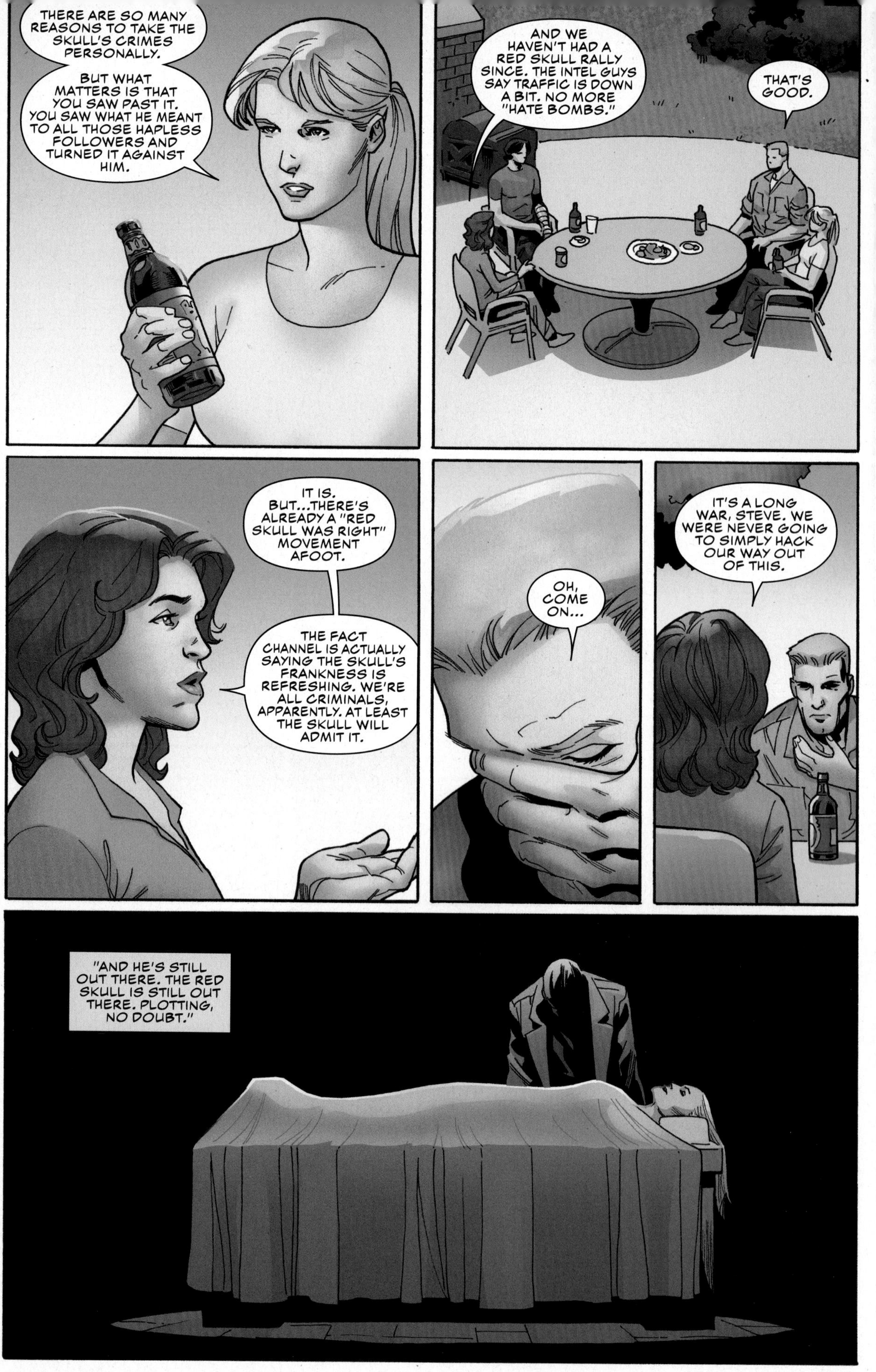
THERE ARE SO MANY REASONS TO TAKE THE SKULL'S CRIMES PERSONALLY.
BUT WHAT MATTERS IS THAT YOU SAW PAST IT. YOU SAW WHAT HE MEANT TO ALL THOSE HAPLESS FOLLOWERS AND TURNED IT AGAINST HIM.
AND WE HAVEN'T HAD A RED SKULL RALLY SINCE. THE INTEL GUYS SAY TRAFFIC IS DOWN A BIT. NO MORE "HATE BOMBS."
THAT'S GOOD.
IT IS. BUT...THERE'S ALREADY A "RED SKULL WAS RIGHT" MOVEMENT AFOOT.
THE FACT CHANNEL IS ACTUALLY SAYING THE SKULL'S FRANKNESS IS REFRESHING. WE'RE ALL CRIMINALS, APPARENTLY. AT LEAST THE SKULL WILL ADMIT IT.
OH, COME ON...
IT'S A LONG WAR, STEVE. WE WERE NEVER GOING TO SIMPLY HACK OUR WAY OUT OF THIS.
"AND HE'S STILL OUT THERE. THE RED SKULL IS STILL OUT THERE. PLOTTING, NO DOUBT."

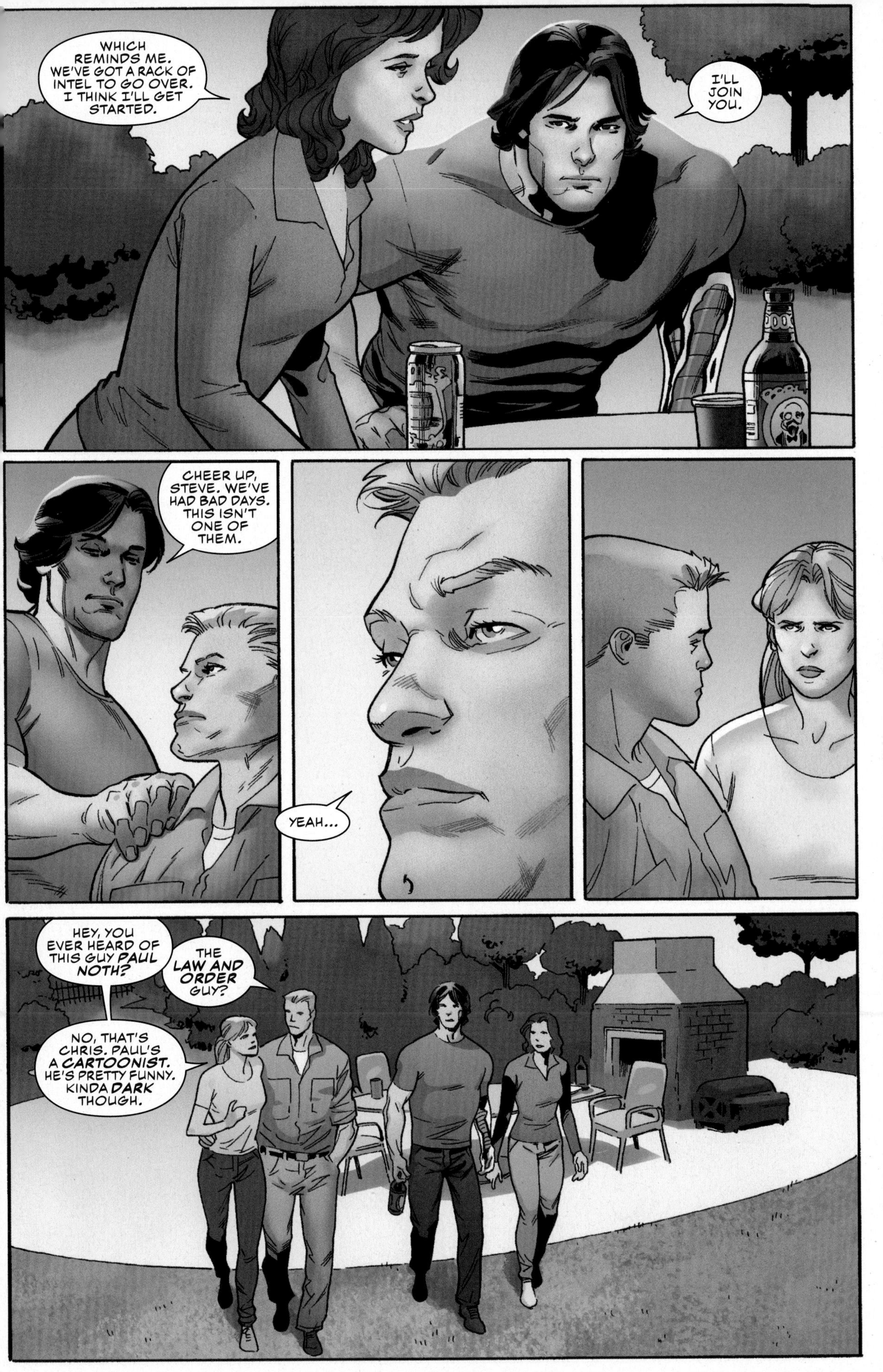
WHICH REMINDS ME. WE'VE GOT A RACK OF INTEL TO GO OVER. I THINK I'LL GET STARTED.
I'LL JOIN YOU.
CHEER UP, STEVE. WE'VE HAD BAD DAYS. THIS ISN'T ONE OF THEM.
YEAH...
HEY, YOU EVER HEARD OF THIS GUY PAUL NOTH?
THE LAW AND ORDER GUY?
NO, THAT'S CHRIS. PAUL'S A CARTOONIST. HE'S PRETTY FUNNY. KINDA DARK THOUGH.

ANYWAY, HE'S GOT THIS ONE WHERE THERE'S A BUNCH OF SHEEP LOOKING AT A CAMPAIGN SIGN.

AND ON THE SIGN, THERE'S A WOLF AND HIS SLOGAN--"I'M GOING TO EAT YOU."

AND YOU KNOW WHAT ONE OF THE SHEEP SAYS IN RESPONSE?

"THAT GUY TELLS IT LIKE IT IS."

WHAT I AM ABOUT TO SAY IS NOT VERY CAPTAIN AMERICA-LIKE.

BUT THE FACT IS, THERE REALLY ARE PEOPLE WHOSE NEED TO BELIEVE IN SOMETHING IS SO STRONG THAT NO FACT WILL SHAKE THEM.

"IT IS DIFFICULT TO GET A MAN TO UNDERSTAND SOMETHING WHEN HIS SALARY DEPENDS ON HIS NOT UNDERSTANDING IT."

UPTON SINCLAIR.

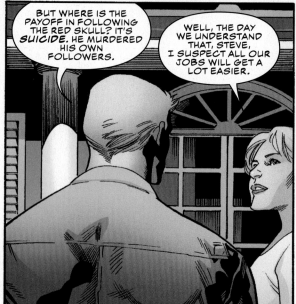

BUT WHERE IS THE PAYOFF IN FOLLOWING THE RED SKULL? IT'S *SUICIDE*. HE MURDERED HIS OWN FOLLOWERS.

WELL, THE DAY WE UNDERSTAND THAT, STEVE, I SUSPECT ALL OUR JOBS WILL GET A LOT EASIER.

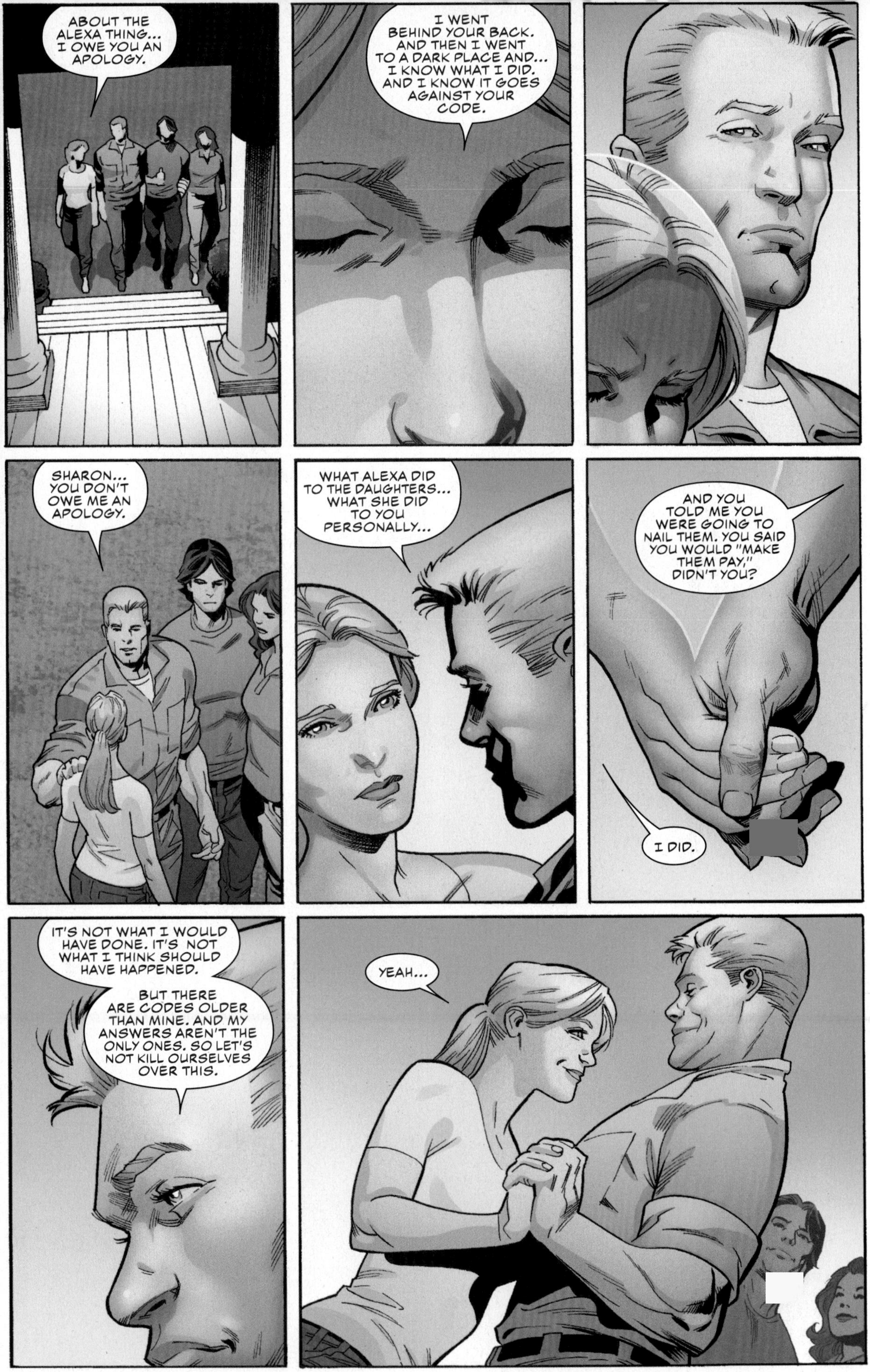
ABOUT THE ALEXA THING... I OWE YOU AN APOLOGY.
I WENT BEHIND YOUR BACK. AND THEN I WENT TO A DARK PLACE AND... I KNOW WHAT I DID. AND I KNOW IT GOES AGAINST YOUR CODE.
SHARON... YOU DON'T OWE ME AN APOLOGY.
WHAT ALEXA DID TO THE DAUGHTERS... WHAT SHE DID TO YOU PERSONALLY...
AND YOU TOLD ME YOU WERE GOING TO NAIL THEM. YOU SAID YOU WOULD "MAKE THEM PAY," DIDN'T YOU?
I DID.
IT'S NOT WHAT I WOULD HAVE DONE. IT'S NOT WHAT I THINK SHOULD HAVE HAPPENED.
BUT THERE ARE CODES OLDER THAN MINE. AND MY ANSWERS AREN'T THE ONLY ONES. SO LET'S NOT KILL OURSELVES OVER THIS.
YEAH...

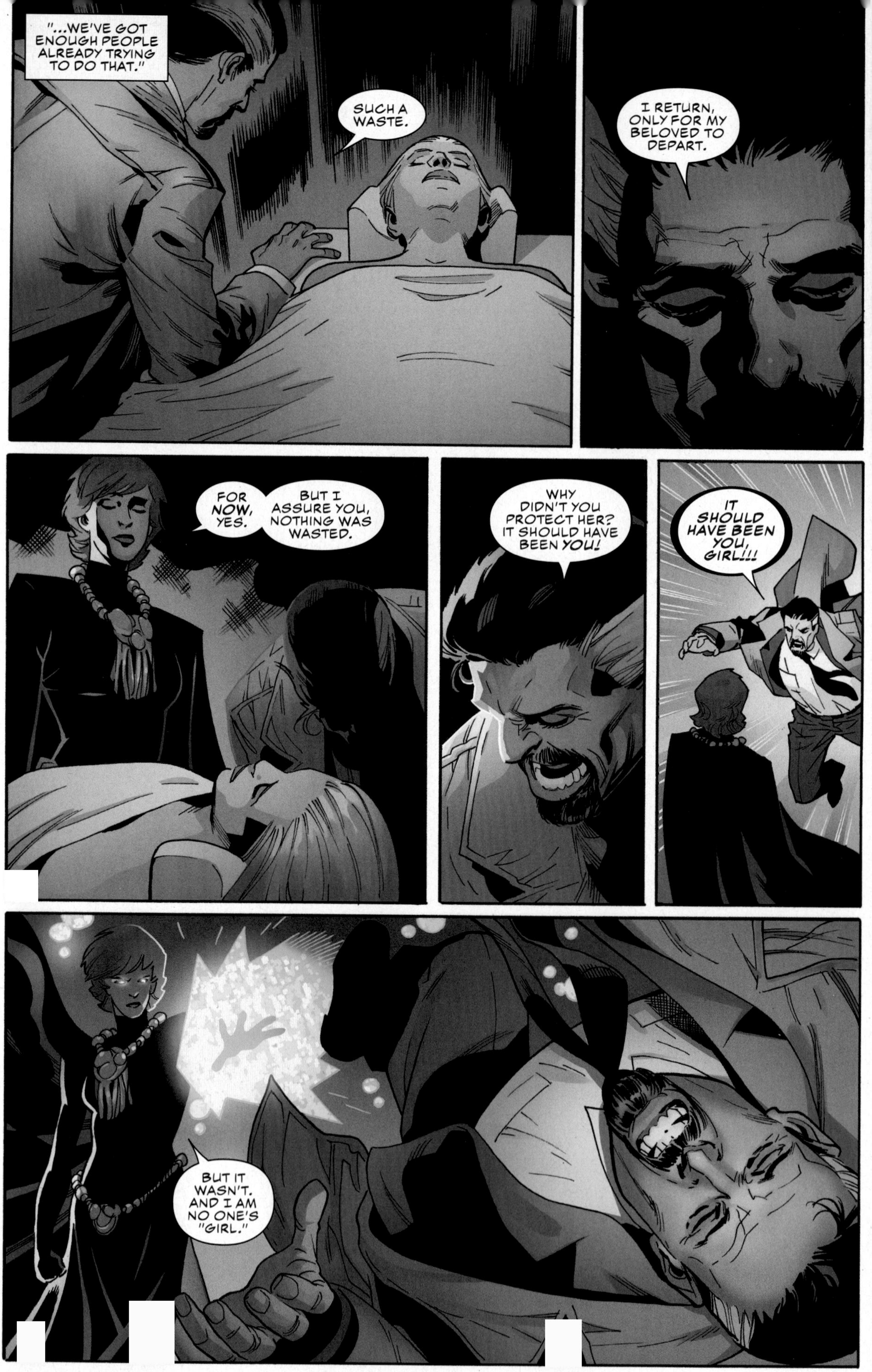
"...WE'VE GOT ENOUGH PEOPLE ALREADY TRYING TO DO THAT."
SUCH A WASTE.
I RETURN, ONLY FOR MY BELOVED TO DEPART.
FOR NOW, YES.
BUT I ASSURE YOU, NOTHING WAS WASTED.
WHY DIDN'T YOU PROTECT HER? IT SHOULD HAVE BEEN YOU!
IT SHOULD HAVE BEEN YOU, GIRL!!!
BUT IT WASN'T. AND I AM NO ONE'S "GIRL."

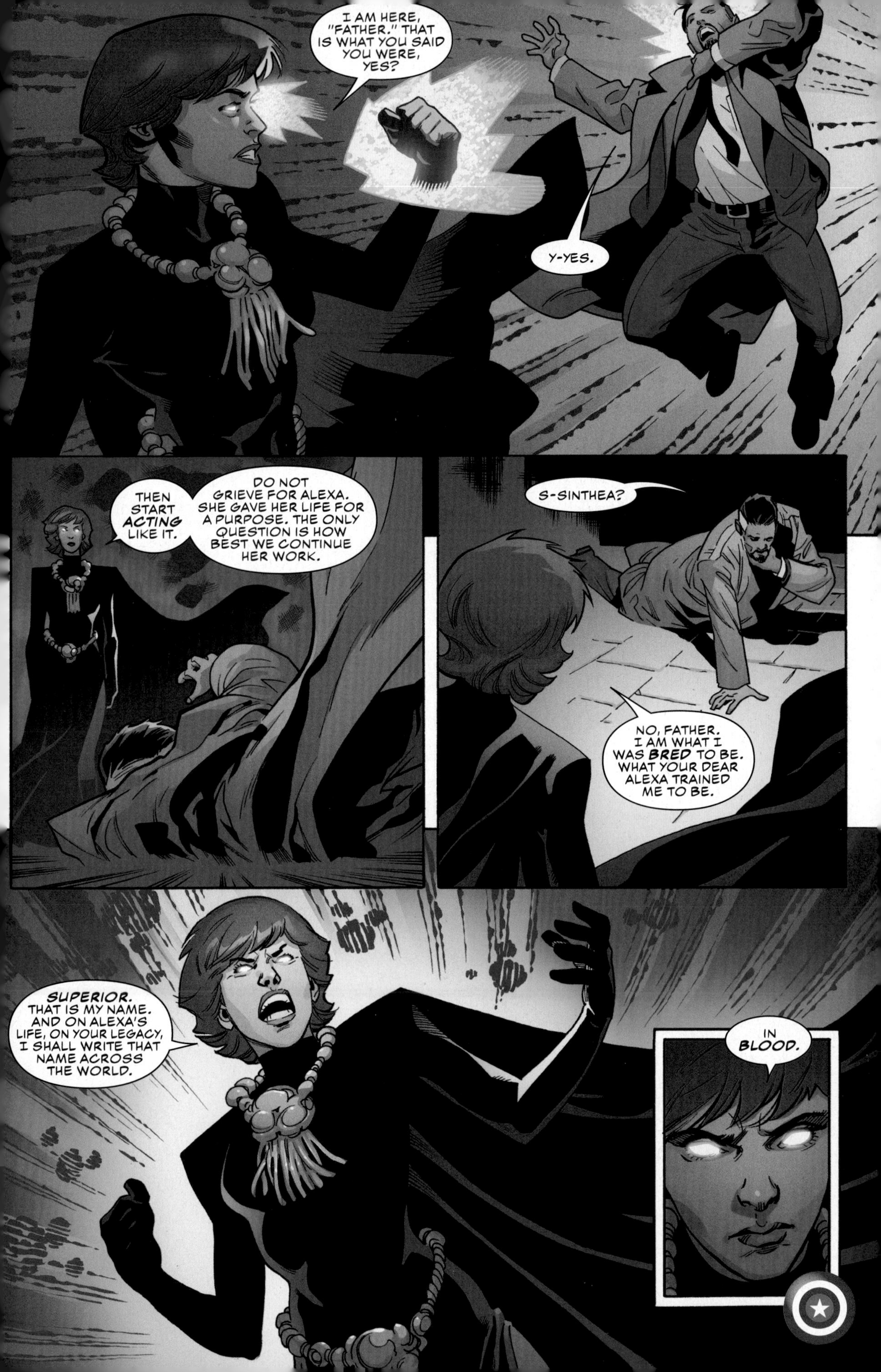
I AM HERE, "FATHER." THAT IS WHAT YOU SAID YOU WERE, YES?
Y-YES.
THEN START ACTING LIKE IT.
DO NOT GRIEVE FOR ALEXA. SHE GAVE HER LIFE FOR A PURPOSE. THE ONLY QUESTION IS HOW BEST WE CONTINUE HER WORK.
S-SINTHEA?
NO, FATHER. I AM WHAT I WAS BRED TO BE. WHAT YOUR DEAR ALEXA TRAINED ME TO BE.
SUPERIOR. THAT IS MY NAME. AND ON ALEXA'S LIFE, ON YOUR LEGACY, I SHALL WRITE THAT NAME ACROSS THE WORLD.
IN BLOOD.

AFTERWORD
BY TA-NEHISI COATES

It's been one of my great honors to fulfill a childhood dream — writing for Marvel Comics and writing two of their premier characters, Black Panther and Captain America. But this was more than a childhood fantasy. Grappling with Steve and T'Challa, trying to understand them as people, and then trying to express that in visual form was a challenge of another order. Novels and memoirs are easier in the sense that one can live in the world of ideas. In comics, like all visual fiction, things must be shown. Five years of doing that work changed me for the better, and it wouldn't have been possible without the diligence of my editors — Tom Brevoort, Wil Moss, Alanna Smith and Sarah Brunstad. It definitely would not have been possible without the truly incredible team of artists I was paired with, from Leonard Kirk to Brian Stelfreeze to Leinil Yu to Sunny Gho to Laura Martin. Throughout it all, I've had a team of veteran creators to help advise and mentor me. They include, but are not limited to, Chip Zdarsky, Christopher Priest, Kieron Gillen, Jamie McKelvie, Ed Brubaker, Matt Fraction, Kelly Sue DeConnick and Greg Pak. Thank you all. And thank you to the fans for reading. I tried to stay true to nothing — except the dream.

— Ta-Nehisi Coates